AN INTRODUCTION TO

FILM
CRITICISM

MAJOR CRITICAL
APPROACHES
TO NARRATIVE FILM

Developed under the advisory editorship of
Thomas W. Bohn, Dean of Communications,
Ithaca College

AN INTRODUCTION TO

FILM CRITICISM

MAJOR CRITICAL APPROACHES TO NARRATIVE FILM

Tim Bywater
Dixie College

Thomas Sobchack
University of Utah

Longman
New York & London

An Introduction to Film Criticism

Longman, 10 Bank Street, White Plains, N.Y. 10606

Associated companies:
Longman Group Ltd., London
Longman Cheshire Pty., Melbourne
Longman Paul Pty., Auckland
Copp Clark Pitman, Toronto
Pitman Publishing Inc., New York

Review of *Year of the Dragon* by Stanley Kaufman from The New Republic, Sept. 16 and 23, 1985, pp. 33-34. Copyright © 1985 by The New Republic. Reprinted by permission of The New Republic.
Excerpts from HOWARD HAWKS by Robin Wood, pp. 42, 55-56, 67-68, and 150. Copyright © 1968, 1981 by Robin Wood. Reprinted by permission of the publisher, the British Film Institute.
Excerpts from BEYOND FORMULA: AMERICAN FILM GENRES by Stanley J. Solomon, pp. 1-2 and 76-77. Copyright © 1976 by Harcourt Brace Jovanovich. Reprinted by permission of the publisher.
Excerpt from Hitchcock by François Truffaut with Helen G. Scott, pp. 247-248. Copyright © 1967 by François Truffaut. Reprinted by permission of Simon & Schuster, Inc., and Martin Secker and Warburg Ltd.
"The Gangster as Tragic Hero" by Robert Warshow, first published in *Partisan Review*, 1948 (from THE IMMEDIATE EXPERIENCE, Atheneum, 1970). Reprinted by permission of Lester C. Migdal on behalf of Robert Warshow's estate.
P. xv, Drawn by Handelsman; copyright © 1986 The New Yorker Magazine, Inc.
Figure 1.1, p. 6, Courtesy of Tri-Star Pictures, Inc.
Figure 1.2, p. 16, Courtesy of Hemdale Film Corporation.
Figure 2.1, p. 36, Reprinted by permission of Tribune Company Syndicate, Inc.

Executive editor: Gordon T. R. Anderson
Production editor: Dee Amir Josephson
Cover design: Anne M. Pompeo
Production supervisor: Judy Millman

Library of Congress Cataloging-in-Publication Data

Bywater, Tim.
    An introduction to film criticism : major critical approaches to
    narrative film / by Tim Bywater and Tom Sobchack.
        p. cm.

    Bibliography: p.
    Includes index.
    ISBN 0-582-28606-9
    1. Film criticism.   I. Sobchack, Thomas.   II. Title.
PN1995.B9   1989   88-17003
791.43′01′5—dc19   CIP

4 5 6 7 8 9 10 DO 95949392

Acknowledgements

Like making a film, this book was a collaborative effort. There are far too many people who have influenced our thinking about the movies to mention here, but a special note of thanks must go to Gordon T. R. Anderson for his unwavering faith in the project, our colleagues and students at Dixie College and the University of Utah for their aid and inspiration, the library staffs at Dixie and the University of Nevada at Las Vegas for their able assistance, Sharon Lee and Josette Price for their super secretarial skills, and our wives, Kathy and Julie, for their encouragement and support.

Contents

Introduction

Nearly everyone watches movies. Viewed in theaters or seen on television, motion pictures are a part of contemporary life. In their surface rush of images and sounds, films present a powerful visual and auditory experience immediately available to all. The mainstream narrative film produced for theatrical release captures the viewer's attention and delivers an emotional payoff. Little thought is required to decipher the images and sounds, to know what's happening in the film or to make a judgment about whether the film was worth seeing. For most viewers, film criticism is simply the expression of satisfaction or dissatisfaction with a current movie. Afterward, one need only say, "I liked it" or "I didn't" to either recommend the film to friends or tell them to save their money. This audience's perception of what makes a narrative film valuable has changed little during the course of film history. If it produces the kind of entertainment viewers expect, then it gets four stars.

But there is another audience with a different idea about films and film criticism. This group of filmgoers finds the movie experience as important and meaningful as literature, painting, dance, and the other fine arts. They take their moviegoing more seriously, extending their pleasure and understanding through the process of discourse—verbal or written—about the movies. This discourse about film's history, theory, and value, though larger in scope than mere evaluation of current films, is only the logical expansion of the basic feeling everyone has, after seeing a film, of wanting to share his or her experiences with others. *An Introduction to Film Criticism* surveys the wide range of the published discourse—the film criticism—available today that centers on the narrative film.

There are alternative modes of film—the documentary, the experimental, the avant-garde—with corresponding modes of criticism that are not covered in this book. This omission does not suggest that such criticism is not an essential part of a well-rounded film student's understanding of the field. It merely attests to the strength and power of the narrative film over the hearts and minds of the mass of filmgoers and the vast majority of people writing about film. Perhaps 95 percent of all published film criticism is about the narrative film: the mainstream, theatrical Hollywood film, whether literally produced in Hollywood or not. Though the concept of film studies implies a concern with all types of films, the vast majority of courses deal with the narrative film.

Although some critics early on championed film as an art as important as the traditional ones and just as worthy of serious consideration, film criticism, as we think of it today—the results of in-depth scholarship, the detailed analysis of style, genre, history, filmmaker, or social impact of the movies—is a relatively recent activity. The process of recommending films, announcing their arrival at the local Bijou, and describing their contents for prospective patrons, however, became formalized in newspaper and magazine reviews soon after the turn of the century and continues to this day. Reviews describe a current film and indicate the writer's evaluation of its quality in order to give readers some basis for deciding whether to see a particular film or not. Though often referred to as "film critics," these writers might more properly be called "reviewers," to distinguish their function from that of film critics whose primary aim is to investigate the medium as an aesthetic, social, and historical phenomenon.

Although a film reviewer and a film critic can be one and the same person—some reviewers in certain magazines or newspapers often go beyond simple reviewing of the latest releases to illuminate particular films and relate them to larger concerns—it is more common for reviewing and criticism to be considered separate activities directed toward different audiences for different purposes. Film reviews appear in the popular press—daily newspapers, weekly and monthly magazines—and are nearly always about films currently playing in theaters. Film criticism, on the other hand, has no particular bond with journalism; indeed, film criticism tends to appear in publications no more immediate than monthlies and is not usually about current releases. Most film criticism of the kind to be examined in this study deals with more specialized subject matter than does the review, even at its broadest. Film critics are usually academics, scholars, and teachers of film history, aesthetics, and theory; their film criticism is most often found in small journals geared to a scholarly audience and in books published by university presses.

The growth of this more detailed and analytical film criticism and scholarship has paralleled the growth of film studies as an academic discipline. The widespread establishment of courses, degree programs, and departments in the last three decades has created a larger audience for serious and specialized writing, and, as well, has added to the ranks of what was once only a handful of publishing scholars. Within the last few years, scholarship within the field has undergone an expansive upheaval, accommodating new areas of inquiry and new critical methods. Structuralism, Marxism, feminism, and the new Freudianism vie with the more traditional historical and aesthetic approaches. The field is crowded with voices clamoring to be heard, all asking for a sympathetic hearing, each aiming to provide increased knowledge about the movies, yet each following a different path toward that objective. *An Introduction to Film Criticism* attempts to outline these various paths pursued by film criticism and scholarship.

Film criticism, as defined in this study, is not merely the negative (or positive) evaluation of particular films. Criticism is an act of ordering, of organizing relationships, of identifying and observing patterns that make the cinematic experience meaningful as well as emotional, comprehensible as well as felt. There are narrower aims and purposes, too, that ultimately define the different critical approaches. The genre approach, for example, examines the familiar groups of films like westerns, horror films, and musicals; the auteur approach concentrates primarily on the filmmaker; the theoretical approach looks closely at the basic elements of the medium.

The general function of this criticism is to deal responsibly with the subject matter so as to increase the possibilities of meaning available in the experiences of viewing and thinking about movies. The critic/scholar writes with logical coherence, clarity, and accuracy in order to support a contention about the subject at hand. Film scholarship and criticism presuppose a literate and serious readership, one familiar with a variety of films and also to varying degrees conversant with film history, theory, and critical methodologies. The style of a critical or scholarly piece is of minor importance compared to the critical strategy, stance, or method the writer takes toward the material under scrutiny. That strategy—what we call here a *critical approach*—is determined by the purpose and intended function of the criticism and by the writer's belief that a certain form of presentation will best reveal the film and related material to the reader.

Because most students' contact with writing about film is in the form of reviews in print and on television, reviewing as a critical approach will be discussed at the beginning of this book, even if, in its standard form, the daily newspaper notice of a new movie cannot be considered a critical approach. At its best, however, the journalistic approach to film, which examines a recently released film as news, can become serious criticism when the writer goes beyond the mere reporting of the cast and plot and analyzes the text or context of the film in some meaningful way. For most of the book, however, we will turn to the body of writing about film that regularly and purposefully goes beyond the simple informational aspect of the review, writing that attempts to explain, analyze, and interpret both individual films and their context, to account for the relations between filmmakers, the production and distribution system, the films, and the audience from a variety of approaches, attempting to make clear the difference and similarities among those approaches.

It should be stated at the outset, however, that the critical approaches are not always as clearly distinguishable in practice as they are in theory. The historical approach, for example, suggests that the critic looks at films from a historical perspective, seeing the relationship between what came before and what came after. But except for the discussion of new releases, in effect, all the other critical approaches have a historical component, because the films under discussion will be those from the past. A genre critic, for instance, may seek to define a category like the western, but inevitably will deal with westerns made in the silent era and the studio years as well as any that may be made today. Thus the student should keep in mind that critical approaches can overlap or borrow from each other, even if the critical approach does define a major emphasis on the part of the writer using that approach.

No matter what the approach, however, film criticism, whether in a review or in a scholarly article, exists as the articulation of writer/reader relationships inherent in any communication about the shared experience of a film. It has to do with seeing films, looking at them closely, reading about them, writing about them, passing thoughts and observations back and forth between consumers of the product, exchanging feelings and ideas about the films seen on the screen, creating a discourse about film. We read the articles and books in order to find out more about a subject of common interest, to compare our own personal responses with those of others who have had the same experience. The critic is "someone who persists in learning to see the film differently and is able to specify the mechanisms which make this possible," as Peter Wollen suggests. "Nor is it the single reading, the one which gives us the true meaning of the film; it is simply a reading which produces more meaning" (p. 169). Film criticism is an ongoing process dedicated to increasing meaning about the subject, valuable to the writer, reader, and, ultimately, the culture at large.

Film, no less than any other cultural artifact, can be "read" in a variety of different ways—as historical document, psychological casebook, philosophical repository, or political example. Whatever we are and whatever we value, consciously or unconsciously, is embodied and preserved in the motion picture. There are disagreements among critics, among schools of criticism, and between critics and the general public over a variety of issues, but the very extent of the discourse, the numbers of people committed to proving one thing or another about film—it is a blight on the land and should be abolished; it is mindless entertainment, nothing more; it is a good/bad model for the young/old to experience; it is the greatest art ever invented by humankind; it has more riches than any other kind of literature or drama; it brainwashes its viewers into accepting the values of the dominant class—suggests that the criticism of film is an important activity of our culture, an activity that is engaged in in a constant, never-ending process of reevaluating human aims and purposes as they are observed and represented in cinema.

This may appear as a lofty ideal for what, at first glance, seems to be a relatively narrow and specialized concern—discourse about movies. But movies, in all their variety, allow for a great many applications of human thinking power. Films dealing with "unimportant" subjects—"Hey, it's just another car chase movie"—may yield surprising, important results from closer viewing. The "car chase" film may reflect our attitude toward the role of automobiles in our lives, or it may indicate our frustration with the whole complex of industrialism. The desire of some critics to note and establish the creative power and control of one person—the director of the film—may reaffirm our notion of the value of the individual in a corporate world. Even the assumption that the mechanical and assembly line process of film production can produce art the equivalent of the novel, the opera, or ballet is an assertion, a demonstration, a validation of a certain kind of human value.

Film criticism, then, is a process that gives value to the reader and writer far beyond the scope of the immediate film or films under discussion, far beyond any influences on the making of future films. It is a process that encourages clear thinking, the weighing of alternatives, the evaluation of evidence, and the risk of having to defend judgment publicly. It is an area where there are no easy answers, only myriad fascinating questions. It is a site, an occasion, an act, a practice where we learn, as in all of life, that there is always more to a subject than meets the eye.

An Introduction to Film Criticism is organized on the basis of complexity of approach and the nature of the intended audience. It moves from the simplest approaches to the most difficult, from material aimed at the general reader and filmgoer to that written for specialists in film study. Part I of the book examines those kinds of writing that focus on immediate responses to individual films—the review found in the popular press and the essay available in publications directed toward the cultured reader familiar with general arts criticism. Evaluation is a strong element of these approaches. This kind of criticism is called *textual* because individual films are usually discussed as whole texts (everything perceived in a single viewing of a single film) whose value is manifested in the immediate experience of the viewer. Little or no consideration is given to other films or to the viewer's observations about the world outside the film. The meaning and value of the film are to be found mainly in the narrow confines of an isolated cultural event.

Part II looks at the auteur and genre approaches. These transitional approaches range from relatively simple material to highly complex; the intended audience is sometimes the general cultured reader and sometimes the student and scholar. Evaluation often is present—this is a director's best film, this is a horror film without equal, and so on—but much of the work is descriptive and analytical. Some of these writings focus on individual films, but most see single films within the context of other films. An individual film by John Ford is viewed in relation to Ford's body of work, or a new science-fiction film is examined as part of the genre of science-fiction films. Thus some of this criticism is textual and some is contextual. Meanings and values of films are found not only within the confines of the text and the viewer's contact with the text but also of the viewer's background and knowledge of other films.

Part III is primarily about scholarly writing aimed at specialized audiences and appearing in professional journals and books. All of this criticism has to be considered contextual because the writers are always aware of and concerned with film's relationship to history, society, philosophy, economics, and film theory. In fact, very little of the writing concerns itself with the individual experience of watching a particular film. Individual films are frequently explicated and interpreted, but as examples to prove a more general or universal proposition. There are, of course, overlaps in intended audience. A recognized sociologist who writes articles on film for other sociologists may also author an article for the *New York Times Magazine* directed at the general cultured reader.

Entry into the kinds of writing discussed in Part III is more difficult, sometimes requiring extensive and specialized background in subject areas other than film, but students taking college courses in film study may be expected to delve into such works. Working through *An Introduction to Film Criticism* from the beginning and moving from the simpler kinds of criticism to the more complex, the student should find the task of reading all kinds of film criticism easier and more fruitful.

At the head of each chapter is a thumbnail description of the set of approaches covered. A more detailed explanation of the basic tenets, audience, practitioners, and function of the approaches follows. Then a brief history of the development of the approach is given, so that the student can see the relationship between the criticism and history in general and film history in particular. Specific critical articles or books are examined next as examples of the approach. Here the attempt has been to show the range and variety in each category as well as to familiarize the student with some of the most well-known pieces of work. This should enable the reader to spot the style and the vocabulary that signal and identify each approach. References in the text to particular works act like an annotated bibliography, pointing the student toward books and articles that will supply further information for those interested in pursuing specific topics.

This format should make it possible for users of *An Introduction to Film Criticism* to increase their knowledge about the body of work that is film criticism. The reader will not only understand the various approaches to narrative film more thoroughly but will also learn something about film itself, since an increase in knowledge about a subject occurs both through the direct experience of the subject—actually watching films—and the indirect experience of reading what people say about the subject—reading film criticism. Students of film should be able to form surer and sounder judgments about their film experiences and to speak and write those judgments with greater clarity and skill as they relate their own impressions of and responses to film to those of professional writers.

Since one of the aims of this book is to help students write better film criticism, a sample student paper using each of the major approaches is included in the appendix. These are average papers from beginning film classes, but many are surprisingly full of unique and fascinating contribu-

Film Critic

tions to the discussions of film undertaken by the individual writers. They show what can be done and, it is hoped, will encourage users of this book to do likewise. To further aid in the writing of specific styles of film criticism, each of the chapters concludes with a set of guidelines outlining the primary and secondary sources for material, the method to follow, and questions the student writer can employ to get the process started.

PART I

Textual Approaches: Description and Analysis of Individual Films

Most viewers are interested only in individual narrative films: the film seen last night, the film for the weekend coming up, the one just released and reviewed in the newspaper or on television. It almost seems simpleminded to remark that a person can only watch one movie at a time—this one, right now, the one on the screen. Even when you take advantage of Video Vern's three-for-a-dollar midweek special and zip through the slow parts of all the movies so you can see all three before returning them to the store the next day, you seldom have two VCR's and two monitors running at the same time. Single, individual films occupy our total viewing attention in any given moment in time, though we can, of course, think about more than one film at a time. Nevertheless, the most common discourse about films, both in speaking and in writing, is about individual narrative films.

It is the text of the particular film—its plot, characters, themes, performers, and technical competence—that first arouses our curiosity. What's it about? Who's in it? Is it worth seeing? Is it a good film? These are the questions most commonly asked by the general moviegoer about a newly released film. The more sophisticated viewer may have different reasons for liking or disliking a film, may be as interested in classic films of the past as contemporary releases, but still may find individual films and their worth the most elemental reason for talking or writing about films. There are occasions, of course, when both general and sophisticated viewers will make references to other films, comparing the current film under discussion with previous films by the same director or performer or noting similarities in several films, spotting a trend or a cycle, yet the predominant interest is in the individual film at hand.

Part I of *An Introduction to Film Criticism* identifies two kinds of film criticism as textual criticism because these approaches to film usually focus on single films. Chapter 1 surveys the *journalistic* approach. Clearly film reviewers in newspapers and weekly magazines devote most of their attention to single, recently released films.

1

Chapter 2 identifies a broad, general approach to film criticism dubbed *humanist*. Writing in a variety of publications that range from monthlies aimed at the general intellectual audience to specialized film journals, humanists are a diverse lot. Though analyses of individual films predominate, the humanistic critic often discusses a particular film in the context of other films, both old and new, and the relationship of the film to social, political, and philosophic issues. Nevertheless, the personal and occasional essays produced by humanists are most often extended, in-depth discussions of individual films.

In one sense, films are never without a context. Films are made and seen in the world, not in a vacuum. But it is the text itself—the very film itself—and the experience of that text that is central to our response to it. In fact, the student examining film criticism for the first time may believe that textual criticism is the only relevant classification, and this is partially true, since thinking and discourse about films, no matter where it may lead, must always start and end with the text. The film must be experienced—seen and heard and digested—and only then can it become an object of critical inquiry. For criticism to have any meaning, there must first be the confrontation between the individual consciousness and the matter revealed in the sights and sounds of a particular film. The experience of a film is the essential first step in the process of developing critical awareness, the aim of all discourse on film. The textual approaches, therefore, are an excellent takeoff point for examining the wide range of film criticism.

CHAPTER 1

The Journalistic Approach: Film Reviews for the Mass Audience

Journalistic Approach Capsule

Audience: General moviegoers who haven't seen the film being discussed.

Functions: Provide information about current releases; suggest relative merit of a film's entertainment value; serve as publicity for film's producers.

Subject: Individual films currently playing in theaters.

Writers: Working journalists writing on a deadline, with no special qualifications except consistent film viewing of new releases.

Publications: Local and national daily and weekly newspapers; weekly and monthly magazines ranging from the widely read, like *Time* and *Newsweek,* to those with smaller circulations, like *The New Yorker* and *The New Republic.*

Journalistic film criticism, primarily in the form of film reviews, supplies information for the mass filmgoing public. These reviews are primarily intended for readers who have not yet seen the films that are the subject matter of the reviews. This certainly doesn't mean they offer nothing of interest to the reader who *has* seen the films, but it does dictate how broad or specific the approach to a given film will be and what kinds of information the review will contain. The reviewer's major functions are to give the unaware reader the information that a specific film has been released and is available (or will be shortly) for viewing, to indicate generally what the film is about and who was involved in its production behind and in front of the cameras, and to evaluate the film so that readers who are sympathetic to the reviewer's tastes have an idea whether or not they wish to spend their time and money to see it.

WORKING JOURNALISTS

Although television reviews have a high degree of visibility, most film reviews appear in daily newspapers. Others appear in weekly papers like New York's *The Village Voice* or in weekly magazines like *The New Republic, The New Yorker,* or *Time.* And reviews of varying lengths, depending upon the orientation of the magazine, also appear in monthly magazines ranging from *Seventeen* to *Esquire* to *McCall's.* Most of these publications have staff reviewers who have no special background in film. Most newspaper editors believe that any working journalist can do the job. Over the years, however, some writers have become identified with their publication and achieved a certain notoriety; for instance, Pauline Kael has represented *The New Yorker* and Stanley Kauffmann *The New Republic* for many years. For thirty years, beginning in the early 1940s, Bosley Crowther was the film critic for the *New York Times.* Because of the paper's reputation, he became the best-known film critic in the country. Currently Vincent Canby and Janet Maslin write the *Times* reviews. Each of these writers has developed personal tastes as well as a personal style, tastes generally suited to those of the periodical's readership and a style generally suited to the dictates of the publication's orientation and time schedule. For some filmgoers these name writers have achieved an authoritative position, dictating the viewing habits of thousands of loyal readers.

Generally, one can identify a certain consistency in a publication's film reviews from day to day or week to week. This consistency depends on how often the publication appears and to whom it is addressed. Film reviews appearing in a daily newspaper are usually written immediately after a film's commercial release. They are, therefore, written for a nearly immediate deadline and do not allow the reviewer time to see the film more than once. The reviewer's first impressions are the ones that count; the time for critical contemplation is limited. In addition, space is limited. Only so much room is allowed a daily newspaper review and the writer must, therefore, keep in mind the allotted space, first answering those questions the reader expects answered in a review and using the remainder of the space—if there is any— for other critical purposes. It is difficult for the daily reviewer to develop what might be identified as a personal style of writing because of the limitations of time and space within which he or she has to work. Indeed, if a newspaper is large and has a staff writing about film, the daily reviewer has less status and usually a lower critical reputation than the reviewer for the Sunday edition, who is given a great deal more space and who is allowed to review the major film of that week's releases. In such an instance, the individual writing for the daily edition is often referred to as a "reviewer," while the individual writing for the Sunday edition is referred to as a "critic." Such a distinction, although casual, is to the point. The film reviewer of a daily, limited by a deadline and by space, can usually do hardly more than synopsize a film's plot, comment briefly on the production, and make a few general statements about the film's worth. Such writing, though difficult to do well, is rarely critical and analytic in nature. But that does not mean criticism never exists. In fact, the most interesting side of the journalistic approach involves those writers whose work transcends the review function.

CRITICS AND REVIEWERS

The writer working for a weekly or monthly publication actually may deserve the title of "critic" rather than "reviewer." Performing the basic function of a reviewer—in some cases discussing a single film and in others a group of recent releases—the writer of a weekly or monthly column will also have both the contemplative time and space necessary to extend that function into critical and analytical areas. There are a good number of "reviewers" for weekly newspapers and magazines who go beyond the basic function that the simple film review serves. Their articles are often perceptive, offering as much to the reader who has already seen the film under discussion as to the reader who hasn't yet seen it.

Indeed, some of the best writing ever published on film has been written by people who would characterize themselves as journalists rather than as critics or scholars, people who have brought a native, experienced, and humane intelligence to the job of reviewing movies and who have, over the years, become known and respected for their critical abilities. Otis Ferguson, James Agee, Pauline Kael, Stanley Kauffmann, and Janet Maslin are only some of those who—even pressed by the editor's deadline—have contributed greatly to our understanding and enjoyment of film, and who have become, in their time, the best of the journalistic film critics. While they always fulfill their primary function as film reviewers, they are also film critics, writing as much to articulate their considered responses to films as to inform a casual reader about a new movie.

HISTORY OF FILM REVIEWING
IN THE POPULAR PRESS

The development of journalistic reviewing and its evolution into serious criticism is tied to the development of film showings to a theater audience. From the turn of the century, these showings were considered newsworthy, so newspaper reporters were assigned to cover them as news events. Early pieces of this so-called criticism were, in reality, a combination of reportage

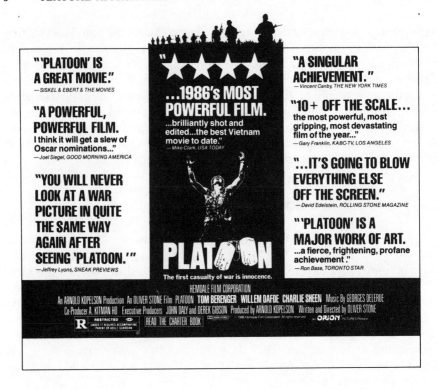

(describing the film event in factual terms) and review (giving the audience, yet to see the film, advice as to its entertainment value). Emphasis is placed on the word *value*. After reading the review, a prospective patron was supposed to be able to determine whether or not the film was worth spending money on, a criterion for a review still valid today.

The first newspaper account in America of a theatrical motion picture showing, written in 1896, is an example of this early film reviewing. The account was four paragraphs long, three of which were allotted to describing the appearance for the first time of Edison's vitascope, "the ingenious inventor's latest toy." (The last paragraph turned back to the theater's regular variety hall entertainment.) The reporter assigned to cover the event treated it as he might have treated any other news story. Using the past tense throughout, he described, in a straightforward, factual manner, the motion picture screen, the projector, and the atmosphere in the theater as the showing began. Then he described the program:

> An unusually bright light fell upon the screen, then came into view two precocious blonde young persons of the variety stage, in pink and blue dresses, doing the umbrella dance with commendable celerity. Their motions were clearly defined. When they vanished, a view of an angry surf breaking on a sandy beach near a stone pier amazed the spectators. The

waves tumbled in furiously and the foam of the breakers flew high in the air. A burlesque boxing match between a tall, thin comedian and a short, fat one, a comic allegory called *The Monroe Doctrine,* an instant of motion in Hoyt's farce, *A Milk White Flag,* repeated over and over again, and a skirt dance by a tall blonde completed the views, which were all wonderfully real and singularly exhilarating. (Kauffmann, Henstell, p. 3)

The reporter also expressed his opinion that this was "an extraordinary exhibition." But he concluded, in his resolutely factual manner, that "there were loud calls for Mr. Edison, but he made no response." This tradition of reporting to a mass audience about the entertainment value of a film, in which factual descriptions of the happenings on the screen and personal opinion concerning the film's merit predominate, still constitutes the bulk of writing about film in newspapers and periodicals.

As the popularity and length of films began to increase, criticism, not simply reviewing, became more important—especially with the development of the narrative film. Longer films containing more substantial subject matter meant longer, more substantial film articles appearing in important literary journals as well as in mass periodicals. The early criticism in journals such as *The Dial* and *The New Republic,* as well as in film journals such as the now defunct *The Moving Picture World,* stressed the film's potential as a higher art form. As early as 1908, in an article entitled "The Moving Picture Drama and the Actual Drama," Rollin Summers observed, "That it has genuine technique, largely in common with acted drama yet in part particular to itself, is a proposition which seems not to be well recognized within the moving picture field itself. It is important to the development of the moving picture that these two propositions be established" (Kauffmann, Henstell, p. 9).

Attempts such as this one to legitimize film as an art form can be seen in articles about film written between 1900 and 1925. During this time period, the best-remembered critics are those who most seriously attempted to legitimize the film and film criticism. Often these critics' background included work in theater and music criticism as well as film. Such a critic is Frank E. Woods, who gained a reputation as the "first major film critic." Writing a column in *The New York Dramatic Mirror,* under the pseudonym "The Spectator," Woods first used his column as an apology for the flaws in current films. Later, however, his columns addressed many important aesthetic/critical film issues) including film's importance as a mode of social criticism. Other important early film critics were Heywood Broun, whose name helped bring respectability to the field of film criticism before the 1920s, since he was also a literary and drama critic for the *New York Tribune* and later a celebrated social critic and columnist, and Kenneth Macgowan, who, after a career as a film and drama critic, became a Broadway and film producer and later chairman of the Theater Arts Department at UCLA.

Important film reviewers of the 1920s include Gilbert Seldes, Harry Potamkin, Robert E. Sherwood, Alexander Woollcott, Edmund Wilson, and

Joseph Wood Krutch—all important writers of the period—who helped to document the impact of film on the audience of that time and who used the role of critic to help establish popular film as an art form to be taken seriously. Here, for example, is Robert E. Sherwood's opening paragraph of his review of Buster Keaton's silent comedy *The Paleface* (1921). "It is strange that the silent drama should have reached its highest level in the comic field. Here, and here alone, it is preeminent. Nothing that is being produced in literature or in drama is as funny as a good Chaplin, Lloyd, or Keaton comedy. The efforts of these three young men approximate art more closely than anything else that the movies have offered" (Kauffmann, Henstell, p. 132). Although reviewing still dominated this early film writing, the attempt to bring critical standards to the process, and thereby to validate film as an art, eventually led to the publication of some highly regarded journalistic critics who, with wit and style, helped establish the credibility of film criticism as a serious enterprise.

STYLISH REVIEWERS: THE EMERGENCE OF JOURNALISTIC CRITICISM

By the 1930s the film had left the silent era and embarked on the experiment of sound. Some critics looked back longingly at those silent film days, believing that the "talkie" could never recapture the artistry of the silent film, destroyed by the advent of sound. But by the mid-1930s, during the heart of the Great Depression, film had become the nation's ticket to a world far removed from the era's grim reality. What the public needed at this time was not an apologist for the film as a credible art form—film was the mass art of the 1930s—or a historian mourning the loss of the silent film. Rather the critic needed to be someone the audience could trust, someone with taste and judgment, who was in a position to see all the new film releases and make some shrewd, enlightened choices concerning which of those releases were worth a moviegoer's hard-earned money. The critic who served as a model in this capacity, beginning in 1934 and continuing until World War II, was Otis Ferguson.

In his introduction to Ferguson's collected film reviews, Andrew Sarris ranks several of Ferguson's film reviews "so close to the top of American journalism that it isn't worth measuring the difference" (Ferguson, p. xii). Sarris goes on to say that a strong claim can be made for Ferguson "as the writer of the best and most subtly influential film criticism ever turned out in America." By "subtly influential," Sarris is referring to Ferguson's influence on later journalistic film critics and their criticism. For in a Ferguson review, wit and style as well as taste and judgment can be seen as central elements. In sampling Ferguson's criticism, one finds none of the self-consciousness of pre-1930s critics, marveling over the medium or attempting to defend films as worthy of serious study and analysis. Clearly, films were, to Ferguson, made to be examined for strengths and weaknesses—the importance of the medium was taken for granted. Ferguson presents himself to the reader as a good friend, someone the literate viewer might enjoy seeing a movie with and discussing it with afterward. He is neither a pedant nor a snob. This persona comes across beautifully in any Ferguson review selected at random. The style is concise and breezily irreverent. The points are witty and directly on target. But most important, the reader is immediately impressed with Ferguson's knowledge of film. His reviews are concise, directly to the point, with never a word wasted. The focus is always on the film as an entertainment, with Ferguson acting as what Dwight Macdonald characterized as a "tipster" writing for a "consumer." His brief review of Howard Hawks's *Bringing Up Baby* (1938) serves as a representative example.

The review begins with an irreverent swipe at the potentially serious philosophical question "Is Humor Best for Us?" To this question Ferguson answers that *Bringing Up Baby* is "funny from the word go, that it has no other meaning to recommend it, nor therapeutic qualities, and that I wouldn't swap it for practically any three things of the current season." At this point Ferguson summarizes the plot in two sentences, followed by a brief description of the performances by Katharine Hepburn and Cary Grant, as well as a word or two concerning the minor characters including "baby," the leopard, who, according to Ferguson (with tongue in cheek), was "better than any of them, but is it art?" Clearly "art" is the last thing on Ferguson's mind. Ferguson ends the review with an overall assessment of the film. This review, written in March 1938, illustrates as well as any the direction that journalistic film criticism would follow for the next forty years. The style is casual, with several insertions of the vernacular: "from the word go," "I wouldn't swap it." Ferguson gets right to the point; immediately, the reader knows the position taken concerning the film's strengths as a comedy, but the critic avoids going into much specific detail. Instead, he relies on descriptive adjectives sprinkled generously through the text. Katharine Hepburn is "breathless, sensitive, headstrong, triumphant in illogic." Cary Grant does a "nice" job. The direction by Hawks "could have been less heavy and more supple." Any thought of an in-depth, lengthy assessment is brushed aside as irrelevant, as evidenced by the final sentence of the review, "All of this [Ferguson's general comments] could be elaborated, techniques analyzed, points cited, etc. But why? *Bringing Up Baby* is hardly a departure; it settles nothing; it is full of an easy inviting humor. So do you want to go or don't you?" (Ferguson, pp. 215–16).

The writer who, according to Sarris, supplanted Ferguson as a journalist critic of importance was James Agee. Sarris goes on to say that Ferguson had an enormous influence on Agee. That influence can be seen most clearly when one examines Agee's casual, concise style and personal point of view. But there the similarity ends. James Agee brought to film criticism a level of intellectual acceptance never before thought possible. Stanley Kauffmann goes so far as to say that the publication of *Agee on Film* (1958) (Agee's collected film criticism) marked the beginning of a new attitude toward serious film criticism.

From 1941 until 1948 James Agee was a film critic for *Time* magazine and from 1942 until 1948 he wrote a film column for *The Nation*. During this period he also wrote selected pieces of film criticism for *Life* magazine, including long essays on silent film comedy and film directors. In 1948 he gave up film journalism to try to break into filmmaking. He wrote film scripts—co-authoring the script for *The African Queen* (1951)—and continually tried to get the backing to make a film by himself. But he never got the chance. He died prematurely, at age forty-five, of a heart attack. So other than a few screenplays, most of which were never produced, Agee's literary reputation rests on his film criticism. In a famous letter to the editors of *The Nation,* W. H. Auden praised Agee's film criticism. What Agee says, writes Auden,

> is of such profound interest, expressed with such extraordinary wit and felicity, and so transcends its ostensible—to me, rather unimportant—subject, that his articles belong in that very select class—the music critiques of Berlioz and Shaw are the only other members I know—of newspaper work which has permanent literary value. (Agee, p. iv)

It's ironic that Auden's praise of Agee comes at the expense of film, but Auden's view represented a common intellectual attitude toward film during the 1940s and 1950s. It's an attitude that Agee rejected. Agee brings to the journalistic approach his personal love of the movies backed by an intellectual's willingness to treat films seriously. The main strength of his film criticism was that even as an intellectual, he never tried to hide that love or his affection for the average moviegoer from his readers. Although Agee may not have been able to change the intellectuals' attitudes about film, his *writing* has had a lasting impact on film criticism.

Beginning as a film reviewer at approximately the same time as James Agee, but not retiring until 1969, Bosley Crowther wrote for the *New York Times* for nearly thirty years. During the 1950s and 1960s he was the most influential film critic writing in America, undoubtedly because of his position with the *Times*. In a Crowther review, one notices how Agee's personal approach to criticism is taken to an extreme. Crowther comes across as emotional and highly opinionated, without the warmth and love of film so evident in Agee's writing. Avoiding the first person makes his individual, subjective point of view appear to be one of unquestioned authority. Crowther's approach can be seen in his review of Arthur Penn's *Bonnie and Clyde* (1967). The review gives the film's title, names the theater in which it is playing, identifies the actors and the director, and outlines the basic plot. Beyond that, the review simply states Crowther's unsupported negative judgments concerning the film. He begins the review by saying that an advertising campaign for the film attempted to put across the idea that it was a "faithful

representation" of the careers of Bonnie and Clyde. To this Crowther responds, "It is nothing of the sort. It is a cheap piece of bald-faced slapstick
comedy that treats the hideous depredations of that sleazy, moronic pair as
though they were as full of fun as the jazz-age cut-ups in *Thoroughly Modern
Millie*" (*The New York Times Film Reviews,* v. 7, p. 6). This is characteristic
of Crowther's personal style, and typical of much film reviewing in general.

THE REVIEWER AS CRITIC

Although most reviewers follow the Crowther tradition, a number of writers
working for weekly or monthly publications have been able to function more
like critics than reviewers. This is particularly true in publications that are
directed at an educated, arts-oriented, and reasonably affluent readership.
Both *The Village Voice* and *The New Yorker,* for instance, often devote three
or four thousand words to a film review. This allows the writer to do more
than merely review a film or films, and the emphasis of the article tends to
change drastically from its daily newspaper counterpart. The reviewer/critic
may, for example, choose to write about a number of films at one time, which
then allows for comparison or for the discussion of some thematic, stylistic,
or generic unity than may exist among a crop of current releases. The
reviewer/critics can, therefore, discuss a new work by a major director in light
of past work. They may draw, in considerable detail, certain cultural and
sociological conclusions from a recognizable trend in current releases. Or
they may be able to select and closely interpret and analyze a single work of
merit, chosen from all the films released in a given period. Because of the
lessened pressure of time and deadlines, the reviewer/critics also have more
time to contemplate the films they write about and, in fact, may even choose
to see them more than once. Their articles are often perceptive and analytic
and offer as much to the reader who has already seen the film under discussion as to the reader who hasn't yet seen it.

These reviewer/critics are often read for their style as well as for their
evaluations and analyses of films. Indeed, such film criticism is often as
entertaining as it is informative. It is not uncommon for a reviewer/critic to be
regarded as a particular kind of personality, whose particular biases and
personal characteristics are revealed in the writing. John Simon, for instance,
is noted for his belief in the moral value of art, his general disdain for most
popular American films, and his acid prose. For example, in a negative review
of *Bonnie and Clyde* (Arthur Penn, 1967), he was scathing in his attack on the
film's violence:

> . . . the whole thing stinks in the manner of a carefully made-up, combed,
> and manicured corpse. Crime may have its funny side, but here, for long
> stretches, it has nothing but funny sides. To switch then, without warning,
> from belly laughs to bloodbaths and produce facile shock effects is added

dishonesty. Between murder as fun and murder as Grand Guignol there is little to choose from.
. . . The acting is good, but slop is slop, even served with a silver ladle. (*Movies into Film,* 168–69)

Andrew Sarris is known for a style that is often epigrammatic and full of alliteration. In Sarris's review of *Rosemary's Baby* (Roman Polanski, 1968), his prose style is as fascinating as is his discussion of the film:

> Ghosts, holy or unholy, have ceased to haunt our dreams in their meta-physical majesty. The devil in *Rosemary's Baby* is reduced to an unimagina-tive rapist performing a ridiculous ritual. It could not be otherwise in an age that proclaims God is Dead. Without God the devil is pure camp, and his followers fugitives from a Charles Addams cartoon. (*Confessions of a Cultist,* pp. 374–75)

Another critic who has transcended the "film reviewer" label and gained a widespread following is Pauline Kael, film critic for *The New Yorker* since the mid-1960s. Kael brings to the journalistic approach an encyclopedic knowledge of film along with a lively, strong, colloquial writing style. She is a serious follower of film who sees taste and judgment as the two most impor-tant attributes of the critic; still, she never forgets to whom she is writing. She, like Agee and Ferguson, identifies with the mass film audience. In describing what she believes to be the qualities of a good film critic, she begins by connecting the critic with the audience:

> The role of the critic is to help people see what is in the work, what is in it that shouldn't be, what is not in it that could be. He is a good critic if he helps people understand more about the work than they could see for themselves; he is a great critic, if by his understanding and feeling for the work, by his passion, he can excite people so they want to experience more of the art that is there, waiting to be seized. (*I Lost It at the Movies,* pp. 277–78)

Often Kael identifies so closely with the audience that when she is not using the first person singular to refer to herself, she uses the first person plural. She compares and associates her reactions with the audience's reac-tions. It may be for this reason she seldom goes to press screenings of films. Instead, she sees films along with the audience.

Kael has great knowledge of the film, but she doesn't become a pedant. She insists that film is a mass medium and should be examined as such. When a group of journalist critics were meeting to choose a name for a film society, she argued for the term "movie critic" as opposed to "film critic." During her years as writer for *The New Republic,* she changed "film" in the title of the column to "movie," because the word "film" was, she felt, too pretentious.

No matter what she calls "motion pictures," her criticism follows in the line of her predecessors, yet transcends them as well. As a journalist, she has space limitations, and sees one of her important roles as that of a reviewer, writing about the film in enough detail so that the reader will have a pretty good idea of what it's about. Her reviews include a brief plot summary and the names of the actors and of other principals. However, when she finds a film that captures her imagination, she seems to get the space to deal with it. On the average, her reviews are longer than most journalists' film reviews and go into greater detail concerning a wider range of topics—all related, sometimes loosely, to the specific film she is discussing. She cannot tolerate less than total artistic dedication in filmmaking; she writes as if a poorly made film were a personal insult. In fact, Kael has taken personal criticism beyond even Crowther in presenting an emotionally charged opinion of a film. A review she wrote in the mid-1960s illustrates well her approach. This was one of her most emotional reviews, one that got her replaced as critic for *McCall's* magazine and brought her national notoriety. The review is of two films, *The Sound of Music* (Robert Wise, 1965) and *The Singing Nun* (Henry Koster, 1966). It is written straight from the lip, with more than a trace of anger. She calls the two films "the sugar-coated lie," the audience who sees them the equivalent of "Pavlov's dogs," crying instead of salivating "as the music swells and the focus blurs." She describes the actors as nothing more than animals in a Disney movie. Of Greer Garson's performance in *The Singing Nun* she says, "With her false eyelashes and her richly condescending manner, Greer Garson can turn any line of dialogue into incomparable cant. It's a gift, of a kind" (*Kiss, Kiss, Bang, Bang,* p. 178). To summarize the entire review, she concludes with the reason for her anger—what she believes to be the state of filmmaking in America in the 1960s:

> Why am I so angry about these movies? Because the shoddy falseness of *The Singing Nun* and the luxuriant falseness of *The Sound of Music* are part of the sentimental American tone that makes honest work almost impossible. It is not only that people who accept this kind of movie tend to resent work which says that this is not the best of all possible worlds, but the people who are gifted give up the effort to say anything. They attune themselves to *The Sound of Money*. (*Kiss, Kiss, Bang, Bang,* p. 178)

Kael can also turn wonderful phrases as she pinpoints aspects of movies she either likes or dislikes. In a review of Stanley Kubrick's *Full Metal Jacket* (1987), she praises the depiction of boot-camp horrors but suggests that Kubrick goes too far:

> He's so narrowly geared to the immediate purpose that he fails to establish the characters who will figure later in the film, but he achieves his effect: the process of turning young boys into robots has a sadistic, pounding compulsiveness. The moviemaking suggests a blunt instrument grinding

into your skull. This can be easily taken for the work of a great director. (*The New Yorker,* July 13, 1987, p. 75)

Though a working journalist, Kael betrays her humanist leanings as she goes on to berate Kubrick for not presenting human beings in his film, merely automatons intended to portray his points of view. She says the best character, the most remembered one in any Kubrick film of the last several years, was Hal, the computer in *2001: A Space Odyssey* (1969). Kael's style is conversational, lucid, to the point. The approach is extremely personal, a chance for the critic to communicate her feelings. It fits snugly in the tradition of the journalistic approach. Pauline Kael is the first to defend the approach. With all the film books being written, it is her opinion that "the only ones that are really fun to read are the ones being written by working critics because only the working critics are capable of giving a direct response to the film" (Mount, p. 32).

Stanley Kauffmann, as opposed to Kael, represents the journalistic approach that tries to be objective about the film under discussion, seeking to make clear the strengths and weaknesses of the individual film. A critic since 1958, he has written reviews as a drama critic for educational TV in New York City, worked as a drama critic for the *New York Times,* written novels and plays, and edited and co-edited film anthologies; his collected film criticism has been published in four volumes. At present, Kauffmann is film and drama reviewer for *The New Republic,* Visiting Professor of drama at Yale, and Distinguished Professor of film at the City University of New York, so he is as much an academic as a journalist. Kauffmann writes:

> I discovered film criticism sometime in 1933. Up to then, although I had already been an avid filmgoer for some ten years, it had not occurred to me that films could be discussed in terms relative to those used by good critics of the theater or literature or music. Then one day in my college library I picked up a copy of *The Nation* and read a review by William Troy—I can't recall the title of the film—in which he compared a sequence in a new picture with a similar sequence in a previous one to show relations in style. I'm not sure that my jaw actually dropped, but that's the feeling I remember. (Murry, p. 142)

The quote is instructive. Kauffmann early on saw the potential of film criticism to go beyond the review, to say something more about a film. A journalistic critic can occasionally use a film as an excuse to discuss tangential matters dear to his or her heart. But Kauffmann attempts at all times to keep the film as the main focus of the critical analysis. For an example of this journalistic approach, one need look no further than the latest issue of *The New Republic.* In 1985 Kauffmann examined *Year of the Dragon,* Michael Cimino's first film since the disaster of *Heaven's Gate* in the late 1970s. The critique contains much that is standard in the average review, including a plot summary and names of the main actors and an opening statement that immediately catches our interest—in this case written in the form of a question. "Who will write the book about *Year of the Dragon?*" This reference to the book chronicling the disaster of *Heaven's Gate, Final Cut* (1985) by Stephen Bach, presumes a literate reader, one aware of recent events in film and literary activity. Immediately we are aware of Kauffmann's point of view concerning the film. Then, with allusions to other films sure to be familiar to intelligent moviegoers, he uses the center of the review to explain why, based on specific and numerous examples from the film, he so dislikes it:

> On one hand, the film is crammed with clichés. On the other, it's crammed with incredible novelty. Cliché: the picture starts with a Chinese New Year's Day celebration, putting such emphasis on the firecrackers that we know the parade is going to be used as a cover for a killing. White (a detective) has marital troubles—he neglects his wife for his job—of so cinematically stale a kind that we wonder how the actors can find the steam to speak the lines. Analogously stale are the quarrels in the police commissioner's office. Sometimes the very words themselves are so trite that we almost gasp. During a lover's quarrel: "Give you an inch and you take a mile." Incredible novelty: the young boss of the Chinatown mafia makes a trip to Thailand and presents the chief of the heroin source with the head of a mafia rival. (I mean, Sam Peckinpah fans, the *head*.) A Chinese gun moll, fleeing the cops, runs into the middle of the street and is buffeted on one side, then the other by passing cabs. Forget the fact that no street in Chinatown has two-way traffic: Wouldn't at least one of the drivers have stopped? The woman newscaster is angry at White when he comes to the studio; she doesn't want to speak to him. Why is she angry? Because she is involved with him, three Chinese men broke into her apartment the day before and raped her. Well, say, that would make any woman angry. The final shoot-out between White and the mafia boss ends with White's victory, after which he hands his gun to the supine boss, risking his own life, so that the Chinese can commit suicide. (A suggestion here of Yojimbo gallantry. Can White have seen that film?)
>
> Loose ends dangle in both plot and theme. Plot: an elderly Chinese forces his way into a Polish funeral, kneels at the coffin, and crosses himself. Who is he? A white man suddenly appears in the mafia boss's retinue to warn him that his office is bugged. Who was that white man? Theme: White blasts loudly at U.S. corruption by TV; the subject is then dropped. Vietnam bitterness—whether pro- or anti-Rambo is not quite clear—is randomly raised and also dropped. (White is a Vietnam veteran.) The need to understand Chinese cultural complexities—White has an armful of books at the start—is raised too, and dropped for the usual fists-and-firearms formula.
>
> In short, which is the wrong term for a picture that runs over two hours, *Year of the Dragon* is a mess. (*The New Republic,* September 16 and 23, 1985, pp. 33–34)

The analysis has the familiar structure of the journalistic approach:

highly readable and lively style, personal comment, and a strong sense of the reader being in the capable hands of someone who knows and understands film. Kauffmann also supports his generalities about the film with specific examples. That strategy is central to his best reviews.

These reviewer/critics, and others who make their living from their written responses to the film, value the English language as much as they do the visual image. They are writers as well as film critics and it shows in their work. Indeed, their reviewing is a kind of literature—the witty and personal critical essay—which can be read for its own sake. At its worst, such writing is so self-centered that it leaves its subject—film—far behind its own devices and, on occasion, it may seem that a film has merely been a pretext for personal exploration. But at its best, the personal response of a skilled writer who is able to share the quest for insight into the film medium adds to the meaning of the work and provides the reader/viewer with food for thought.

TELEVISION FILM REVIEWING

The writings of James Agee, Bosley Crowther, and Pauline Kael provide the reader with examples of the journalistic approach in a highly personal mode. But film reviewing of the 1980s has become more personal yet. *Siskel and Ebert: The Movies,* with Gene Siskel of the *Chicago Tribune* and Roger Ebert of the *Chicago Sun Times,* brings journalistic film criticism to television. These critics provide the ultimate in personal film reviewing

Beginning on public television in the late 1970s as *Sneak Previews,* the program featuring these two critics, one tall and slim, the other short and round—a Laurel and Hardy imitation—provided a forum for discussing and arguing about several recently released movies each week. The format proved to be so popular that in the early 1980s the program was moved to syndicated commercial television while public television kept the title *Sneak Previews* with two new reviewers.

Following in the footsteps of other television critics, such as Gene Shalit of the *Today* program, Siskel and Ebert preview film clips of recently released films and then discuss their strengths and weaknesses. The main difference between *Siskel and Ebert: The Movies* and reviews on other television programs is the time allotted to the reviews. Where Shalit is given approximately five minutes for a reviewing segment, Siskel and Ebert have a half-hour each week. But otherwise the format, with a few exceptions, is the same. Occasionally *Siskel and Ebert: The Movies* will spend a complete program on a single topic such as "Violence in the Movies" or "The Films of Woody Allen," but normally the program previews recently released films each week.

The program's set is made to resemble a movie theater's balcony, with the two critics seated side by side in plush theater seats. At the beginning of each program, there are short clips of the films to be previewed, followed by brief plot summaries by the two critics. Then each film is reviewed in more depth, with Siskel and Ebert taking turns introducing the films. After each film is reviewed, the critics give the films a "yes"—a thumbs-up—or "no"—a thumbs-down—vote. At the end of each program, the critics' votes and their overall opinions of the films are summarized.

The September 21, 1985, edition of the program is a representative example of the journalistic approach as it has been adapted to television. One of the four films reviewed during this program was *Godzilla 1985.* The segment began with Ebert introducing the film, calling it "the sequel that took thirty years to make." Then Siskel took over, noting that he had been "really looking forward" to seeing the film because of his enjoyment of the original *Godzilla,* but found the sequel to be "dumb." At this point, Siskel introduced the clip of the film that included the following lines spoken by Raymond Burr as a Godzilla hunter: "He's [Godzilla] looking for something, searching. If only we can figure out what it is before it's too late." At this point, the clip ended, the lights came on, and for the next five minutes, Siskel and Ebert, in a give-and-take dialogue, reviewed the film. Here is a partial transcript of that review:

> Siskel: (referring back to Burr's line) I was looking for something too. Something with a little bit of fun. That isn't funny. He's just standing there like a stiff. This isn't a mummy picture, you know.
>
> Ebert: Ha, ha, ha.
>
> Siskel: . . . That shot of Godzilla standing in the water—I mean kids with GoBots could have more fun in their bathtubs than that. . . .
>
> Ebert: You're right. You're right. I was waiting for something to happen. . . .
>
> Siskel: You know what this film made me respect, because this one stinks so badly? The remake of *King Kong.* . . .
>
> Ebert: This movie is so bad it made me respect *Inferno Man* and *Invasion of the B Girls.* [This comment was followed by Ebert attempting to discuss the film's failure to accurately portray "the infinite variability of Godzilla's size." Siskel interrupted him with a summary comment: "I think what you're trying to say is this movie stinks."]
>
> Ebert: I don't know what I'm trying to say—this movie stunk; that's what I'm trying to say.

At this point, the reviewers moved on to the next film, the second of four that evening. Though often entertaining, the journalistic approach as practiced on television sometimes seems as shallow as the average review in a daily newspaper: simply the unsupported opinions of the reviewers about a recent film. But it does have its purposes. For one thing, it exposes a vast audience to the fact that reviews of films are available and valuable (surveys have shown that the vast number of moviegoers seldom read *any* reviews before going to the theater). In other words, television critics attempt to raise the audience's standards of critical judgment, suggesting by example that films should not be taken for granted. Despite its current mode of presentation, one can visualize the potential of serious television criticism, with the possibility of using freeze frames, of rerunning a sequence, or of illustrating the points being made with specific film clips. The kind of in-depth analysis provided by reviewer/critics in some weekly and monthly publications might be transferable to the TV screen if the right mix of format and personality were found.

THE JOURNALISTIC APPROACH
IN FAN MAGAZINES, BUFF BIOGRAPHIES,
AND COFFEE TABLE BOOKS

If it is true that any working journalist can write film reviews for a periodical, then it is also true that the same ability can be extended to the creation of longer works. Indeed, many of the well-known reviewers have published collections of their works. Some, like Bosley Crowther, also authored full-length works on aspects of film and the film industry, including *The Lion's Share: The Story of an Entertainment Empire* (1967) about MGM and *Hollywood Rajah: The Life and Times of Louis B. Mayer* (1960). From the 1920s to the present, the mass audience has had a nearly insatiable curiosity about Hollywood and the figures who populated the "dream factory." Journalists have responded by turning out millions of pages of print to satisfy that interest.

The fan magazines, once available everywhere and known to all, like *Photoplay,* were an offshoot of the star system. The public's desire to know what Rudolph Valentino was really like, who was dating Clara Bow, what Douglas Fairbanks liked for dinner, and all the other details of the stars' private lives, kept the studio publicity departments churning out material, most of it exaggerated, much actually fabricated, to fill the pages of the fan magazines and the gossip columns of daily newspapers. With the demise of the studio system, in the 1960s, the public turned elsewhere for its folk heroes, and found them on television. Nevertheless, even today gossip columns and exploitation papers like the *Star* and the *Enquirer* sell copies by featuring lurid and sensational stories about the current crop of movie and television personalities. Accuracy in reporting is not a hallmark of these publications. Nevertheless, one can get a sense of the power that the movie stars once had over the general public by reading back issues of these magazines.

The wish to know something about Hollywood's luminaries continues, of course, and journalists have responded by writing books about the "life and times" of actors, actresses, directors, and producers. Many of these biographies are not well researched and merely reprint all the anecdotes that have circulated orally for years about famous people. Chatty, lively, sometimes sensational—*Mommy, Dearest* (1978), the book about Joan Crawford written by her adopted daughter, revealed a rather perverse family life—such books should be approached as entertainment, with possible value to students but having little in common with criticism. One of the ways to spot a "buff biography"—that is, one intended for consumption by film fans and nostalgia buffs—is that it will probably not have footnotes to document the sources of information about the personality. Another way to detect the spurious from the serious is to be aware that the more accurate investigations of the lives of film people will spend more time analyzing the work produced by the individual than presenting anecdotal material.

Although nearly all books pertaining to film subjects are illustrated by photographs—either publicity stills made during production by a photographer on the set or frame enlargements from the actual release prints of films—some works seem to be all pictures and very little text. These books are often luxuriously bound, sometimes oversize, printed on high-quality paper, and crafted with excellent graphics. "Coffee table books," as they are commonly called because they are purchased primarily for decorative purposes, to be placed on the coffee or end table in the living room to impress guests, seldom contain much in the way of analysis that is of value for the person seriously interested in film.

But coffee table books, like fan magazines and buff biographies, reflect the enormous interest that the general public has in the movies. Sometimes, indeed, the copious photos used to illustrate these books may have been found in some film archive, thus revealing for the first time little-known aspects of the early days of filmmaking or giving a rare view of a forgotten chapter in film history. Though the perceptive reader may have to corroborate the facts through other sources, many of these publications do attempt to be accurate about names, dates, and other matters of record. Thus they cannot be entirely dismissed; they should, however, be read with an awareness of what their function is in regard to the presentation of information of a certain kind to the mass audience.

CURRENT REVIEWS AS EXAMPLES
OF THE JOURNALISTIC APPROACH

Undoubtedly the prime function of the journalistic approach in the public media is to provide the prospective filmgoer with enough information to make an intelligent guess about whether or not the film is worth seeing. But tastes do vary from individual to individual. Bosley Crowther and John Simon hated *Bonnie and Clyde* (1967); Pauline Kael loved it. If you had read these reviews, how would you have made up your mind? In one sense, a reviewer cannot tell you what you will like or won't like. The only thing to do is to see the film for yourself. But in all practicality, no one can see all of the new releases. Thus reviews can serve a useful role in helping the moviegoing public decide what to see and what not to see.

Perhaps the best strategy for a student of film criticism is to get copies of all the major publications' reviews of a particular film before seeing it. Read what *Time* has to say about it, *The New Yorker, The Village Voice,* the *New York Times, Newsweek, Playboy, Harper's, The New Republic, American Film,* and your local newspaper. Then see the film. Then ask the question: Of the reviews you read, which would most closely approximate what you would have said if you had written the review? Perhaps the writer of that review has tastes most similar to your own. Of course, there will be times when you and your favorite reviewer disagree, but there may be enough consistency to make Kael or Sarris or Kauffmann your touchstone journalist critic. From this knowledge you can begin to understand your own strengths and weaknesses when using this approach.

THE INGREDIENTS OF A GOOD REVIEW

It all depends on what the reader wants from the review. Clearly, the review should let the reader know what the film is about, whether it is a mystery or a romance, a comedy or a soap opera, without boring the reader with a recitation of the plot or giving away the ending if that is an important part of the film. The reader probably wants to know who made the film and who's in it, because such information may help in deciding whether to see the film. We all have our personal favorites. And then there should be some judgment about the film's value—the liking or the disliking of it, the feelings aroused by it, whether it was entertaining or not—supported by some specific details from the film. This is the information a prospective filmgoer requires in order to make a sensible decision. A good review need do no more than to fulfill its practical function.

On the other hand, some people enjoy reading reviews for the reviewer's style, just as some viewers may watch Ebert and Siskel for the fun of it, to be entertained; they are not primarily looking for a guide to filmgoing. The best-known reviewer/critics tend to write idiosyncratically, and because they are interesting people, their essays are usually fun to read as well as illuminating. As mentioned earlier in this chapter, John Simon is noted for his acid prose and his general disdain for most films, especially those made in the United States. Andrew Sarris's style is often epigrammatic and alliterative. Pauline Kael, on the other hand, displays a gutsy, streetwise, and highly passionate response to movies.

SUMMARY

By its very nature and function, the journalistic approach, no matter how brilliant, can seldom go beyond a personal and immediate response to a film, based mainly on the writer's individual tastes and background. The work is made convincing by the writer's ability to use the language with wit and style, and to treat the reader like a close friend, who will not be too demanding when it comes to asking for proof of the points being presented. The appeal is always from one person's experience to another's, seeking similarities of taste. "Are your feelings and judgments about the film like mine?" the reader, in effect, asks the reviewer. It is the personal quality that sometimes puts off film students and scholars seeking logic and intellectual rigor in criticism.

Certainly much journalistic writing on film contains simplistic, uninformed, mindless responses typified by "I don't know much about film, but I know what I like." In the process of writing, however, those raw responses of likes and dislikes are often transformed into something more: the heartfelt expression of a community's value system, frequently revealing a consensus about the matters under discussion.

It is clear that the journalistic approach has produced some of the most stimulating writing on film ever written, beginning with the forward-thinking critics of film's infancy and continuing into the present. Today's journalistic critics are readable, knowledgeable, and perceptive. They follow in the footsteps of writers like Otis Ferguson and James Agee, who pioneered the form and style that has been copied from the 1930s to our own day. But in the last analysis, the best of the journalistic critics are not copies—they're originals, each with his or her own style and own eccentricity, but all with the ability to bring freshness, immediacy, and vitality to their analysis of movies.

GUIDELINES FOR WRITING JOURNALISTIC FILM CRITICISM

I. Sources
  A. Primary
  See the film during its initial run, before anyone else can influence your opinion about it. Don't read the publicity hype and avoid negative or positive discussions of the film with friends. View it from a fresh, firsthand perspective. Avoid reading professional reviews of the film until after you've written yours.
  B. Secondary
  See films that are competing with the film you are reviewing, to determine how it compares to other recent releases. Examine other films (on videotape) with similar plots or themes, the same actors or directors to give you deeper understanding of the film's status as member of a genre. Study a variety of film reviews from both male and female reviewers. The reviewers suggested in this chapter would be a good place to start. Also, read reviews in your daily and school newspapers.

II. Method
  Take detailed, accurate notes while viewing the film. Develop your journalistic style by attempting to copy the styles of some of the critics discussed in this chapter. Practice writing confident prose that speaks personally to your reader. Avoid phrases like "it seems to me," "I believe," and "I think." Have fun with your style and with the film being reviewed. Visiting with members of the journalism department of your school or talking with local newspaper film

reviewers to get their insights into the craft of film journalism may prove helpful.

III. **Questions a Writer Using the Journalistic Approach Might Ask**
   1. Who are the actors and what roles do they play in the film?
   2. Who made the film: production company, producer, director, writer, director of cinematography? Have I seen other works by these people? Is it pertinent to mention them?
   3. Do I like the film? Why? Why not?
   4. Have I been fair with the film after only one viewing, or should I see the film a second time to see what I might have missed?
   5. What bias might I have toward the film's star, director, subject matter?
   6. Have I been as objective as possible? used examples to support my views? been prejudiced by my dislike of the film's theme or plot? described the film accurately?

CHAPTER 2

The Humanist Approach: Traditional Aesthetic Responses to the Movies

Even if the movies are produced with machines and are a business subject to corporate and financial pressures, they are also, inevitably, a human enterprise, and it is by their human relevance that they must, in the end, prove their worthiness. (Robinson, p. 9)

Humanist Approach Capsule

Audience: General cultured reader presumed to have seen the film or films under discussion; the intelligentsia who accept film as one of the fine arts.

Functions: Provide in-depth discussion of a particular film's appeal to the intelligent filmgoer; interpret motifs and symbols in difficult films; evaluate films and filmmakers on traditional aesthetic principles.

Subjects: Individual films both recent and classic; filmmakers; genres; trends; the relation of film to contemporary cultural concerns.

Writers: Generalists with experience in literary, philosophical, and fine arts criticism; freelance writers; academics from disciplines other than film; and film scholars writing to the general cultured public.

Publications: High-culture humanities and arts journals like *Critical Inquiry;* Sunday supplements of major newspapers; trade books for the general reader; scholarly books from university presses.

One of the aims of this book is to isolate and identify a set of assumptions, activities, adherents, and audiences that distinguish one critical approach from another. Journalists writing reviews of recent films seem to satisfy this expectation reasonably well. So do professors of film studies writing books about some aspect of film—genres, auteur studies, film history—for other film professors. There are, however, a large number of writers on film who do not neatly fit one of the more specific approaches discussed in later chapters. Generalists rather than specialists, they may be academics in disciplines other than film, professional freelancers who write on speculation, journalists working for a particular publication who have the time and inclination to do more than simply review the latest releases, or students assigned to write a term paper in a film study class. Their reasons for writing criticism vary with the occasion. Intrigued by an experience of seeing films, old or new, silent or sound, American or foreign, or the experience of picking up and reading a book of film criticism, some may simply want to share a discovery, a feeling, a response about some film topic with a wider audience. Others make their living writing, but are free enough from the pressures of a daily deadline to choose topics that interest them. This kind of criticism ranges from very personal and subjective musings to objective and concrete analyses. What unites this group, varied as are the motivations for writing and the subjects undertaken, are two implicit assumptions: (1) that movies are more than simple entertainment and deserve a backward glance, some extra thought, some writing about, in order for us to understand the experience of filmgoing more thoroughly and (2) that since movies are about human experiences, any human who has some interest in intellectual matters in general can write intelligently about the experience of the movies. We call this general way of dealing with film criticism the *humanist* approach. It covers a spectrum from elaborate and well-thought-out reviews in sophisticated magazines like *The New Yorker* and *The New Republic* to complex books like *The World Viewed* by Stanley Cavell (1971), the phenomenological film theory of a practicing philosopher. This approach is called *humanist* because it sees film as an art like other arts, and film criticism as a general human activity practiced by the educated, cultured person. Like the classical humanism of the Renaissance, it asserts the dignity and worth of individuals and the capacity for self-realization through the application of reason to the variety of human endeavors.

Thus the humanist approach to film attempts to make sense of the individual's emotional and intellectual experience of a film (it always begins with that personal encounter with the work), to draw conclusions about the value of that experience, and then to communicate that value to others. Seeing in film the same potential for art that countless generations have traditionally found in painting, music, and literature, the kind that lifts the human spirit and stimulates the human mind, the humanist film critic looks for similar experiences in the movies. What can movies tell us about the human condition? How do they reflect current intellectual interests in politics, religion, history, philosophy, or art? What kinds of ideas are hidden beneath the surface of a film? How shall we interpret the symbols? How do form and content interact to convey the filmmaker's meaning? Is there an artist behind the creation of a film? What relations are there between this film or this kind of film and the world outside the theater? How shall we rank the quality of this film compared to some ideal excellence compared to the best that has been produced in the past? The questions are familiar. They are the same ones asked of any art form. They are not specific to film, but specific to aesthetic inquiry in general.

Because of the widespread interest in film criticism displayed by people from a variety of fields, the humanist approach presupposes that writer and reader have a certain familiarity with the general principles of aesthetic inquiry that have been articulated by Western culture from the time of the Greeks to the present. Film is simply assumed to be of the same order as other art forms and, therefore, subject to similar investigation. This was not always the case, of course, because traditional definitions of art imply a high moral purpose and a complex aesthetic scheme. In short, art has always been defined as something qualitatively different from entertainment, and, as we shall see in the historical discussion of this approach, most commentators, at least in America, saw movies as nothing more than entertainment until after World War II.

W. R. Robinson, writing in the 1960s, examplifies the change of view that had taken place and that still characterizes the way the intellectual community looks at film today. He justifies critical inquiry of movies by suggesting they make the same appeal to the spectator as do the other arts, an assertion which also implies that the spectator is a cultured individual familiar with such appeals. He states that a movie engages the viewer in a moral and aesthetic dialogue that demands some sort of response, even if only to decide whether the movie was worth attending:

> In short, everyone instinctively recognizes that a movie—all art, in fact—invites him to exercise his taste in making a value judgment. He senses that a value assertion has been made and that a reply is demanded of him. And except for the most diffident, everybody also senses that he is qualified to reply. (p. 119)

Surely everyone seeing a film will make that first value judgment, even if it is only based on immediate emotional grounds; the humanist simply goes further, probing more deeply those initial responses, recognizing the potential for moral and aesthetic interchange. The humanist is largely self-defined, perhaps simply a person who takes an interest in the subject at hand—here, film. A general knowledge of literature, drama, and the fine arts is useful to relate the film experience to other art experiences. For the humanist, critical inquiry, intellectual curiosity, and logical analysis of all aspects of experience are habitual responses to life. Looking closely at the movie experience and trying to discern there the mark of human excellence is no different from looking closely at the experience of reading novels, viewing paintings, or listening to music. The humanist seeks to understand human nature and humankind's place in the scheme of things, asking the traditional questions— who are we and what is life all about? And as Robert Richardson points out, the answers may be found in movies:

Perhaps man is no longer the measure of all things, but man remains the measure of the world on film. The films of Jean Renoir, for example, show just this emphasis on the desirability of being human; it is the main theme of *The Grand Illusion* and of other films. *La Strada,* revolving around three people whom psychology would call abnormal, nevertheless manages to find and then insist on humanness in the animal Zampano, in the half-wit Gelsomina, and in the Fool. The film has the pace and power of a Greek tragedy; its theme, like that of Sophocles's *Ajax,* might be said to be an examination of what it is to be human. (pp. 128–29)

The humanist looks for representations in film of general human values, the truths of human experience as they relate to the common and universal aspects of existence—birth, death, love, aggression, happiness, sorrow— seeking the answer to the question "What is there in this film or in my experience of it that will help me understand the variety and complexity of the human heart and mind?" Finding out more about a particular film, a genre, a director's concerns and interests, or the influences of society on the production of the movies makes the moviegoing experience more meaningful. The alchemy of the mind enlarges and expands the merely physical and emotional sensation of watching shadows in the dark.

It should be mentioned here that the very broadness and generalness of the humanist approach, the emphasis on an individual's intuitive insight and sensitive interpretation of a film, is also its major weakness. Though possibly leading to enrichment of the movie experience for those who read the criticism and then go back to a film and see it in a new light, the humanist method is often criticized for its lack of intellectual rigor and for its theoretically unfounded, unscientific, and sentimental assertions. Many feel it is not a method at all, not an approach, but simply elevated taste, only as good as the sensibility of the critic, only as convincing as the rhetoric of the prose. The approach raises problems for those who see the aim of criticism as the creation of an orderly, systematic body of knowledge about a subject aimed at achieving consensus of all informed participants. After all, one can always disagree with someone's attempts to justify an intuitive vision of what such-and-such a film "really meant," or what makes a film "great," by simply saying, "It didn't strike me that way at all." Truly objective criteria upon which to base such claims are not part of the humanist approach.

Nevertheless, when an article or a book makes intelligent sense, when we read someone's thoughts and feelings about a particular film, and the spark of recognition occurs—"Oh, sure, now I see. I was thinking it had to be something like that, but this says it all. Hits the nail right on the head!"—we feel the force of agreement. And despite the claims of the more methodical approaches, perhaps that's all we can ask for in the world of the arts, in which human experience is the primary area of activity. Physics may be able to argue for a certain kind of objective quality in the aspects of the world that it assesses, but the perception of a film seems likely always to have some subjective element to it. And here, perhaps, is where the humanist may be right in more ways than other, more specialized writers of film criticism.

HISTORY OF FILM WRITING
FOR CULTURED AUDIENCES

By the time the movies became a reality, at the end of the nineteenth century, the intellectual community had clearly demarked the difference between highbrow art and lowbrow art, between artworks seriously aimed at discerning audiences and those aimed at the unwashed masses. Movies were popular entertainment similar in form and function to dime novels, circuses, and the music hall, and thus not worth either experiencing or commenting upon. Nevertheless, over the years, there appeared a few cultured individuals who found in the movies something of human relevance for the discerning mind.

Vachel Lindsay, an American poet, wrote a book-length study, *The Art of the Moving Picture*, in 1915, in which he attempted to distinguish the properties of film from those of other arts and to synthesize the properties of other arts within the one art of cinema. In the following year, Hugo Münsterberg, an eminent psychologist on the faculty of Harvard, explored the psychological relationship between the film viewer and the screen image in his book *The Photoplay: A Psychological Study*. Writing at the very beginning of the history of the motion picture, Münsterberg was aware of the way early films recorded the activities of the world in front of the camera, providing an educational or instructional function. But he makes a great case for the position that the motion picture's greatest strength lies in its ability to portray human emotions. "To picture emotions must be the central aim of the photoplay" (p. 48). He also goes on to suggest that, as in some of the other arts, the representation of the human mind in the film necessarily raises moral issues. For him the film narrative presents the opportunity for making moral judgments, both on the part of the filmmaker and of the audience. The truth of the representation must be tested against the truth of the viewer's own experience of the world. Though, in one sense, these early books by a poet and a psychologist might be classed as works of film theory, rather than evaluations of specific films, they were both written by cultured individuals who were not primarily film scholars or critics. And in both cases they were impelled to argue in the face of continued neglect by the intellectual community that cinema deserved a place alongside the time-honored arts.

For the most part, their rhetoric failed to convince their peers—at least in America. In Europe, on the other hand, intellectuals had been attracted to filmmaking from the birth of the medium. (France, for example, had initiated the extensive filming of classic stage plays and novels well before the First World War.) So it is not surprising that all over Europe—in Paris, Berlin, Moscow—during the 1920s, intellectuals and artists devoted to all aspects of the arts gathered and talked and wrote about the movies as the equivalent of the other arts. Between the world wars in America, however, intellectuals scarcely noted the existence of the medium. There were, of course, some thoughtful reviews of specific films in major periodicals by critics more commonly given to writing about high-class literature. Edmund Wilson, Aldous Huxley, and Robert E. Sherwood were a few who occasionally did not condescend when writing about current films in the 1920s and 1930s.

Other reviewers who wrote regularly about specific films from the 1930s through the 1950s, in magazines intended for a cultured readership, who accepted films as worthy of intellectual scrutiny, included Harry Alan Potamkin, Otis Ferguson, Robert Warshow, and James Agee. These writers, though clearly identifiable under the title of "reviewers"—they all wrote about current films in periodicals—also wrote what can be considered humanist criticism, since their perceptions of film include thoughtful references to contemporary concepts about psychology, sociology, politics, and aesthetics generally understood by a cultured audience. They did not simply give the plot of the film and say whether they liked it or not, but went further in trying to relate their experiences of individual films to the intellectual concerns of the day.

Robert Warshow, for example, in his 1954 essay on the "The Westerner," the hero of western movies, discusses not simply a number of movies, but the American fascination with violence. He compares two movie incarnations of that fascination—the gangster and the cowboy gunfighter—in great detail, but always in the context of what was then, as now, a great concern about the nature of American culture. Just what is this fascination we have with the gun and the use of force to gain our ends? Thus his movie criticism goes beyond simply reviewing films or identifying the characteristics of a genre figure. He suggests that the educated observer of the time automatically abhorred the images of violence found in popular literature, television, and film and, by avoiding an examination of the problem, allowed the producers of these media free rein. "The celebration of acts of violence is left more and more to the irresponsible: on the higher cultural levels to writers like Celine, and lower down to Mickey Spillane or Horace McCoy, or to the comic books, television, and the movies" (p. 152). Warshow makes an appeal for closer scrutiny by the humanist of the artifacts of the age.

Nevertheless, the intellectual community as a whole did not make film one of its concerns until after World War II. In part because of the pressure of returning veterans, some of whom had seen non-Hollywood films while stationed abroad, and in part because of an increase in experimental and avant-garde filmmaking by members of the art community who were situated in academic departments, film societies sprang up on college campuses all over the country. In addition to providing inexpensive entertainment to students making do on the G.I. Bill, the film societies introduced Americans to foreign films, films that attempted to treat postwar problems realistically and to present life as it was lived and not as it was depicted in most Hollywood films, glamorized and dramatized in the well-known and predictable genres. The film societies also filled out their programs with silent films from all countries, thereby suggesting the existence of a body of work, a history of classic films, whose value was sufficient to pass the test of time. They had been preserved because they had enduring aesthetic and moral values; they were worth viewing because those values were still relevant. The experience of watching old movies not for their camp appeal but for honest intellectual satisfaction invited more organization. Soon this random exposure to the classics of world cinema became codified into college courses.

By the late 1950s and early 1960s, a large number of college-educated Americans had come to realize that movies existed that were not simply escapist entertainment but that held possibilities for human enrichment similar to the other, more traditional arts of drama, dance, painting, and literature. The early films of Ingmar Bergman (*The Seventh Seal,* 1956) and Federico Fellini (*La Strada,* 1954) were the first to be reviewed and praised by highbrow critics in prestigious journals. The first films of the French New Wave—François Truffaut's *The Four Hundred Blows,* Jean-Luc Godard's *Breathless,* and Alain Resnais's *Hiroshima, Mon Amour*—won prizes at Cannes in 1959. Anyone who claimed to be an intellectual, a cultured individual who was aware of the trends in contemporary life, had to see these films. They were the talk of the town and the campus. Hollywood films were fit for the lowbrow, the average, run-of-the-mill person, but these foreign films were deemed high-class art. A circuit of movie houses appeared that featured such films; they were distributed all over the country. The popcorn, candy, and soda pop counters were abandoned for espresso machines and natural foods. People came not to forget their cares, but to think about the difficulties and problems of living in the nuclear age. And a lively and informed criticism of these films began to appear in print. From the 1960s to the present, intellectual magazines like *Harper's* and *Atlantic Monthly* have carried articles on film. New journals aimed at the cultured reader/filmgoer like *Film Comment* and *American Film* were formed. Older established academic quarterlies like *The Yale Review* and *Critical Inquiry* published essays on cinema. Several universities sponsored new journals devoted to a wide-ranging film criticism, like *Literature/Film Quarterly* and *Postscript.* Thousands of highly literate books by writers from a wide variety of disciplines were published as the intellectual community sought to map out this new area of human study. In 1969 W. R. Robinson, a professor of English, titled his collection of essays written by poets, novelists, script writers, and academics who were not primarily teachers of film, *Man and the Movies.* Covering a wide range of film subjects and personal views, the articles are connected by the notion that film matters deeply to anyone who is involved with contemporary ideas. T. J. Ross's anthology *Film and the Liberal Arts* (1970) also brought together a diversity of cogent essays on a variety of film topics from many disciplines.

During the late 1970s and into the 1980s, as film studies in the academic world became more specialized, evolving on many campuses into doctorate-granting departments, fewer writers from other disciplines felt comfortable about making the crossover. Yet the humanist approach is still alive and well anywhere and any time the generalist decides to analyze the movies. Vincent Canby, Charles Champlin, and Pauline Kael, nominally reviewers, often write lengthy essays for their publications which discuss current films, directors, and trends. Nonspecialized intellectual journals like *The New York Review of Books, Partisan Review,* and *Critical Inquiry* run articles on film subjects. *American Film* and *Film Comment,* though dealing entirely with film, accept articles by nonspecialists. And, in any given year, books on film written by people in literature, philosophy, or history make their way to the public.

And one cannot forget the thriving interest in humanist film criticism registered by the countless numbers of students in general introductory film classes who write papers. For the most part, these students are generalists, who are familiar with the terms of humanist inquiry. Their speculations and intuitions about film topics, as any film teacher can attest, are often as eye-opening and enlightening as any professional's. Film criticism of this sort is truly democratic. All students should be encouraged to realize they might, upon some careful reflection, come up with something very original and very good.

COMMUNICATING REFLECTIONS ABOUT FILMS ALREADY VIEWED

One of the distinguishing features of humanistic writing about film is the assumption that the reader has seen the film or films under discussion. Even if it appears in a monthly magazine, the article's primary function is not to guide people to see or not to see the film, but rather to comment on an event that writer and readers have shared. Presumably, then, the film chosen is one judged to have some lasting value. Either it has been around for a while—it is an older classic that is shown frequently in revival theaters or in film classes—or, if it is a new film, the writer is hazarding a guess that it will be around in the future. There is the implicit assumption that the writer has seen the film several times, that the judgments and analysis are not vaguely recalled from a single viewing, and that the reader may verify the claims made by the writer by seeing the film again—that is, the reader may disagree with the writer and can return to see the film and, if inclined to do so, offer a rebuttal. In short, there is the assumption that the reader and the writer have a common body of experience and knowledge within which the discussion can take place. Both reader and writer usually take the subject of discussion seriously.

What Robin Wood wrote about Alfred Hitchcock's *Psycho* (1960) in a book in 1967 implied that the film would be seen again and again, not only because it was a Hitchcock film but because it is "one of the key works of our age. Its themes are not new—obvious forerunners include *Macbeth* and Conrad's *Heart of Darkness*—but the intensity and horror of their treatment place them in an age that has witnessed both the discoveries of Freud and the Nazi concentration camps." (p. 113) Wood sees in the film a restatement of a modern cliché: all people have a dark and violent unconscious part of their being. But he suggests that *Psycho* forces us to feel the reality of that statement, not just to understand it. He says that the end of the film cannot

> remove our sense of complicity. We have been led to accept Norman Bates as a potential extension of ourselves. That we all carry within us somewhere every human potentiality for good or evil, so that we all share in a common guilt, may be, intellectually, a truism; the greatness of *Psycho* lies in its ability, not merely to *tell* us this, but to make us experience it. (p. 112)

It is clear that Wood is serious about this film and he expects his readers to be also. And since *Psycho* is still a popular and oft-reseen film today, this analysis of the film written in the 1960s is still relevant reading for a richer understanding of its complexities.

One can also point out that writing serious, in-depth criticism about particular films suggests that the films are more difficult than other films—that they, in fact, need interpretation. Like other forms of modern literature, the films that attract intellectual inquiry appear to hide their deeper meanings, to be puzzling to the casual viewer who needs the guidance of a critic to help in the discovery of the truths lying beneath the surface. In a certain sense, then, the films chosen for analysis are self-selecting: they make use of symbolism; they work by analogy and allegory. The easy pleasures of thrills, chills, and laughter provided by Hollywood genre films, evident to even a child viewer, may not need a gloss, but films about existential characters lost in the maze of the modern urban environment, unable to find hope and comfort in traditional religious verities, frequently cry out for interpretation.

Ingmar Bergman's films, of course, have always struck most viewers as films with deeper, hidden meanings that need interpretation, and humanist critics have spent a lot of time unweaving the threads of his discourse. *The Seventh Seal*—a story set during the Middle Ages in the time of the plague, in which Death appears as a character—is hard to understand unless one sees it as an allegory. Michael Pressler, in an article in *Literature/Film Quarterly,* describes one way of interpreting the actions of Block, the knight, and Jons, his squire, as they move through the landscape of the plague-blasted world:

> For Block, Death first appears on the beach—suddenly and fittingly—as an allegorical personification, standing slightly atilt, like a black post, a suitable opponent for a game of chess. For Jons, Death's appearance is characteristically material, arising from an unexpected encounter with the rotting corpse of a plague victim—a figure which the squire would of course find "most eloquent." Similarly, the knight's troubled matins are set against the squire's own brand of morning service, a bawdy song. The antithesis of the two characters, reflecting the early Christian debate between the soul and the body, develops in the course of the screenplay into a full-scale moral dialogue and provides it with its major structural motif. (p. 98)

Curiously enough, once the intellectual community took up the complex, subtle, and obtuse films of European and Asian filmmakers flooding our shores in the 1950s and 1960s, they also, through the writings of French critics (see Chapter 3), learned that Hollywood films might have deeper hidden meanings, too, that John Ford films might be more than just good westerns. Analysis of a character's movements, gestures, and activities, lighting schemes, graphic composition, and consistent narrative situations often resulted in the uncovering of underlying motifs in American films. The writer Brandon French shows how a tiny action, easily overlooked by the casual viewer, can reflect the major theme of a film. *Sunset Boulevard* (Billy Wilder, 1950) is about a young would-be screenwriter in Hollywood who becomes involved with an aging actress from the silent film days who is hoping to make a comeback. The two of them grow to live off each other's fantasies. Joe tries desperately to shake off her influence, but fails. Living in her house, on her money, doing whatever she tells him, he has lost his self-respect. At a bizarre New Year's Eve party in the grand ballroom of the old mansion where Norma Desmond has secreted herself all these years, Joe is so humiliated that he breaks away from Norma and heads for the door. He's going to see Betty, a girl of his own age whom he has met earlier in the film. "And as Joe tries to leave the house a moment later, the golden watch chain Norma bought for him catches on the door handle, symbolically suggesting the umbilical dependence Joe has on Norma as her kept man and the guilt that makes leaving her impossible" (p. 9). Thus humanist interpretation skills, close reading of the filmic text, often learned through literary study, can be applied to any film, old or new, American or foreign.

MORAL AND PHILOSOPHICAL VALUES

Traditional humanist criticism, formulated over the centuries in the West, has assumed that there are universal truths about life that the inquiring mind—the fine light of reason—can discover intuitively. Close reading of texts and rational observation of life can yield access to such truths. The questions that humankind asks are universal: Who am I? Why am I here? What gives meaning to life? What is the good life? Each generation seeks new formulations of the questions in response to the changing conditions of history. Answers that satisfy everyone for all time are never found, so the questions must be rethought over and over again. Assertions are made, of course, but the pronouncements of the past are always open to argument and discussion. Plato came up with a great many conclusions about the nature of things; his pupil Aristotle disagreed with nearly all of them. As someone once said, the history of philosophy has been merely footnotes to that basic disagreement.

Plato believed that the world of change we inhabit materially was ephemeral; he looked for a solid intelligible reality behind the fleeting impressions of the senses. Ever since, Western society has mulled over this theme. What can we know through sense perceptions? What can we know through intellect? Is there something behind or beyond the sensually apprehensible world? Is what we take for real, simply an illusion? But if the so-called real world is an illusion, as Plato assumed, how much more so must representational art be, since it is just an imitation of an imitation! The movies are almost a paradigm of the problem, because they literally give us only appearances of the "real" world, nothing but shadows on the screen. And yet we sense a reality of some sort being represented. And of course our experience of the movie is a real one; it takes place in time and space. But what good is it? Is there value in representations at all, whether we are talking about stories in print, on the stage or on the screen, or paintings or sculptures?

Humanist writers have tried to justify movies, just as they have had to defend all art from Plato's challenge that art is too ephemeral to provide anything more than momentary, perhaps even harmful—i.e. immoral—distraction. In his essay "The Movies, Too, Will Make You Free," W. R. Robinson writes: "From this traditional distaste for the ephemeral emerges the most persistent theme in Western art—the problem of appearance and reality—and the artist's most persistent challenge—to counterbalance transitoriness by formal strategies capable of articulating the truths behind the mask, a realm beyond change" (p. 114). Film is a transitory art attempting to express the immutable. And it does so because every film is "the end result of a deliberate human act, it is imbued with all the intangible emotional, intellectual, and moral attitudes man necessarily expresses in everything he does" (p. 115).

Robinson goes on to say that movies may be a distinct phenomenon, clearly distinguishable from literature or stage drama, but that what is important about the medium is the way it gives us the possibility of engaging with represented human action and of reacting to the vicissitudes of existence. Movies have their identity not in what they are physically but in what meanings they embody. What is important is

what one chooses to do with them. Film per se is just celluloid strips, as useful for decorating posters, starting fires, or recording information as for making visual narratives. It becomes art when a choice is made to employ it for aesthetic ends. When those ends . . . are regarded as worth trying for, a movie becomes an end in itself, a vehicle by which the human spirit becomes free. (p. 117)

Nevertheless, the humanist is aware that every assertion about what constitutes value in life can be challenged, even the simplest statements about the value of narrative in general. Human beings have been telling stories to each other since the dawn of history. What is the purpose of this practice? Clearly, we like stories, but what good are they? Are some better than others? And what criteria do we use to make such judgments? All of these questions have led to a large body of thinking and writing about narratives. Plato and Aristotle both addressed the issue, Plato finding the power of stories reprehensible unless they taught morality, Aristotle finding the mere experience of narratives a powerful social good even if they didn't teach particular moral lessons. The humanist film critic, aware of this tradition of literary criticism, steeped in the terms of the debate over literary values, simply applies the same principles to the most modern form of storytelling.

What are those principles? First of all is the notion that the experiencer of an artwork is looking for excellence in its construction or presentation. With the proper attention and concentration on the part of the spectator, excellence of achievement in the making of a film can be observed. Every particular example, each individual film, needs to be measured against the ideal potential inherent in the materials available to the medium. Movies, like any other form of creative endeavor, can be evaluated on the basis of their craftsmanship—that is, how well the perceptual elements of sight and sound have been organized to relay the intended meaning. Is the form of a film, its pictorial effects, its sound qualities, its editing, recognizably superior? Is meaning created as much through the deployment of visual and aural devices as through dialogue and action? If so, the film will be considered more cinematic, less like a filmed play, and hence of a higher artistic accomplishment. The second principle that follows is that if there is excellence achieved in a work of art, then this should be attributed to an artist, not to a production system. To recognize or appreciate the skill of the filmmaker is a desirable end; the humanist believes in recognizing individual human achievement.

It may have been this necessary corollary to artistic achievement that prevented intellectuals in America from granting the movies artistic stature earlier. Film production in America seemed like an assembly line system, with no single person responsible for a film's integrity. Unlike playwrights or novelists, who seem totally responsible for the works they put their names to, who "authors" a film? There were studio decisions that determined what scripts would be produced, who would direct the actors, and who would play the parts. And then there were the camera crew, the editors, the composers

of the music, special effects technicians, second unit photograpers, and so on, whose presence in the production of any film seemed to blur the issue. Although certain directors achieved legendary status for making their own unique films before World War I, like D. W. Griffith, it wasn't until the early 1960s that critics wholeheartedly came to embrace the idea that the director was the "author" (French writers used the term *auteur*) of the film. At last the humanist could feel comfortable about locating an artist responsible for the creativity of film, just as there had always been an artist for drama, literature, painting, and music. Not only did the acceptance of the director as the author of a film attract humanists from other fields to film criticism, but the extensive research that followed led to the reevaluation of many movies that at first viewing had been dismissed as mere products of the Hollywood genre machine.

Raymond Durgnat, a British freelance writer, has published several books on film subjects, including studies of Chaplin and Hitchcock. Here were two clear-cut cases of film artists who fit the mold of people like Shakespeare, Dickens, or Wagner. But Durgnat was also able to find the artist in the work of a Max Ophuls, who made fewer films and films without the obvious elevation of theme and style that marks directors like Chaplin and Hitchcock. Ophuls concentrated on films about beautiful women who were unhappy in love; they appear to be typical "weepies," or soap operas. Durgnat makes the case, however, that Max Ophuls's films achieve a high degree of sophistication and provide great visual pleasure because Ophuls used a moving camera where another, less imaginative director would not:

> By his camera movements, Ophuls gives both visual life and emotional dynamism to the stuffy, hierarchicalized, static decor—and society—of Vienna 1900. His camera moves past screens, flunkeys, fans, candles, whispered conversations, much as a Henry James sentence winds its way through innumerable reservations, concessions, and hesitations to its final tentative assertion. Ophuls' films are full of symbols of movement—staircases, spiral staircases, immensely long corridors, the can-can in *Le Plaisir,* coaches, the lovers waltzing in *Madame De.* . . . In *Lola Montes,*

even the ship waltzed under the stars, and when Lola and Liszt live together, it is in two coaches, traveling. (p. 56)

In this passage, the first two humanist aesthetic principles combine as the critic cites excellence of form issuing from an artist of great skill and imagination whose chief value lies in his unique ability to make meaning arise from the form itself.

The third basic principle of the great tradition of humanist literary inquiry is that the experiencing of an artwork should bring about in the audience member some increase in moral understanding. Exactly what kind of knowledge this is, is harder to define than creating in a spectator an awareness of formal craftsmanship either in the work or on the part of the artist. It does not simply imply a lesson in common sense morality such as "It is wrong to steal." The terms used are vague. And yet somehow there is a thread of consistency. All commentators have suggested the best films are those that somehow transmit effectively the knowledge of what it means to be human. Whether comic or tragic in form, whether realistic or ex-pressionistic in style, films of the highest order are those in which the spectator learns something about the complex nature of human existence, finds a world represented that makes one think of the world outside the theater, shows us the way the world really is, and not simply the way we'd like it to be. And the humanist contends that some films are designed to do that, while others aren't. Genre films, for the most part, don't try to represent the way things are, but merely substitute a fantasy world in which simply defined good and evil contend and good always wins out. The humanist believes that the way the world really is, the way it feels to us when we stop and think about it, is much more complicated and ambiguous. To be able to participate vicariously in stories about characters who play out possible lives, confront possible situations, who have moral conflicts and who must make choices, is to learn such truths about life, not through personal experi-ence but through a kind of *super* experience—that is, an experience that one might never be able to have oneself, except through the story. In other words, the viewer of a film can share in a way what it feels like to be another human being.

Jonathan Baumbach locates in Michelangelo Antonioni's films of the early 1960s a parallel between a way of being-in-the-world which his charac-ters portray and the way the world behaves. By identifying with these characters, Baumbach suggests, the viewer will be able to reorganize in a more positive fashion old ways of being-in-the-world. He particularly focuses on *Red Desert* (1964), which appeared to represent the ugliness and de-humanization inherent in modern industrial society. Most critics saw the debasement and slow descent into madness of its protagonist, Guiliana, as a result of this pressure. But what Baumbach finds so fascinating about the film is that it literally, visually, shows the beauty of the modern world and the inability of the heroine to accommodate herself to it. We, like the heroine, may not be happy with the world of today, but the film forces us to understand it, to see it in a different light. The same thing applies to basic human relationships revealed in the film. "An Antonioni movie presents us with a new way of seeing—that is, forces us to see against our preconception of the way things are. No other artist deals with the hang-ups and delusions and possibilities of love, which is to say life, in our time as profoundly and truthfully as Antonioni" (Robinson, p. 179).

Thus the kinds of stories and characters that a humanist values are those that work out the universal problems of human existence. These stories, though fictions, seem to provide a place or point in time where the viewer is invited to make comparisons between the story on the screen and the world in which the viewer exists. The work of the film narrative is to give expression to human concerns about personal identity, social institutions, political responsibility, and aesthetic and moral value. How does one deal with the conflicting demands of individual expression and social conformity? At what point does the desire for success become unbridled and ruthless ambition? How should an individual relate to the state? Is there an absolute moral code or is it relative? Does capitalism derive its energy from human exploitation? Do humans have the capacity to choose their destinies, or are they determined by forces outside of their control? These may sound like essay topics, but in fact they are themes which are depicted in films through action and dialogue. The humanist critic gives such films high praise.

John Fletcher, for example, while demonstrating Strindberg's influence on Ingmar Bergman's work, shows how Bergman's films capture a sense of the intellectual problems of the day:

> . . . Bergman's characters . . . appear to suffer from a more generalized feeling of guilt over existence itself, at what Calderon called *"el delito mayor del hombre,"* the sin of having been born. As we might expect, the whole atmosphere of *The Silence* and *Shame* is redolent of an oppressive sense of guilt—guilt at living in this world at all and guilt on the part of the artist for imagining such horrors:
> EVA: Sometimes everything seems like a long strange dream. It's not my dream, it's someone else's, that I'm forced to take part in. Nothing is properly real. It's all made up. What do you think will happen when the person who has dreamed us wakes up and is ashamed of his dream?
> This is much more akin to the existential *angst* of the mid-twentieth century and to the Schopenhauerian stoicism of Beckett than it is to the more personal torments of Strindberg, which smack of late Romanticism rather than the hard-headed Modernism which pervades the work of Kafka's heirs. (pp. 183–84)

Fletcher is clearly relating Bergman's intellectual concerns to the mainstream of literary and cultural history which connects the ideas of the past with the present. Schopenhauer and Strindberg of the 19th century are seen as instrumental in creating Bergman's 20th-century views.

LITERARY VALUES—THE SEARCH FOR THEMES AND CHARACTERS

Although much literary study has concentrated on the analysis of style, for most readers the value of literature lies in its ability to reveal the breadth and depth of the human condition. The inexhaustible variety of human characters—from hunchbacks to martyrs, inarticulate mechanics to sophisticated artists, housekeepers to dynamic leaders, fools and saviors—suggests the ordinary, everyday world as well as the extraordinary, the commonplace and the unique, as fit subjects for representation. The stories of these people, their conflicts, their joys, their losses should be portrayed in such a way that witnesses to their lives should be moved deeply by the experience, whether to tears or laughter. Identification and empathy with the characters should be strong, what happens to them a matter of great import for the reader. For many filmgoers the same expectations apply to the movies.

The humanist film critic searches out those films which, like Shakespeare's plays, Tolstoy's novels, or Frost's poetry, present important themes as portrayed by fully developed characters. The great themes of drama, prose, poetry, and film are very general when written down: how do members of the human race relate to each other? to the environment? to history? to God or the gods? to mortality? Abstracting these themes from the works in which they are embedded often reveals commonplace human understanding: "Art is long, life is short." "Humans must suffer to win redemption." "Heroes are made, not born." "Everyone has a dark or evil side." "Men and women are alone in an empty universe." It is the working out of these themes in a dramatic context, however, the elaboration of these themes within the fiction of representative characters in conflict, that makes such works resonate with profound meaning.

It is the self-imposed task of the humanist critic first of all to view a film and then decide whether or not the film in question has, indeed, been able to communicate such meanings. If the critic has been moved by the experience of viewing to appreciate or understand these themes, then there is a great desire to relate this to others. Thus the first function of the humanist is to identify, from out of the mass of ordinary films, the exceptional ones that do share in this process of dealing with the human condition. The next task is to evaluate how well the film has succeeded in its intention. For the most part, the basis for such judgment is subjective. The critic observes, the critic has responses. The humanist assumes that what he or she feels and observes is what most people feel and observe. But even if that were not so, the humanist has no other recourse, no rigorous theoretical structure, no special, narrow viewfinder upon which to ground his or her perceptions, only the immediate experience of the film filtered through rational thought. And yet such criticism can open up a work, make a film seem more comprehensible to the discerning viewer.

Writing about Hitchcock's deployment of theme and plot, O. B. Hardison makes some cogent remarks about *Marnie* (1964), a film that at first viewing left even Hitchcock fans cold. Hardison's criticism, in a sense, saves the film from obscurity. By casting it in a new light, he gives it an amazing structural complexity. He says that the plot appears to be a return to a simple melodrama formula "of the dependent female and *noblesse oblige*" on the part of the male character, one that Hitchcock had used earlier in his career. For example, in *The Thirty Nine Steps* (1935), the male figure brings help and aid to troubled females even while being hunted by the police. In *Marnie,* the young woman is presented to the audience as a self-possessed, sexually experienced, and highly successful thief, a counterpart to Cary Grant in *To Catch a Thief* (1955). Caught in the act, however, by the wealthy hero, she agrees to marry him, rather than go to prison. The audience and the hero eventually find out that Marnie is, in fact, a virgin and sexually frigid, her thieving a neurotic compulsion. "As in *Spellbound,* an informal psychoanalysis ensues." The husband talks to Marnie and uncovers her past. She has a "breakthrough"; the neurosis seems gone and she presumably will go on to a healthy and happy life. This apparently innocent fantasy, Hardison suggests, has perverse overtones, however. "The hero's marriage to a woman whom he knows to be a thief is curious, to say the least. The suggestion of perverse relations is further underscored by the overt jealousy of the hero's sister. If the film is considered fantasy, it is a playing out of the Electra complex. But if it is judged on any other basis, the hero is at least as sick as the woman he is trying to cure" (Robinson, p. 149). Thus what looked like a cut-and-dried story of "man saves woman from her worst self" has more to it. Hardison's criticism certainly makes the film well worth a second, more thoughtful, glance. He is able to show the viewer that the characters are not what they appear to be on the surface, that there are resonances here that make the characters richer and more complex. What appears to be a formula thriller with a clichéd chauvinist theme turns out to be a lesson in aberrant psychology.

AESTHETIC PREOCCUPATIONS

In addition to searching for meaningful themes, the humanist critic looks for excellence in the deployment of aesthetic elements. As mentioned above, a theme of profound significance simply stated is a cliché. It is the effective treatment of that theme within the limits of the medium that distinguishes the excellent film from the commonplace. The choices made by the script writer, the exact configuration of the plot, the details of characters, and the dialogue they will speak are important aesthetic decisions. With a film, however, the process is complicated by the material aspects of the form. Filmmakers must make manifold choices in translating the script into the finished film. Casting the right performers plays an essential part in determining the success of a film. Not only must the actors be able to "act" successfully, but their very physical appearances and voice qualities must be suitable to the best projection of their characters. Erwin Panofsky, in an essay frequently anthologized, said that characters produced by playwrights are definite substantial figures who can be played badly or well but who exist even when they are not played at all. Film characters, on the other hand, only exist as they are played by specific flesh-and-blood humans. Clint Eastwood is the embodiment of "Dirty Harry"; Orson Welles is "Charles Foster Kane." "Conversely, if a movie role is badly played there remains literally nothing of it, no matter how interesting the character's psychology or how elaborate the words" (Ross, p. 390).

Then the filmmaker must choose the most appropriate camera angles to show the action, lighting that reveals or conceals the world framed, and an editing pattern that provides the mood, tone, or style most suitable to bringing out the nuances of the characters and themes; and, finally, a composite sound track must be organized with the selected noises and music amplifying or minimizing the impact of the images and dialogue. All of this makes a film a very complicated set of aesthetic materials that filmmakers must orchestrate to create the intended effect. The humanist film critic works under the assumption that both the intention and the success or failure of the filmmaker and the film in realizing that intention are discernible to the person who looks closely at the film. Form and content work together to produce meaning.

Speaking of Luis Buñuel's films, Leo Braudy finds that the surrealism of the films, their often striking liberties with the material world and the conventions of narrative cinema, all come together to express Buñuel's attitudes toward freedom and repression. In all of Buñuel's films, from *Un Chien Andalou* (1928) to *That Obscure Object of Desire* (1977), the level of narrative suggests that no order or meaning is innate. "Buñuel's subject is less the story than the expectations of the audience about film form, how a story is told, what objects mean, and what suspense leads to." From the beginning of his career, Buñuel has attacked the bourgeois obsessions with food, money, and manners that are institutionalized. "His hatred of the bourgeois springs not so much from any concerted political philosophy as it does from an aesthetic one, founded on the belief that religious modes of patterned meaning and bourgeois modes of possessive meaning are oppressions of the eye, the mind, and the spirit. Institutionalized belief is not belief but tyranny" (p. 72). Thus Buñuel's film technique forces new meanings on the content, because, for Buñuel, meaning is arbitrary.

V. F. Perkins, on the other hand, in an analysis of the shower scene from Hitchcock's *Psycho* (1960), finds meaning in form more explicitly:

> Within the sequence the downward impetus is felt variously as crushing, being crushed, sinking, falling. It embodies the mad relentlessness of the assault and the ineluctable erosion of Marion's life. The scene's compositionally and emotionally most powerful elements—the knife, the flow of water, Marion's body and hand in their lurching slide down the tiled wall, the tearing and falling shower curtain—these are opposed only by Marion's will: her arm reaching out for the curtain's support asserts a momentary, tentative upward movement. But this is swiftly overruled by the curtain's collapse and Marion's fall. (p. 111)

Such humanist exploration of the interrelationship between form and content in film has often been attacked for its dependence on literary tradition, its use of imprecise vocabulary which tends to be intuitive, emotional, and impressionistic. The best humanist criticism, however, shows a heart and a mind working together, connecting art and life as it examines all kinds of films. Thus as Gerald Mast demonstrates in a comparison of Buster Keaton's *The General* (1925) and Chaplin's *The Gold Rush* (1925), specific analysis of a film is used to reveal not only the film's aesthetic devices but also its moral and philosophic perspective:

> That heroism becomes an accident in *The General* is at the center of its moral thrust. It is an accident that the cannon, aimed squarely at Johnny, does not go off until the train rounds a curve, discharging its huge ball at the enemy instead of at the protagonist. It is an accident that Buster's train comes to a rail switch just in time to help it detour the pursuing Union train. Whereas wealth, material success, is accidental in *The Gold Rush* (and an accident not worth waiting for), heroism and successful military strategy are accidental in *The General*. And just as Charlie's character exposes the folly of the accidents of wealth, Buster's character exposes the folly of the accidents of heroism. For how less heroic, how less aspiring, less grand can a man be than little Buster? Buster merely uses this shrewd common sense against impossible odds, and he is lucky to get away with it. (p. 156)

THE PLEASURES OF INTUITIVE INTERPRETATION: THE PERSONAL ESSAY

The humanist approach to film criticism is open to all. It requires only a general background in the arts, the experience of filmgoing, and the habit of reading and writing. It presupposes that criticism, looking rationally and logically at things, seeking to understand the world and its inhabitants more completely, is an important human function. At the same time there is an awareness of the great pleasure to be had, the very human pleasure, of discovering something about a film (or films) that is new and original, a pleasure that achieves its highest level during the critical act when a person sits down to organize the vague and ephemeral impressions of the actual experience in written form. Writing it down is hard work and sometimes it doesn't reach the highest level; great thoughts and insights don't always come. But they seldom come at all unless there is writing. Something about the concentration necessary for writing often coalesces and distills vague impressions and feelings into substantial thought.

The first step, of course, is to think of films as something more than mere escapist entertainment for the mass audience, with the conclusion drawn that more than a cursory glance at the movies can yield intellectual satisfactions. From this perspective, the humanist critic can find important things to say not only about the obviously complex films made by foreign filmmakers but about mainstream entertainment films as well. The important thing is that humanists look inward, examine their own responses in more than a cursory way, and try to understand what it was that produced the initial response to the film. People usually know whether they liked or disliked a particular movie; the humanist is not satisfied by this simple response, but wants to know more precisely why. What was it, in particular, that made the film good or bad? Or what made the film so boring, pretentious, thrilling, saddening, hysterical, or rewarding? The humanist trusts intuition first, and then tries to elaborate a more rational way of describing the effects which produced that first intuitive response. It is the very articulation of responses and the sharing of responses to films at a more cultivated level that distinguish humanist film criticism from simple reviewing.

Paul Ricoeur, a noted French philosopher, has described the process of immersion in a text which leads to a richer, more complete relationship with that text, as a movement through three stages. The first he calls "understanding." This is the movement when a text makes its power clear to the experiencer. Having seen a particular film, for example, the viewer is struck by the insistence the text has in the viewer's life of meaning. We are all aware that some films do not have such an appeal; we see them, pass the time, and forget them. When this recognition of understanding does take place, however, the text demands some "explanation." This is Ricoeur's second stage. Dudley Andrew, in *Concepts in Film Theory* (1984), says this is necessarily a reductive process, breaking down the text into its various parts to unlock its hold on us. "The text is situated in its various contexts (biographical, generic, historical) and is subjected to linguistic study, psychoanalysis, and ideological critique until the particularity of its appeal is explained as an effect of these generating forces" (p. 181). In a sense this analysis, the second stage, may remove us from the power of the text felt during the moment of understanding, the first stage. But Ricoeur goes on to say that a third stage, "comprehension," follows. Here a return to the work, bolstered and enlarged by the explanatory process, renews, in a stronger and more comprehensive way, the initial sense that the text has importance in the spectator's life of meaning. "Comprehension," Andrew suggests, "is synthetic in that it listens to the wholeness of the text rather than breaking it down into parts: further it responds to the cues it finds in the work, initiating a project of meaning which is never complete" (p. 182). The relationship of the text and the spectator becomes a living one. One can return to certain films again and again because they never lose their ability to yield meaning. It is these kinds of films that humanist critics write about.

Because the form of humanist film criticism is the personal essay and because humanists are such a diverse lot, this criticism can often be found in anthologies. Some of the essays in *Man and the Movies* (1969), for example, were written specifically for this anthology; others had appeared in scholarly journals. The topics vary widely from personal reminiscences to close analysis of film rhetoric. George Garrett, a novelist and poet, who went to Hollywood and wrote screenplays for what turned out to be unmemorable films, discusses with wit and humor the problems of being of a literary mind in the midst of the crass commercialism of the movie capital of the world. After all, he co-authored the screenplay for *Frankenstein Meets the Spacemonster* (Robert Gaffney, 1965). R. H. W. Dillard, a poet, looks closely at horror films and suggests that "they teach us an acceptance of the natural order of things and an affirmation of man's ability to cope with and even prevail over the evil of life" (p. 65) which can never be understood. Martin C. Battestin, an eminent scholar of eighteenth-century British literature, compares the film version of Fielding's *Tom Jones* (Tony Richardson, 1963) with the novel and shows how the filmmaker did an excellent job of capturing not only the essence of the book but also its ironic and distancing devices. There are articles on Hitchcock's thrillers; on Federico Fellini, the Italian director noted for his use of dream sequences, as a psychoanalyst; on skin flicks, D. W. Griffith, and more. Each of these articles, starting from a personal perspective on the subject, ends by making pointed insights into both the nature of film and the nature of human beings.

T. J. Ross's anthology, *Film and the Liberal Arts* (1970), collected a number of essays that had appeared elsewhere. Most of them were written by academics and others who were not film specialists; they address a wide range of issues and topics of interest to the cultured reader. For example, Ross reprints Susan Sontag's illuminating article on science-fiction films called "The Imagination of Disaster," in which she maintains that genre films formulate and materialize attitudes and ideas held by a broad spectrum of the body politic. Sontag is a good example of a writer, essentially a social scientist, who turns her critical gaze on a variety of topics that relate to contemporary life. Then there's a fascinating study of adaptation by J. Blumenthal, a professor of literature, who compares Kurosawa's *Throne of Blood* (1957) with Shakespeare's *Macbeth,* upon which the Japanese film was based. Arnold Hauser and Erwin Panofsky, both art historians, are represented by cogent articles on film's link with the visual arts. Even the Beat novelist Jack Kerouac is represented by an essay about the original vampire film, *Nosferatu* (F. W. Murnau, 1922).

Mention of these anthologies and their contents serves to demonstrate the wide variety of positions and topics that arise when the cultivated mind takes up the world of the motion picture and our involvement with it. Though published many years ago, the critical remarks are still worth reading today. Sometimes the impulse of the personal essay grows to book length. Stanley Cavell, a philosopher by trade, wrote about the nature of the medium in his book *The World Viewed* (1971), in which he explains a phenomenology of film. (Phenomenology examines the relations between subjective and objective accounts of the world, the connection between the perceiver and the perceived.) More recently Professor Cavell examined the "screwball comedy," that group of films popular in the late 1930s and dealing with male/female relationships, in a book entitled *Pursuits of Happiness: The Hollywood Comedy of Remarriage* (1981). Leo Braudy, trained in literary studies, covers nearly all aspects of film—style, history, auteurs, genres—in his work *The World in a Frame* (1976). Frank McConnell, another teacher of literature, probes the relationship between metaphor and narrative, whether literary or filmic, in *The Spoken Seen* (1975). Michael Wood, from a similar perspective but taking a closer look at the audience, examines aspects of the American character as represented in film in his book *America at the Movies* (1975). He finds that cultural attitudes about life in a given period (here the 1940s through the 1960s) are clearly represented on the silver screen. For Wood, and for all the humanist critics, movies tell us in conscious and unconscious ways who we are as human beings.

THE STUDENT AS HUMANIST FILM CRITIC

Every student taking a beginning film class is, in effect, a humanist critic when asked to write a paper about a film or to compare and contrast several films. Sometimes such courses are called "Appreciation of Film." The intention is to increase the student's awareness of the complexity of the medium and how it can be viewed as an art. Writing coherent analyses of intuitive responses to films tends to sharpen the ability to see and understand more, to enrich the experience of watching film. Reading the responses of other students or essays published in general film magazines and journals also adds much to the experience of seeing films.

To show that it can be done, we have reprinted actual student essays in an appendix at the end of this book; they were written on assignment in beginning film classes and are printed unedited. Each, in its own way, has something to say about the topic discussed. These are not primarily research papers in the sense that the ideas were found in other books, quoted, and stitched together to make a paper. Rather they are humanist responses to films, thoughts and feelings formalized through the writing process by each of the writers as they tried to make sense of the experience of the movies. It is hoped that the example of these papers will encourage students reading this book to feel positive toward the task of writing about film.

In general, humanist film critics like the movies they write about, but evaluation is usually not the most important objective of the writers. Rather they are trying to understand more fully what the viewing experience is all about and why it gets to them the way it does. At the same time they can experience a sense of achievement in coming up with an interpretation of a film that may open up the work to others, just as they themselves may have been awakened to the meaning of a certain movie by a thought-provoking lecture, article, or book. Readers, writers, and filmgoers unite in one task, to enlarge the experience of this twentieth-century art—the movies.

GUIDELINES FOR WRITING HUMANIST FILM CRITICISM

I. Sources
  A. Primary

    All films are potential subjects for humanist criticism. Think of films that have had a powerful effect, made a distinct impression, especially those that caused you to think or wonder about their meanings. Though mainstream Hollywood films can be investigated in this way, don't fail to seek out foreign films, cult films, documentaries, and experimental films. See films of the past as well as the current releases. Films shown in class are always a good bet.

  B. Secondary

    Read the film criticism of the highbrow journals mentioned in the chapter. Go to the library and look into film journals like *Sight and Sound, Film Comment,* or *Literature/Film Quarterly.* Use the card catalogue to find books related to your films.

II. Method
  See the film or films you want to write about more than once. Videocassette versions are very helpful here. For example, it is easy to go over a passage you wish to describe by rewinding the tape or searching backward and reviewing the appropriate scene. This will help locate the aesthetic devices or the way themes are developed in specific detail. This kind of close analysis of passages is the best way to support your generalizations about the film's merits or flaws. Observation of the film and intuitive responses come first. Then comes the writing itself, the process of setting down your impressions with some sort of logical support. For instance, you might decide on the thesis that Bergman's *Fanny and Alexander* (1982) portrays the reality of childhood accurately. Then you would list and describe in detail the scenes in the film that depict this idea.

III. Questions the Writer Using the Humanist Approach Might Ask
  1. Did the film provoke a powerful emotional response either for or against the film? Why?

2. What was the film's theme? Was it important or trivial? How did the film reveal the theme?
3. Was the film complex, full of ambiguity in terms of its plot resolution? Was it ironic? paradoxical? straightforward?
4. Were the characters stereotypes or well-rounded figures?
5. Did the film's formal aspect—the lighting, composition, editing pattern, and so on—add to the film's impact? Why or why not?
6. Who made the film? Is this person a noted film artist? What about the film suggests that it was made by an artist?
7. If the film is an older movie, is it still worth seeing today? Why is it (or isn't it) still a memorable film experience?
8. Does the film reflect the human condition, show us something authentic about human relationships?
9. If it is a Hollywood genre film, does it transcend its genre to become art?
10. Does the film tell us something about the mass audience, popular assumptions, American values, or foreign points of view?

PART II

Textual/Contextual Approaches: Analysis of Individual Narrative Films in Relation to Groups of Films

"When you've seen one, you've seen 'em all," says a character in *Singin' in the Rain* (Gene Kelly–Stanley Donen, 1952), implying that all Hollywood movies are the same—the familiar formula plots of adventure, horror, and romance—in contrast to drama, in which individuality and uniqueness supposedly rule supreme. It is an obvious remark because films do beget films. Hardly a viewer has not had the experience of thinking. "This is very familiar," when confronted with a new movie. In the last several years, remakes of older films and follow-ups of newer successful films have crowded theater screens. It seems only natural to compare the film of the moment with those enshrined in our memories.

Upon inspection, we realize that this phenomenon is not restricted to certain types of films. Not only do all westerns appear very much alike, for instance, but all Humphrey Bogart pictures appear similar, all MGM films seem to have something in common. This sense of repetition in Hollywood films, the vision of the "dream factory" turning out interchangeable movies on an assembly line, produced by anonymous workers for the mass audience, has led to the identification and close examination of the various groups of films and the way any one particular film fits or departs from the characteristics of a definable group.

Part II of *An Introduction to Film Criticism* identifies two major critical approaches in which particular films are nearly always viewed within the context of other films. Chapter 3 outlines the assumptions and values of the *auteur* approach. An auteurist is interested in locating individual creative achievement amid all the pressures of conformity inherent in the mass production of movies. The auteurist examines the individual films of a performer, screenwriter, or director in the context of other films made by the same person to see if a consistent body of artistic excellence has been achieved. The value of any single experience of an Alfred Hitchcock film, for example—its specific themes and motifs, its technical virtuosity—is enhanced by the viewer's knowledge of other Hitchcock films, the recognition of recurring themes, motifs, and style in a body of work over a period of time. Though the individual film experience is powerful and memorable, it is amplified by understanding the way it fits into the whole.

Chapter 4 surveys the genre approach. The character in *Singin' in the Rain* mentioned above was complaining about repetition in movies, finding that it made films trivial and boring for the intelligent observer. The genre critic, on the other hand, is fascinated by the phenomenon. Why are these films so similar in character, setting, and plot? What are the potential variations that can be tolerated? What are the dominant aesthetic and thematic elements of the western? the musical? the horror film? Are there hidden meanings playing beneath the surface of these seemingly simple-minded fantasies relating the conflict of good and evil? For the genre critic, a particular film may be moving and forceful—one of the best sci-fi films ever made— but the way in which the individual film represents the genre, how it continues to redefine the limits of the genre, is of greater importance.

Thus for both auteur and genre approaches the individual film has little critical importance by itself. It must be compared and contrasted with similar films: with other works by the same auteur or with other works in the genre. In both approaches, relating the text of particular films to the context of other films may broaden out into a discussion of more general social and historical contexts. For example, the western film seems to reflect, even if obliquely, a vision of the actual history of the American frontier experience. Musicals and gangster films were very popular in the early 1930s, and writers have connected this fact with the actualities of the Great Depression. Filmmakers, too, have an actual history, the facts of their biographies as well as their relations to the artistic, political, and social currents of their eras. Many auteurist critics also delve into the psychological propensities of their subjects.

The approaches covered in Part II revolve about the interplay between the experience of individual films (the text) and the cumulative experience of many films either in a genre or by a specific filmmaker (the context in which the films were made). Such approaches demand a wide and diverse spectrum of film viewing as well as immersion in the literature of films and filmmakers.

CHAPTER 3

The Auteurist Approach: Analysis of Filmmakers and Their Films

Auteurist Approach Capsule

Audience: General reader interested in film craftsmanship; film students and film scholars.

Functions: Identify the person most responsible for the creation of a film, usually the director; describe and evaluate the work in terms of uniqueness or consistency of content, style, or excellence of craftsmanship.

Subject: Body of films attributable to a single individual—for instance, all the films directed by Alfred Hitchcock.

Writers: Freelance professionals: film scholars.

Publications: Highbrow journals; specialized film journals; trade and scholarly books.

Auteur criticism can be placed about midpoint on the spectrum bound by textual criticism and contextual criticism. On one hand, the auteurist critic is primarily engaged in identifying formal and rhetorical patterns in single films (individual texts), in discovering and describing cinematic structures and personal visions that are consistent from film to film in the work of a single film artist. On the other hand, auteurism is connected to the extratextual (contextual) consideration of film as an intersection of social and personal history, through questions of authorship, artistic influence, and biography.

Auteur critics are intent on characterizing and illuminating the style of a single artist through a consideration of formal elements and the recurring attitudes and ideas expressed through plot, character, and theme, but these critics are also drawn into a description and interpretation of the forces, both personal and public, that surround the production of the films under consideration.

Given the fact that most feature-length narrative films made during the entire history of the cinema are clearly the result of a collaborative effort between studio representatives, writers, directors, camera crews, lighting experts, editors, composers, sound technicians, art directors, costumers, and performers, all contributing to the end product—one western is like another, one MGM color spectacular is like any other—and that the filmgoing public usually identified films with performers—the stars of the picture—the development of a critical approach that sought out a single individual to praise or blame for the appeal of a film may seem odd, to say the least, if not actually impossible. To be sure, traditional criticism of the other arts has always been interested in the creator. But plays and paintings and operas are more frequently brought into being by a single person. Though many experimental short films are still made entirely by one person who thinks of the idea, runs the camera, does the editing, makes the titles, selects the music, and sends it off to film festivals for public screening, everyone knows that movies are made by the film industry.

The credits of a film speak for themselves: except for such multitalented figures like Chaplin, who could indeed write a screenplay, finance the production, cast and direct the performers during shooting, write and play the musical score, and ultimately distribute the film, every element of a film's production, distribution, and exhibition is in the hands of many different people. Surely from such a group of practitioners one is more likely to get a product that represents the values and attitudes of a cross section of the public for whom such a product is made. The field does not look like one conducive to individual expression. Corporate decisions based on market findings rather than personal feelings seem more likely to affect the shape and texture of the finished product, just as they do, for example, in the auto industry.

But if this is true for the vast majority of movies ever made, certain directors in the past were known to have overseen every aspect of production to make films that were uniquely theirs. This was particularly true in the silent era. D. W. Griffith, Sergei Eisenstein, Friedrich Murnau, Erich von Stroheim, and others were all recognized by their peers and the public to be totally responsible for the films they made. With the coming of sound, however, and the increased need for technicians and capital to make films, studios took control, and the power of individual directors diminished. The general public seemed not to notice. They went to see what and who was on the screen: they had little interest in who had made the film.

After World War II, however, the Italian Neorealist directors like

Roberto Rossellini and Vittorio De Sica emerged to grasp artistic control for the director once again. In the 1950s, American intellectuals took an interest in movies coming from Europe and began to notice that Fellini films and Bergman films, for example, were unique and extremely individualized and consistent in style and theme. Such films were often called "art films," perhaps because they had such identifiable artists. Movies of this kind made moviegoing and the discussion of movies an acceptable and even necessary part of contemporary intellectual life. The same audience who found art in European films, who began to read translations of writings about film from Europe, where film had traditionally been considered an area for personal artistic expression, turned to the American films—which up to that time had appeared to be no more than commercial, mass entertainment—with the intention of seeing if there were any artists there. The French critics had already discovered this. We followed suit. By the late 1960s, the intelligentsia was convinced that certain directors like John Ford, Alfred Hitchcock, and Howard Hawks, though working within the restrictive Hollywood studio system, had, by dint of their own personal convictions, put as clear an imprint on seemingly simple generic comedies or westerns or thrillers as any European directors had on their self-conscious art films. One of the aims, then, of auteur criticism is to justify an intellectual interest in an area that had previously been considered simply mass culture, the products of which, like paperback romances and detective fiction, were formerly beneath intellectual scrutiny. Where there's an artist, there must be an art.

The basis of auteurism is a belief that the art of film resides in its employment as a medium for personal rather than public expression. While granting that the production of a film is a collaborative effort, the auteur critic singles out the dominant personality who has made that effort cohere and whose force and creative vision have chiefly shaped the finished film. This dominant personality—the film artist—can be identified and his or her power and creativity confirmed by a controlling presence in a number of films, films whose other production personnel shift and change but in which the auteur— the film "author"—remains constant. Initially, critics discussed only directors as auteurs; they were the persons whose articulated role in the production process seemed to involve the most absolute control over the total film. Recently, however, auteur critics have singled out the creative and "authorial" presence and force of screenwriters, cinematographers, actors, and editors. On occasion, even producers have been seen as artistically and creatively shaping the style of films; producer Irving Thalberg of MGM is a classic example.

Auteurist criticism has a value system founded on the presence or absence of a personal style manifested in a body of film work. Thus the critical hierarchy of film artists is topped by those whose thematic interests or cinematic techniques are consistent and recognizable as elements of style, like John Ford and Alfred Hitchcock. At the bottom of such a hierarchy are those chameleon-like filmmakers who change their style from film to film and who do not seem to reveal a world view or thematic preoccupation; examples include John Huston and Mervyn LeRoy. Since the auteurist highly values consistency, unity, and the harmonious coherence and evolution of a body of work, auteur criticism often ignores significant single films that are not part of an *oeuvre*. It ignores, too, those filmmakers whose fine individual films seem to have no stylistic connective tissue between them. Conversely, the auteurist occasionally overvalues a particular filmmaker's work because of its consistent, identifiable style—even when it is aesthetically unremarkable or thematically uninteresting. Thus an auteurtist critic may find director/performer Jerry Lewis more cinematically significant and valuable a film artist than, say, the allegedly styleless studio director—William Dieterle—although Lewis's films have been commonly dismissed as minor comic works, while many of Dieterle's films, like *The Life of Emile Zola*, (1937) have been highly praised for their individual artistry and formal coherence. Generally, those auteurs most valued are consistent and identifiable in *both* style and thematic preoccupation, such as Alfred Hitchcock, John Ford, Howard Hawks, Ingmar Bergman, Federico Fellini, and Woody Allen. Robin Wood, for example, introduces his auteur study of Hitchcock by recognizing the director's work as an organic whole:

> First, then, one might point to the *unity* of Hitchcock's work, and the nature of that unity. I mean of course something much deeper than the fact that he frequently reverts to mystery-thrillers for his material; I also mean something broader and more complex than the fact that certain themes—such as the celebrated "exchange of guilt"—turn up again and again, although that is a part of it. Not only in theme—in style, method, moral attitude, assumptions about the nature of life—Hitchcock's mature films reveal, on inspection, a consistent development, deepening in clarification. (*Hitchcock's Films*, p. 18)

Most auteur criticism, then, traces the continuity and evolution of style and theme in a substantial body of a given film artist's work. The two predominant methods of auteur criticism are straightforward. The auteur critic examines a group of films, pointing out their stylistic and thematic continuity in order to identify the film artist responsible for them as a significant auteur, or closely analyzes a single film so as to show how it relates to an already established auteur's thematic and stylistic preoccupations. The analysis of formal cinematic elements such as camera movement, composition, lighting, and editing are central to both critical methods, and close attention to the visual as well as literary nature of film has most likely been auteurism's greatest contribution to film criticism. Specifically, auteur criticism has resurrected and reconsidered forgotten film artists previously thought too insignificant to warrant consideration; when their work is seen as a coherent whole rather than in isolated units, it takes on value and reveals a conscious and forceful artist. At its best, auteurism has placed such filmmakers as Nicholas Ray and Don Siegel and their films in aesthetic and historical perspective, redeemed the low-budget, "B" movie from its previous snobbish neglect, insisted that a collaborative and commercial medium can also be a personal medium in the hands of a strong and visionary artist, and stressed the importance of close visual analysis and formal observation of the films themselves.

At its least effective level, however, auteur criticism falls victim to what has been called the cult of personality, a form of adulation that attempts to elevate the most patently awful of a filmmaker's works because that filmmaker has been deemed an auteur. The auteur critic can be guilty also of dogmatically attempting to make singly idiosyncratic films fit into an otherwise obviously coherent body of work, ignoring their individual qualities or, finally, dismissing them as "minor" and "atypical." This value placed on coherence and consistency, on the unity of a body of work, may have consequences beyond the neglect of those films that are either not part of an established artist's body of work or that don't fit into an identifiable stylistic or thematic scheme. Marxist critics, for example, charge auteurism and its search for coherence and harmony as essentially myopic; they suggest that auteur critics fail to see the way social and economic forces determine what eventually is produced, distributed, and exhibited.

Despite such criticisms, the auteurist approach to film is still popular and as widely practiced a form of criticism as any other. Like most humans, film critics enjoy seeing the traces of human individuality and creativity in the objects of their contemplation, even when the manufacture of those objects most often appears mechanical and anonymous. Like the biographer, a critic using an auteur approach focuses on a specific member of the filmmaking team—usually the director—and, like the historian, tries to discover that member's place in film history. But unlike the biographer or the historian, the auteur critic puts less emphasis on the filmmaker's life or place in film history. Primarily concerned with the films themselves, the auteurist seeks out the individual creative force behind the films, in order to demonstrate through critical analysis that there indeed exists someone who is the film's author. In addition, the auteurist's work provides an up-to-date filmography of the filmmaker, in the form of a careful description and a critical analysis of several films in the filmmaker's *oeuvre*.

HISTORY OF THE AUTEUR CONCEPT

From the infancy of film history, critics have acknowledged the importance of certain film artists in creating the finished film. The public first associated films with the companies that made them—Biograph, Vitagraph, and Essanay, for example—but the individual director of a particular film soon received screen credit. As early as 1911, in a review in *The Moving Picture World,* Epes Winthrop Sargent remarks that "more than one company has been given its first uplift by a director who could make good pictures, and even when the field broadened until there were plenty of able directors, the superstition that it was bad luck to cross a director still obtained and still does obtain in many studios." In this essay, Sargent advocates limiting the power of the director, but inherent in his remarks is a belief in the director's importance to the success of the film and his or her control over all phases of the production:

> The director is not human who will not avail himself of this position to do precisely as he thinks best, even though his ideas of best are the exploitation of his personal beliefs as opposed to dramatic rule, common sense, and the change in the fashion of films. Hundreds of films are spoiled each year because directors are permitted without restraint to make a picture precisely as they please, owing to the belief that a director must not be interfered with. (Kauffmann, Henstell, p. 53)

Sargent is championing the screenwriter as the central creative figure in the filmmaking process, but from the time of that essay to the present day, writers examining film history have acknowledged the film director's power to assert creative influence over the screenwriter's work.

During the golden era of the silent film, critics automatically conceded film authorship to directors like Griffith, Chaplin, and Keaton because of their control over every stage of film production. With the release of *The Birth of a Nation,* in 1915, the name D. W. Griffith became a household word. As early as 1917, Chaplin had become a subject of serious critical discussion. "Charlie Chaplin's Art," a brief essay in the February 3, 1917, issue of *The New Republic,* praises Chaplin as a "restrained and naturalistic" actor whose "work has become more and more delicate and finished as the medium of its reproduction has improved to admit of delicate and finished work. There is no doubt . . . that he is a great artist (Kauffmann, Henstell, p. 104). But as is obvious from the review, the reasons for his greatness, according to the critic, had to do with acting, not with the other functions of the filmmaking process, such as writing and directing, in which Chaplin was also involved. Both critics and audiences considered most films to be vehicles primarily for the actors' artistic expression, with the other members of the filmmaking team filling the role of artisans, not artists.

From World War I on, the studios saw the profitability of turning the actor—the figure most visible to the audience—into the "star." At this time, the focus shifted from publicity for the company making the film to the actor starring in it. As a result, filmmaking and marketing based on the star system became synonymous with the Hollywood studio system, which created the star. With a few exceptions like Cecil B. De Mille, the director's name was no longer a selling point with the general public.

During the 1930s and 1940s, at the height of the studio system's power, directors like Ford, William Wyler, and Hawks—no matter how important their creative efforts were to the studio and no matter how much that work was acknowledged behind the scenes—remained as background figures, looked upon, by critic and audience alike, as nothing more than competent technicians using the assembly line methods of Hollywood formula filmmaking. In film reviews of the period, directors and writers were thought of only as craftsmen working within the confines of the Hollywood tradition. From this tradition, for example, Hitchcock became known as the "master of suspense"; John Ford, as a maker of fine westerns. Exceptions, like the publicity surrounding the "boy wonder" Orson Welles's move to Hollywood from the Broadway stage to direct *Citizen Kane* (1941), and his rise and subsequent fall from grace when he bucked the studio system, point out the relative obscurity in which most directors were working during this period. Only the stars, and the pictures they starred in, regardless of who actually made them, were considered worthy of public promotion. And because of this promotion, some literate critics often ignored the Hollywood product or refused to take it seriously, seriousness being reserved for foreign films and their directors, who were often acknowledged as film artists.

Then, in the 1950s, came the auteur theory. This tenet, formulated by a group of French critics, including Jean-Luc Godard, Albert Astruc, François Truffaut, Jacques Rivette, and Claude Chabrol, writing for the French film periodical *Cahiers du Cinéma,* had as its foundation the belief that many neglected film directors, mostly Americans making commercial films, were worth studying in depth. A crucial date in the development of this theory would have to be the publication in January 1954 of Truffaut's article *"Une certaine tendance du cinéma français."* In this piece, as Doniol-Valcroze, a critic who wrote for *Cahiers,* points out, "a leap had been made, a trial begun with which we were all in solidarity, something bound us together. From then on, it was known that we were for Renoir, Rossellini, Hitchcock, Cocteau, Bresson . . . and against X, Y and Z. From then on there was a doctrine, the 'politique des auteurs,' even if it lacked flexibility. From then on, it was quite natural that the series of interviews with great directors would begin and a real contact established between them and us" (Talbot, p. 118). The American film critic Andrew Sarris, who promoted the auteur theory in his book *The American Cinema* (1968), in discussing the early French auteur critics, points out they were "obsessed with the wholeness of art and the artist." Their primary concern was to look "at a film as a whole, a director as a whole." The parts of the film, Sarris notes, "however entertaining individually, must cohere meaningfully." Geoffrey Nowell-Smith's definition serves as an adequate summary of the tenets of the auteur theory as it developed into critical practice:

The purpose of auteur criticism . . . becomes to uncover behind the superficial contrasts of subject and treatment a hard core of basic and often recondite motifs. The pattern formed by these motifs . . . is what gives an

> author's work its particular structure, both defining it internally and dis-
> tinguishing one body of work from another. (Wollen, p. 80)

The auteur theory as described here was, no doubt, initially responsible for
the flurry of personal interest in and the number of critical works on the films
of neglected American directors.

As described by Sarris and Nowell-Smith, the general premises of
auteur theory seem reasonable, but as put into practice by Truffaut and
Godard, among others, the theory produced some extreme judgments based
on what seems to be nothing more than personal opinion. For example, on
Godard's list of all-time great American sound films, Hawks's *Scarface* (1932)
is number one. This may be what provokes Sarris to note "a certain perversity" in the extreme auteurist position.

Naturally, personal opinion enters into all criticism to some extent, but
critics usually try to minimize its influence. However, Truffaut and Godard in
France, and Sarris and Peter Bogdanovich in America, relied heavily on their
personal taste in selecting directors to be elevated to star status. Autobiographical accounts and interviews with directors then were used to back
up evaluative judgments and to reinforce the principles behind auteurism. It
was in the form of those interviews and in the cult of personality evidenced
by the intense interest in biographical material that the auteur theory began
to have an impact on film criticism in general.

THE PLACE OF INTERVIEWS AND THE CULT OF PERSONALITY IN AUTEUR CRITICISM

In most critical approaches, the film critic tries to maintain the stance of
objectivity while examining a film for evidence of authorship or for its
historical and biographical relevance, or while trying to discover the film's
value as a piece of propaganda or as a work of art. In contrast, the use of
personal documents such as letters, memos, and journals, as well as interviews with the parties involved—sources of data that are often less than
objective—sometimes begins the critical process that ends as auteur criticism. Insights culled from these sources, although often far from objective,
can help the critic and student become better acquainted with the filmmaker,
determine who is responsible for what in the finished film, gain some knowledge of filmmaking techniques, and deepen understanding of the ideas and
intentions of the filmmaker. In these ways this very personal and seemingly
random method helped contribute to the development of a comprehensive
auteur theory. (Andrew Sarris has called auteur theory "not so much a theory
as an attitude, a table of values that converts film history into directorial
autobiography.")

Robin Wood, for example, uses personal information gained from interviews in his 1968 auteur study of Howard Hawks's films to refute the com-

monly made charge that Hawks restricted himself to subjects like auto racing and flying because of their guaranteed box office appeal. Knowing Hawks's genuine interest in these activities, Wood convincingly argues that Hawks's personal concerns were more important than box office statistics. "There is no sense anywhere in his work," Wood writes, "that box-office considerations have compelled him against his will to make films about flying, motor racing. . . ."

In discussing the meaning of specific films, Wood uses Hawks's own pronouncements of his intentions to provide insight. For example, having read Hawks's statement that he made *Rio Bravo* (1959) partly in reaction to Fred Zinneman's *High Noon* (1952) enables Wood to observe thematic differences in the two films by comparing their plots and structures. Wood also used personal information to point out some of Hawks's shortcomings. In his meetings with Hawks, Wood found him to be unpretentious as an artist and, as Wood makes clear, "unaware that people are likely to look at his *oeuvre* as a whole." From these meetings he concluded that Hawks's unconcern for his films as art, "although inextricably bound up with the kind of artist he is and therefore with his great qualities, has had a detrimental effect on his work" (Wood, p. 15).

Naturally, the constant flow of personal information in the form of interviews, gossip, and autobiographical detail has led some critics to see the personal information provided by the filmmakers involved as nothing more than self-serving propaganda. Adding to this image has been the publication of several anthologies of interviews, such as *Encountering Directors* (1972), *The Director as Superstar* (1970), and *Directors at Work* (1970). Although these interviews can be helpful, they often read like what one critic called "snatches of conversation overheard while drifting through a cocktail party." The American Film Institute's Dialogue on Film program, the Public Broadcasting System's series of interviews with American film directors, and the continuous supply of interviews in film periodicals such as *Film Comment* and *Cahiers du Cinéma* have also added to the abundance of personal information concerning film directors, producers, screenwriters, actors, and their films.

Three Personal Visions

The collection of personal information is not systematic criticism, however. When used by knowledgeable critic/film directors like François Truffaut, Peter Bogdanovich, and Jean-Luc Godard, who helped develop and refine auteur theory, the technique compensates for what it loses in objectivity. It gives readers a sense of actual participation in the filmmaking process by acquainting them with the personalities involved. Most important, it makes clear how complicated a task it is, to get a film made. While supposedly glorifying the director as creative artist, the interviews often reveal the real world of conflict, pressure, and compromise that characterize feature filmmaking. In the following examples, the interviews with major directors conducted by critic/directors, though not precisely formal criticism, do reveal a lot about the subjects and their films because the critics, steeped in the auteur concept, know what questions to ask. The information also serves as raw material for other auteur critics to digest and use in further analyses of these directors and their films.

François Truffaut, whose interviews with Alfred Hitchcock in 1963 set a precedent for many of the interviews since that time, has placed the value of the interview in perspective. In his introduction to the Hitchcock interviews, he offers as his defense for conducting such long, in-depth conversations— fifty hours of recording sessions covering subjects that span Hitchcock's notable and, at the time, neglected films—the following rationale: "There is no question here of fatuous admiration, nor am I suggesting that all of Hitchcock's work is perfect and beyond reproach. But inasmuch as his achievements have, until now, been grossly underrated, I feel it is high time Hitchcock was granted the leading position he deserves. Only then can we go on to appraise his work; indeed, his own critical comments in the pages that follow set the tone for such an objective examination" (Truffaut, Scott, p. 20). By beginning with Hitchcock's own comments, Truffaut believed he could influence later critics to make a more objective examination of Hitchcock's films. Since these interviews were collected and published in book form in 1966, and revised in 1983 not long before Truffaut's death, several critical reevaluations of Hitchcock have been made, resulting in new understanding and appreciation of Hitchcock's films. In his introduction to the revised version of the interviews, Truffaut points out the importance of those films in light of Hitchcock's death: "The man was dead but not the filmmaker. For his pictures, made with loving care, an exclusive passion, and deep emotions concealed by exceptional technical mastery, are destined to circulate throughout the world, competing with newer productions, defying the test of time." It is clear that Truffaut believed that his interviews with Hitchcock helped insure a more accurate critical assessment of those films. But it is also obvious that Truffaut believed that the interviews were only a first step toward a critical analysis. This seems to be an accurate description of the value of personal information such as interviews.

The Hitchcock interviews are organized chronologically, beginning with the earliest films. But beyond this organizational strategy, the information is a potpourri of gossip, personal opinion, anecdote, and reminiscence, with a fair amount of technical and critical insight concerning the films. A sample taken of the interviews from the discussion of the film *Vertigo* (1958) is representative:

FT: . . . I feel you really like *Vertigo.*

AH: One of the things that bothers me is a flaw in the story. The husband was planning to throw his wife down from the top of the tower. But how could he know that James Stewart wouldn't make it up those stairs? How could he be sure of that!

FT: That's true, but I saw it as one of those assumptions you felt people would accept. I understand that the picture was neither a hit nor a failure.

AH: It has made money by now.

FT: In your terms, wouldn't that be considered a flop?

AH: I suppose so. One of our whimsies when a picture isn't doing too well is to blame it on the faulty exploitation. So let's live up to the tradition and say they just didn't handle the sales properly! Do you know that I had Vera Miles in mind for *Vertigo,* and we had done the whole wardrobe and the final tests with her?

FT: Didn't Paramount want her?

AH: Paramount was perfectly willing to have her, but she became pregnant just before the part that was going to turn her into a star. After that I lost interest; I couldn't get the rhythm going with her again.

FT: I take it, from some of your interviews, that you weren't too happy with Kim Novak, but I thought she was perfect for the picture. There was a passive, animal quality about her that was exactly right for the part.

AH: Miss Novak arrived on the set with all sorts of preconceived notions that I couldn't possibly go along with. You know, I don't like to argue with a performer on the set; there's no reason to bring the electricians in on our troubles. I went to Kim Novak's dressing room and told her about the dress and hairdos that I had been planning for several months. I also explained that the story was of less importance to me than the over-all visual impact on the screen, once the picture is completed.

FT: It seems to me these unpleasant formalities make you unfair in assessing the whole picture. I can assure you that those who admire *Vertigo* like Kim Novak in it. Very few American actresses are quite as carnal on the screen. When you see Judy walking on the street, the tawny hair and makeup convey an animal-like sensuality. That quality is accentuated, I suppose, by the fact that she wears no brassiere.

AH: That's right, she doesn't wear a brassiere. As a matter of fact, she's particularly proud of that! (Truffaut, Scott, pp. 247–48)

These interviews are not film criticism, but raw material: they do provide valid insight into the filmmaker's world, in the hope, according to Truffaut, that they "might modify the American critics' approach to Hitchcock." In this case much of what Hitchcock says is idle gossip. But the discerning critic can uncover valuable information. Hitchcock admitted that he had chosen the clothes and hairdo of his star himself, months in advance—sure indicator of Hitchcock's painstaking approach to all aspects of production.

Peter Bogdanovich has used the personal material successfully in book-length interviews with Howard Hawks, Fritz Lang, John Ford, and Alan Dwan as well as in a book on Hitchcock. His analysis of Orson Welles's films, published in *Esquire* magazine (October 1972), uses interviews and other personal sources to examine Welles's life as a filmmaker. Bogdanovich says his reason for writing about Welles is to take the empty legend of Welles's working life and "get it right at last." Bogdanovich believes this task is important in Welles's case because "much has been written about the so-called 'boy wonder,' some favorable, some damning, much apocryphal."

For example, in the *Esquire* article, Bogdanovich attempts to refute certain criticism of Welles in Pauline Kael's book-length introduction to the published version of the *Citizen Kane* film script. In the introduction Kael argues that Welles tried to take total credit for the *Kane* project himself, giving none to his co-writer, Herman J. Mankiewicz, or to cameraman Gregg Toland. Kael's intent is to diminish the importance of Welles, consistent with her general dislike of auteur theory and specifically with those critics who champion the director at the expense of the script writer. Bogdanovich, to refute her thesis, offers firsthand sources to back up his claims for Welles.

His interviews with Welles were held in 1969, 1970, and 1971, long before Kael's introduction went to press. During those interviews he asked Welles of Mankiewicz's role in making the film. Welles told him it was "enormous." The interview includes the following exchange:

PB: You want to talk about him [Mankiewicz]?
OW: I'd love to. I loved *him*. People did. He was much admired, you know.

Bogdanovich calls this "a fair sample of Welles's feeling about Mankiewicz." Concerning Mankiewicz's contributions to the *Kane* script, Bogdanovich records this exchange between Welles and himself in which he asks Welles about a crucial scene in the film between Bernstein and the reporter:

OW: That was all Mank—it's my favorite scene.
PB: And the story about the girl: "One day, back in 1896, I was crossing over to Jersey on a ferry . . . there was another ferry . . . and a girl waiting to get off. A white dress she had on . . . I only saw her for a second, but I'll bet a month hasn't gone by since that I haven't thought of that girl. . . ."
OW: It goes on longer than that.
PB: Yes, but who wrote it?
OW: Mankiewicz, and it's the best thing in the movie. "A month hasn't gone by that I haven't thought of that girl." That's Mankiewicz. I *wish* it was me.
PB: Great scene.
OW: If I were in hell and they gave me a day off and said what part of any movie you ever made do you want to see, I'd say that scene of Mank's about Bernstein. All the rest could have been better, but that was just right. (Bogdanovich, pp. 103–104)

The Bogdanovich interview illustrates, again, the weakness of using the interview as part of critical analysis. Welles is the spokesman giving his view of the relationship he had with others working on the film many years after the fact. Authors—here a film director—may not always know the truth about their own work or may distort it or view it from a narrow, subjective perspective. In this instance, Welles remained the only personal source, for Herman Mankiewicz died before the Bogdanovich interview took place or the Kael article was written. Still, Bogdanovich's perceptive questions coming from his own film-viewing experience and understanding—quoting lines of dialogue from *Citizen Kane*—bring the interview to life, making it crackle with Welles's interesting remarks.

Bogdanovich sought to widen his base of factual information by also interviewing different people who worked with Welles on the film to find out their response to Kael's introduction. One of the people interviewed was Charles Lederer, a screenwriter, who described Mankiewicz's script before Welles got hold of it as "pretty dull," which is not to say he thought the finished film was dull. According to Lederer, "Orson vivified the material, changed it a lot and . . . transcended it with his direction." The argument that Mankiewicz should get credit for the final film script is challenged in Lederer's remarks.

Bogdanovich also did research to uncover memos, telegrams, and affidavits to call into question the validity of Kael's many statements. For example, Kael asserts that the *Kane* opera sequence was taken from the Marx Brothers' film *A Night at the Opera* (1935), with which Mankiewicz was involved. Bogdanovich quotes a telegram dated July 18, 1940, sent from Welles to the composer Bernard Herrmann concerning the writing of the *Kane* opera sequence. Welles asks Herrmann to create an original opera—a parody on a Mary Garden vehicle. When Bogdanovich asked Herrmann about the opera sequence, Herrmann said:

> Pauline Kael was never in touch with me while the book was being written. . . . If the rest of her opinions are as accurate as her statements about the music, none of it is to be taken very seriously. . . . It had nothing to do with the Brothers Marx. (Bogdanovich, p. 181)

Finally, long after the original interviews, Bogdanovich asked Welles to comment on his reaction to Kael's book. A letter from Welles to Bogdanovich concerning his status in that book sheds light on Welles as the human behind the legend:

> I hate to think . . . what my grandchildren, if I ever get any, and if they should ever bother to look into [Kael's book], are going to think of their ancestor: something rather special in the line of megalomaniac lice. . . . If there's anything that could maybe be dealt with in clear terms, it's the greasy smoke coming out of the book version of *Kane*. A low endeavor, worked without a spark of fire, but how to scrape off all that smudge? The job would take more time than you've got, more words than anybody will print, and what's worse—to be totally convincing—it's bound to be unreadable. Cleaning up after Miss Kael is going to take a lot of scrubbing. (Bogdanovich, p. 190)

Although usually not critical in nature, personal interviews can also be used to explicate critically a specific film. Directors of a film can often shed light on their own work by separating critical speculations from their intentions. In Jean-Luc Godard's interview with Michelangelo Antonioni, Godard's questions focus on Antonioni's intent in making the film *Red Desert* (1964). The interview has critical application because Antonioni's interpretation of his film differs from the general critical interpretation. Many critics have argued that the film condemns the industrial society in which a sensitive woman, Giuliana, lives. To this Antonioni says, "It simplifies things too much (as many have done) to say that I accuse this inhuman, industrialized world in which the individual is crushed and led to neurosis."

Antonioni reveals that he intended to show the beauty of the industrial world. "The line . . . the curves of factories and their smokestacks," he says, "are perhaps more beautiful than a row of trees. . . . It's a rich world—living, useful." Antonioni's intent, as he sees it, is to show Giuliana's neurosis as caused by her failure to adapt to the reality of the industrial society, and not the society's failure to make a place for her. Antonioni believes she is "too tied to life rhythms that are now out of date" (Ross, pp. 331–32).

Knowing something of the director's intentions gives the critic new perspective from which to interpret the film. The critic need not accept this interpretation, but it still can be useful to his or her own search for a balanced and complete understanding of a film. Most often the critic is forced to judge a new release on the evidence of only one or, at the most, two screenings. Directors, whether they comprehend fully their own intentions or not, cannot help but be much closer to the mechanics of the film—the choice of film stock, specific uses of sound, and reasons for including certain scenes—than the critics.

To get at these subtleties in *Red Desert*, Godard questions Antonioni about specific scenes that have puzzled critics. For example, one of the most obscure scenes in the film involves a story Giuliana tells her son. The story of a young girl who lives alone on an island is acted out on the screen in a vivid dream sequence. Antonioni interprets this story as reinforcing the idea that Giuliana, not her society, is sick. Antonioni argues that Giuliana's psychology is such that the story becomes "for her—unconsciously—an evasion of the reality surrounding her."

From the interview the reader learns much, not only about the film but about Antonioni's personal vision that prompted him to make it. In this vision he sees a world dominated by industry and technology. For human beings to remain healthy, they must adapt to the reality of increasingly expanding technology, which will eventually replace today's fast-declining humanism, and he anticipates the coming of this event "with a great deal of envy." Antonioni's comments are a switch from those of artists who decry the loss of tradition and the takeover by technology. If the critic accepts Antonioni's statement as sincere—there is always the possibility of irony— the film *Red Desert* may take on new meaning.

Since *Red Desert* was Antonioni's first color film, the question of his use of color photography arises. Antonioni says that during filming he found that color and camera movement had to be matched. He says, for example, that "a rapid panoramic sweep is efficacious on brilliant red, but it does nothing for sour green, unless you're looking for a new contrast." Also, Antonioni is aware of the psychology of color in choosing certain colors for certain shooting locations: "I wanted this contrast between warm colors and cool colors. . . . I dyed the grass around the shed on the edge of the marsh in order to reinforce the sense of desolation, of death. . . . I would never have done the scene in the shack when they talk about drugs, aphrodisiacs, without using reds" (Ross, pp. 339–40).

The interview provides precise information about the making of *Red Desert* from a man closer to that process than anyone else. Godard, as interviewer, keeps Antonioni on the subject of the film. No superfluous talk about actors' personalities, shooting atmosphere, or other gossip detracts from the subject. Godard is interested, as critic and filmmaker, in film aesthetics, and, happily, Antonioni's answers prove enlightening. The result: sharp critical insight into the film's construction.

The examination of personal materials has one final application: in the hands of certain great filmmakers—as in those of all great artists—the finished film can provide the filmmaker's own critical point of view. For example, a director/critic like Jean-Luc Godard uses his knowledge as a director when conducting a personal interview. Conversely, Godard's films can be seen as pieces of film criticism as well as essays about life, love, and politics. For example, his first film, *Breathless* (1959), was a radical departure from the theatricality of many popular French films made in the 1940s and 1950s. The film works not only on a narrative, artistic level, but also on a critical level because it shows up the pretensions of the standard commercial films of the period. Godard achieved these results by experimenting with radically different filmmaking methods. He used *cinema verité* camera work and location filming, in contrast to the stationary camera and studio location favored at the time by the more conservative, traditional French filmmakers. But besides showing up the more pretentious methods of filmmaking, Godard made clear which filmmakers he admired. *Breathless,* as many critics have pointed out, is a loose adaptation of Howard Hawks's *Scarface,* containing allusions to other films and filmmakers Godard esteemed.

Godard's statement concerning his stance as filmmaker and critic illustrates his personal basis for both occupations:

> As a critic, I thought of myself as a filmmaker. Today I still think of myself as a critic, and in a sense I am, more than ever before. Instead of writing criticism, I make a film, but the critical dimension is subsumed. . . . For there is a clear continuity between all forms of expression. It's all one. The important thing is to approach it from the side which suits you best. (Narboni, Milne, p. 171)

BIOGRAPHICAL AND
AUTOBIOGRAPHICAL MATERIAL

Though highly personal material is valuable when used by perceptive writers like Truffaut, Bogdanovich, and Godard, it is only one important source for the critic and student trying to understand the role of people in the impersonal world of filmmaking. Beyond the interview there are the traditional forms of memoir, personal correspondence, and autobiography and biography which have long been used in literary criticism. It was only with the advent of auteur criticism and the artistic credibility it provided for filmmakers, however, that these tools took on real significance. When used to explicate filmmakers and their films, such materials helped to confirm the importance of the director as the head of the filmmaking team.

Frank Capra's autobiographical memoir affords an outstanding example of how a director's own account of his career can produce more extensive material than that found in an interview. James Childs, interviewing Capra in *Film Comment* (November–December 1972), asked the crucial question: Are you espousing the auteur theory? Capra, whose answer as a film director should be obvious, said, "Yes. [Film] is an art form and one man must create that form." Childs tried to get Capra to elaborate by asking if he believed his consciousness is imprinted on his films as Milton's is on his poetry. Capra's cryptic reply was, simply, "Yes. This has been so with my films. My films have been one man, one film" (pp. 385–86).

To someone unfamiliar with Capra's life and work, this exchange can mean little. But after reading Capra's own account of his career in film, one realizes that he provides proof of the director's importance to almost every aspect of the filmmaking process and, therefore, tends to validate the claims made by those who support the auteur theory. Capra's autobiography offers not simply an offhand remark that the critic must develop into a theory, but the record of experience of a man who devoted his life to a certain filmmaking approach. The autobiography enables the critic to view filmmaking from the perspective of the filmmaker himself. Equally important is Capra's creation of the whole milieu in which he works—casting, production, dealing with actors, distribution of the film—which can all have influence on the completed work. John Ford said of the scope of Capra's autobiography that it brings to the monumental task of describing film production in Hollywood "the sure sense of the professional and accomplishes the only definitive record I've ever read on the subject" (Capra, p. viii).

Capra's memoir is full of anecdotes about his years making films, but it also adds considerable evidence for auteur speculations about the role of the director in Hollywood filmmaking. Without arguing a thesis, Capra's account of his work establishes the idea that film, like literature, must have a single author to succeed. Throughout, he insists on the validity of the auteur theory without ever mentioning the word. For instance, in describing his first attempt at making a film, Capra claims almost total responsibility for the finished film—from writing the script to final editing.

For him, this experience confirmed his belief that film could be used for an individual to speak directly to the "heart and mind of man." This experience also made unthinkable the idea of turning over any part of the film to someone else. Capra felt this would be the equivalent of Beethoven giving his themes to an arranger to orchestrate for him. Capra says his guiding principle—"one man, one film"—became for him "a fixation, an article of faith."

The anti-auteur critic who believes that the director is an overrated member of a film team might accuse Capra of self-aggrandizement in emphasizing the importance of "one man, one film." But, from reading Capra's accounts of his film projects, one gets a sense that Capra is being absolutely honest and candid. He readily admits that it was Harry Cohn, founder of Columbia Pictures, who made Capra's "one man" pictures a reality. Cohn's method was to let proven directors choose their own script, cast, and crew, making personal creativity possible even within a studio atmosphere. Capra insists that he was allowed to do anything he wanted as long as he stayed within allotted time and budget—and as long as his films made a profit. Capra accepted these restrictions as part of the ground rules and never saw them as curbing his freedom of expression.

Capra, as a director, of course, has a stake in his claim for the director's supreme importance to the filmmaking process. For personal accounts describing the importance of other members of the filmmaking team, one need only read the following: *Memo from David O. Selznick* (1972), a collection of Selznick's private and public correspondences and pronouncements which illuminate the producer's role in making commercial films; *The Hollywood Screenwriters* (1973), interviews with screenwriters, as well as critical essays and a screenwriters' symposium, which help to clarify the contribution of the writer; and *The Movies, Mr. Griffith and Me* (1969), Lillian Gish's autobiography in which she describes her work with D. W. Griffith and the growth of the Hollywood star system.

Film biographies have flourished almost from the beginning of the rise of film. Many of these biographies are merely gossip and anecdote, but some have important critical value. In the latter category would be placed the biography detailing Griffith's life and work by Robert Henderson. Henderson states his intention in his introduction: "The substance of Griffith's creation was derived from his experience and life. To understand the nature of his films is to understand his vision" (Henderson, p. vii).

Henderson begins the biography by describing Griffith's early career at Biograph Studio, first as an actor, then as a director. The chapters portraying those years alternate with those that detail Griffith's childhood and family life. From the experience at Biograph, Griffith is shown to have gained great skill and confidence as a filmmaker. From his family, especially his father, as Henderson endeavors at some length to show, Griffith gained a love and respect for the South's cause in the Civil War, a sense of the dramatic and theatrical, and a keen understanding of the Southern code of honor.

Henderson's introduction helps the reader better understand some of the ingredients that went into the creation of what has been universally hailed as one of the greatest films of all time, *The Birth of a Nation* (1915). The need to justify *The Birth of a Nation* as a work of art or Griffith as an artist never arises. Henderson simply describes this film, which was adapted from a novel, *The Clansman,* by Thomas Dixon, as Griffith's attempt to tell what he considered to be the truth about the losing side in the Civil War.

The outcry by civil rights groups against *The Birth of a Nation* served, according to Henderson, as a stimulant to Griffith and led him into his next film project, *Intolerance* (1918). Griffith was outraged by attempts made to censor certain scenes in *The Birth of a Nation* that were considered racist. He believed that these were attacks against his presentation of truth, and he responded with a lengthy essay on free speech in America. In the essay Griffith attacks the "powers of intolerance as an excuse for an assault on our liberties." The "powers of intolerance" became the focus for Griffith's theme, which Henderson describes as a "counterattack . . . to defend mankind against the inhumanity and intolerance of others."

The Birth of a Nation and the even more spectacular *Intolerance* were made as mass entertainments, but they were created from one man's personal vision, at least according to Henderson's biography. An awareness of Griffith's vision, his gift for the dramatic, his Southern background, his love of the romantic, and his early years perfecting his art at Biograph make both Griffith's artistic achievement and his one-sided view of history easier to perceive.

At one level, auteur criticism is the attempt to identify the personal element in filmmaking in order to acknowledge someone as "author" of a film, much as we associate an individual author with a particular book or series of books—for instance, Louis L'Amour's westerns. This urge has its roots in the informal, undeveloped, immediate response to film. If we like or dislike a film, we want to praise or blame someone—someone specific. Filmgoers also like the potential satisfaction implied by the name above the title: a Steven Spielberg film, a Brian DePalma film, an Ingmar Bergman film can be seen as an assurance of a particular kind of positive experience. Hollywood has used this identification to market films, even when the star director has only produced the film but not directed it—for example, George Lucas's *Star Wars* series made after the first one. But this initial response for simple identification can be made much more complex.

THE AUTEUR THEORY IN PRACTICE

In order to illustrate more complex applications of auteur theory to film criticism, let's examine the films of the American director Howard Hawks as seen by Peter Wollen, a British critic who explains auteur theory primarily through analysis of filmic structures; and by Robin Wood, another British critic, who explains auteur theory as the result of consistent and conscious artistic activity visible in the work of such directors as Hitchcock, Bergman, Arthur Penn, and, of course, Hawks. Hawks's films are important because, in describing those films, Wollen has called them "a test case for the auteur theory." By this he means that Hawks has made films in every popular genre, has always worked inside the studio system, and has never been considered, by most critics, to be more than a competent film technician.

Wollen's analysis of Hawks as an auteur, in *Signs and Meaning in the Cinema* (1972), demonstrates how an auteur critic, interested mainly in repeated structural motifs and themes, might go about constructing, out of the films the director has made, the ideal film, which because of financial and artistic restrictions could never be made in the real world of Hollywood genre filmmaking. At the heart of this ideal film is what Wollen calls "homo Hawksianus," "the protagonist of Hawksian values in the problematic Hawksian world." The auteur critic finds meaning in Hawks's films by pointing out, in each of the films, structural characteristics common to all.

Wollen begins by grouping Hawks's films into two categories: (1) adventure dramas and (2) crazy comedies. Within these two categories he points out some Hawksian motifs, beginning with those in the adventure dramas. According to Wollen, these films usually center on a group of men isolated from society. The strongest emotion of these men is camaraderie, which, along with a resistance to outside pressure and the performance of rituals, binds the group together. Tension exists only when a member of the group lets the group down or when a woman intrudes. Of Hawks's attitude toward women, Wollen says: "Man is woman's 'prey.' Women are admitted to the male group only after much disquiet, and a long ritual courtship, phased round the offering, lighting and exchange of cigarettes, during which they prove themselves worthy of entry" (Wollen, p. 86).

As a further example of the method of structural auteur criticism, Wollen describes the composite character traits of Hawks's adventure drama hero. He notes that time and again Hawks's heroes are outcasts associated with other outcasts (racing drivers, pilots, cattlemen, marlin fishermen). He says that it is the group that determines the hero's actions. The hero must first become a member of the group in which, at this point, all the members are equal. Wollen acknowledges that the hero as he is to be found in a Hawks adventure drama may seem to some critics to be "cruelly stunted." But that judgment, as regards Hawks, the auteur, is too hasty, for Wollen argues that the adventure dramas by themselves give a limited view of Hawks's intent. It is in juxtaposing the crazy comedies with the adventure dramas that both film types become more meaningful. Wollen believes that Hawks was aware of the shortcomings of the adventure film and that his "real claim as an author lies in the presence, together with the dramas, of their inverse, the crazy comedies," which, he says, are "the agonized exposure of the underlying tensions of the heroic dramas." In the dramas we see men, who pose as heroes, really acting like children, and women disguising their femininity in order to be accepted as men. On the other hand, in the comedies the two principal themes are the hero's "regression to childhood" and "sex and role reversal."

Wollen brilliantly points out this contrast: "whereas the dramas show the mastery of man over nature, over women, over the animal and childish; the comedies show his humiliation, his regression. The heroes become victims; society, instead of being excluded and despised, breaks in with irruptions of monstrous farce" (Wollen, p. 91). Wollen places the comedies in opposition to the dramas to set up a satiric Hawksian universe in which the characters in the dramas are mocked by those in the comedies. He says to appreciate Hawks's characters, "we must be aware of a phantom, stripped of mastery, humiliated, inverted," which walks as a shadow to every dramatic hero.

This description of the films might lead one to conclude that viewing a Hawks adventure film must be a flat, dull experience—and some of Hawks's films bear this out. They *need* to be shored up with theory. However, when the good films are analyzed for more than structural similarities, a richness emerges that does not have to be explained or enlarged upon. In Robin Wood's auteur-based *Howard Hawks* (1968), his description of Feathers, Chance's girl in *Rio Bravo* (1959), illustrates this quality in Hawks at his best. It also exemplifies Wood's more humanistic version of the auteur approach. Here he interprets the character as a respository of Hawksian values:

> Feathers is the product of the union of her basic "type"—the saloon girl— and the Hawks woman, sturdy, and independent yet sensitive and vulnerable, the equal of any man yet not in the least masculine. The tension between background (convention) and foreground (actual character) is nowhere more evident. We are very far here from the brash "entertainer" with the heart of gold who dies (more often than not) stopping a bullet intended for the hero. Angie Dickenson's marvelous performance gives us the perfect embodiment of the Hawksian woman, intelligent, resilient, and responsive. There is a continual sense of a woman who really grasps what is important to her. One is struck by the beauty of the character, the beauty of a living individual responding spontaneously to every situation from a secure center of self. It is not so much a matter of characterisation as the communication of a life-quality (a much rarer thing). What one most loves about Hawks, finally, is the aliveness of so many of his people. (Wood, p. 42)

Finding touches of humanity in Hawks's characters is important to Wood, as is setting apart the hero from the Hawksian group. Wood says that in the good films, no matter how important the group is, there is always a group leader—a man who transcends the group to become a complete personality. He is not a stereotyped hero but, as Wood describes him, an individual hero in a unique situation living in the Hawksian universe.

In *Rio Bravo,* for example, Wood notes that the hero (Chance) is definitely part of the group—as Wollen has pointed out. But he goes on to say that the hero's role is more important than just being an outcast member, completely dependent on the group:

> Without the cripple, the drunk, the comic Mexican, the teenage boy, a girl on hand to fling a well timed flower pot, the superman would be defeated before he had the chance to perform a single decisive action. Yet if the others are physically indispensable to him, remove him from the film, and you would be left largely with the human wreckage; for it is abundantly clear that it is Chance, partly by direct influence, partly by example, by the very fact of his existence, who gives meaning, coherence, and integrity to the lives of those around him. As a concrete embodiment of the Hawksian values, he is the nucleus round which the others can organise themselves, without which there would be no possibility of order. (Wood, pp. 55–56)

The isolated group is a fine example of a repeated Hawks motif. But it is the hero who brings the film *Rio Bravo* to life; it is because of the hero that the group coheres.

In Wood's analysis of another Hawks adventure film, *To Have and Have Not* (1945), Humphrey Bogart, as Morgan, is offered as a striking example of the Hawks hero. Yet, as Wood points out, Morgan is a man in isolation—the group plays no role at all. Wood believes that here Bogart's performance "is arguably at once the completest realisation of the actor's personality and the most perfect embodiment of the Hawks hero."

When looking at a specific film, Wood does not rely on auteur theory alone. Coming originally from a humanist position, Wood combines the auteur approach with close analysis of character and plot imagery that is reminiscent of the New Criticism in literature. He focuses, therefore, on the individual hero in the specific film. Wollen, in explaining the structural nature of auteur theory, is more concerned with those structural elements of Hawks's films that prove Hawks to be an auteur. He does not concern himself with specific heroes in the adventure dramas. He simply concludes that, if Hawks were judged only on the merit of these films as a group, "it would seem that Hawks's work is flaccid, lacking in dynamism." As has been mentioned, he finds richness and depth in Hawks's films only by juxtaposing the adventure dramas with the crazy comedies, only by looking at the entire body of work.

Wood, too, is aware of certain opposition between the adventure dramas and the comedies. He is concerned, however, first of all, with the individual comedy films and secondly with the way they relate to the director's work. As with the heroes of the adventure dramas, Wood discusses the comic characters in depth. An example is his explication of the heroine, Susan, in the film *Bringing Up Baby.* Only through a close analysis does one become aware of her importance to the film, for, according to Wood, the comic excellence of the film depends to a large extent on the complexity of Susan's character.

He points out that Hawks infuses her character with a number of possible interpretations that work on different levels of meaning. The first is that she is the female equivalent of Hawks's hero. She is a unique, truly remarkable screen heroine—not because she is a shadow to some "stunted" hero but because, like Chance and Morgan, she refuses to accept the constraints of society. She trusts completely her own spontaneous impulses of attraction and repulsion. She has a sense of identity beyond her alliances (with high society), and she is committed only to those personal ties she wishes to acknowledge.

Naturally, a woman with these qualities dominates men and serves as a reminder of the limitation of the Hawks hero. Still, she is more than a shadow or a symbol. On the screen, according to Wood, she is an alive, vibrant girl, who brings a second level of meaning to the comedy: the reversal of the cliché courtship story of boy meets girl. In *Bringing Up Baby* girl meets boy, girl chases boy, girl loses boy, but in the end girl gets boy.

On a third level she represents the life force itself, closely associated with animal instinct. (She is identified with a tame leopard). This level can be seen in the contrast between Susan and Dr. Huxley's fiancée, who is willing to forgo their honeymoon so Huxley can complete his work, the reconstruction of a dinosaur. The fiancée is as lifeless as the dinosaur. Wood believes that this contrast is crucial to the meaning of the film on this level. Here the film works as an initiation rite in which Huxley goes from the world of the superego (the world of reason and order represented by the fiancée and by the completed dinosaur) into the world of id (represented by Susan and the leopard). Though this kind of analysis enlarges the meaning of the film, Wood himself admits that the film is not "as crudely schematic as I make it sound."

A close look at Wood's analysis of a single Hawks film, *Scarface,* will demonstrate that Wood relies heavily on the basic structural premise of auteur theory to uncover new insights concerning this complex film mode early in Hawks's career. But it should also be clear that auteur criticism serves as a springboard for Wood's eclectic critical method of placing this film in relation to others in Hawks's *oeuvre*.

Using the premises of auteur theory, Wood classifies Hawks's films according to theme. For example, the theme "the lure of irresponsibility" includes *Bringing Up Baby* (1938), *His Girl Friday* (1940), *I Was a Male War Bride* (1949), and *Monkey Business* (1952), but it also includes *Scarface* (1932). In organizing films around an elemental Hawksian theme, Wood discovers motifs in *Scarface* that are repeated in the later comedies. For example, he says:

> The overlapping and combining of farce and horror points ahead to *His Girl Friday,* Tony's destructive innocence to that of Lorelei Lee; in *Monkey Business,* the juxtapositions of ape, savages and children are clearly related

to the presentation of the gangsters in *Scarface*. Above all, *Scarface* gives us the essential theme of Hawks's most characteristic comedies. If the adventure films place high value on the sense of responsibility, the comedies derive much of their tension and intensity from the fascination exerted by irresponsibility. (Wood, pp. 67–68)

Wood has discovered structural similarities that had not been considered before. But he is not content simply to describe motifs and relate them to themes, even though the insights are new and valuable. To clarify further the film's meaning, he compares the main character in *Scarface* with the main character in Godard's *Les Carabiniers* (1963). He argues that although many of the methods and styles of the two films are different, the main characters— Tony Camonte in *Scarface* and Michelango in *Les Carabiniers*—are both child-like primitives, "innocent, immune from moral judgment," because neither has developed a moral awareness. It is as they discover their moral nature that they become vulnerable and fall.

Tony, the primitive, is identified with animals—he is introduced as a squat, ape-like shadow. The aspects of childlike primitivism are important thematic elements of both films. To reinforce the primitivism, all the gangsters in *Scarface* are portrayed as childlike or animalistic or both. Like children, they boast extravagantly, treat women as a commodity, and perform childish acts—cutting out paper dolls, for example. As animals they kill without remorse and with a sense of exhilaration that is terrifyingly communicated to the audience.

The exhilarating sense of freedom and excitement associated with the killings, and the humor contained in the childlike behavior of the gangsters, cannot hide Hawks's and Godard's theme as Wood sees it, "the frightening discrepancy between the achievements of civilisation and the actual level of culture attained by the individuals who are its byproducts." For example, Tony's male secretary is shown throughout the film to be afraid of telephones. At one point he even tries to shoot one. He is killed, at the telephone, never able to understand it, the society, or his nature.

Though Wood still focuses on the director's role in the creation of a film, his emphasis on moral values and symbolic images shows his use of the humanistic approach to the work. In discussing Hawks's moral stance in the film, Wood claims that while Hawks never preaches that the gangsters' life is wrong—because as primitives they are seemingly beyond society's rules—he does show a revulsion to the gangsters' subversion of the social order. Yet Wood realizes that often Hawks's characters—even those tied to society— must struggle against the attractive pull of irresponsibility.

Like the comedy characters—Susan in *Bringing Up Baby,* for example—the gangsters are associated with the naturalistic world of animals and children. In this light they are humorous, sympathetic characters. But by using images, like the cross, Hawks tells us that total lack of responsibility is to be deplored; moreover, according to Wood, the "values appealed to are absolute rather than social; our horror derives from deeper sources than violation of social stability" (Wood, p. 64).

Wood argues that the film gains terrific moral force near the end even though it has been criticized for its immorality. Tony, who has been unknowingly attracted to his sister, has become dimly aware that this is an erotic attraction and it has shaken him. It is only as he gains this awareness that a sense of moral confusion is awakened. This awakening is pictured metaphorically by the police attack on Tony's fortress. He disintegrates into blind panic as gas bombs explode around him. According to Wood, the smoke from these bombs proves "the perfect visual expression for his bewildered state of mind." As Tony's protective innocence crumbles, his fortress is punctured and his death is inevitable. Tony's death stands as a judgment of his entire life.

At this point in the essay, Wood again turns to the comparison between *Scarface* and *Les Carabiniers,* saying that the strengths and weaknesses of Hawks are revealed in this comparison. It is Wood's understanding, not only of Hawks's films but of other films of the genre as well, that makes this analysis possible:

> At first sight *Scarface* seems richer than *Les Carabiniers.* It works brilliantly on a popular narrative level, a dimension that Godard's film doesn't pretend to. Beyond this is the essential stability of Hawks's characters and the traditional nature of his art: his successful films are preceded by a robustness derived from stable values—loyalty, courage, endurance, mastery of self and environment—whereas the emotion underlying and characterising *Les Carabiniers* is a terrible despair, arising from Godard's exposure to the complexities and confusions, the disintegration of accepted values, inherent in contemporary society. *Les Carabiniers* is a statement about the modern world of a kind Hawks nowhere attempts. This defines him as an artist—it doesn't invalidate him. Hawks takes the state of civilisation for granted in a way that has become increasingly difficult for the modern artist, and he has been helped in this by the availability to him of cinematic traditions which manifest themselves in the genres. . . . (Wood, p. 150)

An auteur critic like Wood recognizes, identifies, and classifies motifs and themes in a director's films, yet never relies completely on such typical auteur methods. Rather, he combines elements of structuralist auteur criticism with a humanist perspective: literary criticism and genre criticism, as well as biographical, historical, and autobiographical insights, aid him in analyzing the films of a director's entire career.

Since authentic auteurs, as the French identified them, worked mainly in the Hollywood studio system making genre films, it is not surprising that genre studies and auteur studies often overlap. In *Horizons West,* Jim Kitses examines the western film genre, as it has been interpreted by three Hollywood directors who, until this critical analysis, were little understood or appreciated by the serious film critic and student: Anthony Mann, Budd Boetticher, and Sam Peckinpah. Here the auteur theory becomes a critical tool, used along with the tool of genre criticism (discussed at length in Chapter 4), to explicate specific films that draw their strengths from their directors and the genre in which they worked. In this way Kitses attempts to show that the director and the genre can form a symbiotic relationship that has a positive influence on both.

The opening chapter of *Horizons West* is entitled "Authorship and Genre: Notes on the Western," and in it Kitses points out that, in the years preceding the book's publication (1970), the western genre had received "scant critical attention," while, at the same time, the director had "occupied critical energies." In Kitses's view, this emphasis on auteur theory based on the study of directors had the positive effect of bringing about "the beginnings of a systematic critical approach; the foundation for a subject with its own body of knowledge." But while endorsing auteur theory as his way to "rescue three talented men from the neglect forced upon them," he is also aware that adhering to a narrow auteurist approach is a mistake. Kitses believes that the way to build a "body of film scholarship that is both vigorous and educationally valid" is to "explore the inner workings of the genre." Thus the critical coupling of genre criticism with auteur criticism is explained theoretically for the first time, even though it had been used to a lesser extent by Wood and others. Up to this time the main focus for auteur critics had been to show how auteur directors had been able to work within the confines of the genre and to transcend its seemingly narrow limits. The idea implicit in this view was that the genre material was not worthy of the director but had been imposed by the Hollywood production (and value) system. Even Wood, who attempted to broaden the narrow focus of auteur theory, wrote somewhat apologetically about Hawks's and Hitchcock's subject matter, never seeing in it a main reason for their success.

Kitses, on the other hand, suggests that "in place of the reactionary notion that Hollywood directors function like the charismatic heroes of their films," in reality the strength of the work of genre filmmakers is tied to the tradition inherent in the genres, "of which the western seems . . . an admirable and central model." To begin his study, Kitses presents a survey of the western genre founded on the idea of the American west that is part of every American's mythic consciousness. He then lists the elements that make up the genre, concluding that the western is a

> complex variable, its peculiar alchemy allowing a wide range of intervention, choice and experiment by script-writer and director. History provides a source of epics, spectacle and action films, pictures sympathetic to the Indian, "realistic" films, even anti-westerns (Delmer Daves's *Cowboy*). From the archetypal base flow revenge films, fables, tragedies, pastorals, and a juvenile stream of product. Of course, the dialectic is always at work and the elements are never pure. Much that is produced, the great bulk of it

inevitably undistinguished, occupies a blurred middle ground. But for the artist of vision in *rapport* with the genre, it offers a great freedom for local concentration and imaginative play." (Kitses, p. 20)

It is in this context that Kitses begins to explore "the contributions of three of [the western's] finest champions in the post-war era": Anthony Mann, in whose work is "a constant drive towards mythic quality in the hero"; Sam Peckinpah, who provides "a rich creative play with romantic potential"; and Budd Boetticher, in whom "the ironic mode . . . dominates."

The close of Kitses's first chapter states well the symbiotic role of auteur theory and genre theory as they can be used to explicate the work of Hollywood-based filmmakers: "The western is not just the men who have worked within it. Rather than an empty vessel breathed into by the film-maker, the genre is a vital structure through which flow a myriad of themes and concepts. As such the form can provide a director with a range of possible connections and the space in which to experiment, to shape and refine the kind of effects and meanings he is working towards. We must be prepared to entertain the idea that *auteurs* grow, and that genre can help to crystallize preoccupations and contribute actively to development" (pp. 26–27).

Kitses then examines in detail the major films of each director as they can be seen to make unique artistic statements, necessary for the directors to be considered as auteurs, while at the same time working within the limitations imposed by the genre—which turn out to be few or no limitations at all. For example, the films of Anthony Mann are first broken down into the genre elements, including the hero, the villain, the community, and the landscape. In describing these common genre devices as they are used by Mann, Kitses explores the ways in which Mann plays off against the stereotypical genre patterns in order to come up with his own, unique artistic vision, which validates him as an auteur. He begins, however, by indicating Mann's indebtedness to the western genre; he quotes Mann himself: "A western is a wonderful thing to do because you take a group of actors who have acted on the stage or who have acted in rooms and now you take them out into the elements, and you throw them against the elements and the elements make them greater as actors than if they were in a room. Because they have to shout above the winds, they have to suffer, they have to climb mountains . . ." (p. 66). This quote is vitally important because it shows the director in harmony with one of the major elements of the genre in which he works. In fact, this director goes to the extreme of suggesting that the landscape of the western genre brings out greatness in actors, a concern normally considered the job of the director. With this as a background, Kitses examines the way that Mann uses the western genre landscape in his own unique way: "Where the traditional imagery of the western intersected with Mann's preoccupations, offering an image through which he could express and focus his themes, was in the recurrent visual motif of a man alone in the landscape. But for Mann the landscape was a specific, the man, time and again, on a *mountain*. Great height is always important in Mann, a clue to the reach and conflict of his characters on the one hand, the transcendent forces of justice which they defy on the other" (p. 70). Kitses then gives examples of this particular use of the landscape in a specific Mann picture, *Bend of the River*. "Study of the topography of *Bend in the River* repays itself, illuminating the deceptive movement of the film in which Cole, by his act of defying the community—leaving his better impulses in the form of the savagely beaten McLyntock to perish atop snowy Mount Hood—becomes a tragic figure. The hero in turn becomes an omnipotent force firing down from high up in the terrain, blocking Cole's every step. Creating him only as gunfire, movement, and a voice in the landscape, Mann suggests the spirit of implacable justice working itself out through the figure of McLyntock." (pp. 70–71). Kitses, in this example, has shown how the stereotypical landscape of the western genre is used by Mann for specific thematic reasons that reinforce the director as an auteur and the film as a genre western.

The movement in critics like Kitses and Wood is away from the restrictive application of auteur theory to a broader, more eclectic criticism, where auteur approaches serve as the starting point for a more encompassing, richer film criticism.

THE QUESTION OF ART AND THE ARTIST

In the final analysis, auteur approaches have proved valuable for two reasons. First, by describing and analyzing major films of one director, the auteur critic serves the needs of the film student who usually must face the problem of gaining access to a large number of a single director's films. In literary study solving this problem is not difficult. A library in any fairly large university or city will have the collected works of most major authors and, if not, can obtain them through interlibrary loan. But because of distribution rights and expenses involved, seeing a film director's major works or, ideally, the "collected works" often proves impossible for anyone outside Washington, D.C., New York City, or Los Angeles. With the advent of the video recorder and cassettes, however, more and more films are becoming available. But many so-called minor works of a director may never appear profitable enough to ever appear in this format.

The auteur critic, then, provides a major source of insight into a large group of a single artist's creative production. The critic who has access to a nearly complete collection of a director's films does the film student an invaluable service by bringing together, cataloguing, describing, and analyzing the films in detail. Of course the critic's description of the films will never take the place of the films themselves; it can, however, shed new light on films not immediately available for viewing.

The second contribution of the approach is that it has tended in some ways to validate the theatrical film as, potentially, an art object and in some ways to modify the general public's view that mainstream films are incapable of being art. Until auteur theory made it fashionable to critically examine their works, most Hollywood filmmakers were viewed as popular entertainers, not as artists working in the most representative art form of the twentieth century. But because of auteur theory, that view has been able to gain intellectual currency. Without the theory, for example, William Rothman's wonderfully detailed, scholarly study of Hitchcock's films, *Hitchcock: The Murderous Gaze* (1982), could not have been written. An art form, and the critic who examines that art form, needs an artist, and auteur theory supplied the artists—discovered mainly in the commercial ranks of Hollywood genre directors.

The problems with the extreme application of auteur theory are not to be discounted, especially by beginning film students. The auteur approach may lead critics to overvalue the director who accumulates a body of film in which recurring motifs are evident, may distort critics' judgment of an individual film because of its connection with a director's total work, and may cause critics to become preoccupied with finding and identifying the motifs in a director's work for their own sake, seeing the making of films as an isolated instance of personal creativity, without reference to the social and economic forces at work in film production and distribution.

Obviously, calling attention to these problems is not intended to invalidate auteur criticism or the personal approaches that it implies. It has performed a singular service by insisting that filmmakers, working in a commercial arena, can be taken seriously, and that the films they create can be the subject of insightful, in-depth criticism.

GUIDELINES FOR WRITING
AUTEURIST FILM CRITICISM

I. **Sources**
 A. Primary
  Think about a film you really enjoyed. Find out who directed the film. Locate several others directed by the same person (most likely on videotape). Or find and see several films by a well-known director, one whose name has been mentioned in your reading or in a film class. It might also be possible to find several films by the same screenwriter.
 B. Secondary
  Read all the criticism of your chosen auteur's films that you can find in both popular and specialized magazines, journals, and texts. If you choose an established director, you should be able to find some biographical material. Check the *Readers' Guide to Periodical Liter-*

ature for the location of film reviews, interviews, and biographical information.

II. Method

Examine three or more films by the same director, screenwriter, or even film star. Choosing a director who also wrote and maybe even acted in the film, like Sylvester Stallone, Sydney Pollack, Woody Allen, or Barbra Streisand, might be helpful. Or you might examine the work of an established auteur, concentrating on films or themes that have been ignored. Examine films for thematic concerns, camera style (expressionistic/realistic), characterization, dialogue, and settings. Try to narrow the focus of the essay to just one or two major similarities that you find in all the films. Though an actual interview with your auteur figure may be impossible, sending a list of questions to his or her publicity address might get a response—and a surefire paper topic.

III. Questions a Writer Using the Auteurist Approach Might Ask

1. Does the auteur's life (social class, politics, education, professional training) contribute to the thematic preoccupations of his or her films?
2. Does the auteur collaborate with the same people, including actors, from film to film?
3. Are interviews, biographies, or autobiographical information concerning the auteur available?
4. Does the auteur consistently use the same themes or work in the same genre? Does the auteur favor certain shots (close-up, high-angle, extreme long shot, and so on) or other filmmaking techniques?
5. What is the personal stamp exhibited in all the auteur's films that I examined?

CHAPTER 4

The Genre Approach: Analysis of Formula Films

Genre Approach Capsule

Audience: General readers familiar with film subjects; film scholars and students.

Functions: Describe film forms and types; classify and analyze the elements found in formula films.

Subject: Groups of popular films that use similar plots, characters, and settings—for example, horror films, westerns, science-fiction films.

Writers: Freelance professionals; film scholars.

Publications: Highbrow general magazines; film journals; trade and scholarly books.

As American film developed in Hollywood, there grew up a number of popular film types similar in form, style, imagery, and subject matter which became established as *genres*—the family melodrama, the horror film, the western, sci-fi, and so on. Genres that immediately caught the mass audience's imagination and gained instant popularity included the western, the crime film, and the slapstick comedy. *The Great Train Robbery,* directed by Edwin S. Porter in 1903, is a landmark movie, not only for its technical innovations such as sophisticated editing methods and the first use of the close-up, but also because it brought the western from the pages of the dime novel to the screen for the first time. The crime film was pioneered by D. W. Griffith in films like *Musketeers of Pig Alley* (1912), the forerunner of the gangster film. The slapstick comedy film, begun in the form of the great silent shorts of Mack Sennett, soon developed into the well-known features made by Chaplin, Keaton, and Harold Lloyd. These film types, although all had their roots in other mediums, such as the short story and novel, theater and pantomime, were used in a unique way by the filmmakers. They took advantage of the medium's capacity to capture physical movement and rhythmic timing, its ability to emphasize insignificant detail in the close-up shot, and its power to transport viewers to exotic locales where heroic actions and dramatic events appear plausible.

While early filmmakers were exploring the possibilities of these genres, film critics were ignoring the generic aspect of Hollywood films entirely, analyzing them for other than genre considerations, such as acting, directing, and script writing—or condemning the use of genres out of hand. This is not surprising, because most people writing about films in magazines and newspapers in the first half of the twentieth century would have been applying traditional humanistic criteria toward their subject. In traditional views of art, uniqueness and novelty are desirable; imitation and repetition are not. Genre films surely depend far more on repetition for their effects than on novelty. Since the vast majority of Hollywood films are genre films, members of the critical establishment gave short shrift to the product, unless they could find the uniqueness of individual achievement in a particular genre film attributable to the performers, the director, the composer of the score, or even the costumer. There was no notion of seeing in the genres some signs of the culture which made them or seeing them as reflections of the world outside the theater.

The critics' neglect or chastisement of the genre impulse did not bother Hollywood. For an industry dedicated to maximizing the profits of the business, the genres worked as cost-cutting procedures. The same western street or Middle European village square could be used over and over again for picture after picture. "Unique" sets did not have to be built for each film. Because the public appeared to like certain genres and not others, the industry concentrated on selling those genres that had proved popular. In time, standardization of product became the norm. As mentioned earlier, a character in *Singin' in the Rain* (Gene Kelly–Stanley Donen, 1952) remarks about Hollywood films, "When you've seen one, you've seen 'em all." To be sure, each instance of genre film had to have a surface that gave the appearance of difference, but the basic structures beneath the surface were essentially the same.

Modern genre criticism is first concerned with locating and describing those basic structures—for instance, how does the good man/bad man opposition work in a western, and what do the two figures represent in the context of the individual film and the genre as a whole? This approach can be termed textual criticism, since it examines the text or texts closely. But genre criticism also explores the relationship between the genre and the condition of the world surrounding it—we might ask, for example, why westerns and musicals, once so popular, are not being made anymore; who is responsible for the invention and maintenance of a genre, the audience or the industry; or what messages are being relayed between the manufacturer and the consumer, between society and its members. This approach can be termed contextual criticism, since it examines the history, politics, economics, and ideology surrounding the films. For the most part, genre criticism is descriptive and not evaluative, taking as its field any and all examples of a genre, whether considered "good" or "bad" by other criteria. Often a sixty-minute "B" western or a quickie drive-in horror film can illustrate aspects of genre more clearly than an expensive production with name stars.

HISTORY OF GENRE CRITICISM

One of the major goals of film reviewers writing before World War I seems to have been to provide film with some credibility by voicing disapproval of Hollywood genre films, and by using their positions, usually as members of the press, of critic to teach the audience the errors of its poor taste and judgment. To many early writers, the audience represented the great unwashed who were in need of large doses of cultural training. If, in the writer's view, this so-called training took hold, the audience's standards could be raised so that films would take their rightful place as a serious art form. These writers believed they could then gain the respect they felt they deserved in being gifted enough to recognize the potential of that form and to document how it was being wasted. Obviously, the repetition of formula subjects and trite thematic material, the emphasis on the chase and shoot-'em-up violence of the western, and the tacked-on happy ending and sentimental, superficial emotion of the social drama seemed to these critics to be evidence of that waste.

For example, in a December 1910 essay entitled "How to Improve the Business," Louis Reeves Harrison criticized genre film elements in terms that have been echoed many times over the years. He makes the case that directors are mostly studio hacks given a mass of bad material containing few ideas, the result of which is "monotony of production, a feeble sameness of idea, where vigor and variety are needed. The cowboy chases the Indian, the sheriff pursues the villain, the hero embraces the heroine at the end, or the pianist plays the wedding march at the foreseen conclusion until the steady patron grows sick and weary of the motion pictures as a form of entertainment" (Kauffmann, Henstell, pp. 46–47).

During the same year that Harrison wrote those words, an anonymous critic, writing in *The Moving Picture World*, observed that "there seems to be amongst exhibitors, among whom we have made inquiry, a strong and increasing demand for Indian and Western subjects" (Kauffmann, Henstell, p. 36). So on one hand a writer like Harrison, one of the better known of the early film critics, saw the genre film as a stale dead end, while, on the other hand, audiences were clamoring for more. When, if at all, genres were mentioned, it was to articulate the critic's belief that the mass audience's taste was faulty and needed to be elevated. Harrison, again writing in *The Moving Picture World,* April 22, 1911, in an article entitled "Violence and Bloodshed," had this to say about the western genre:

> The accumulation of abhorrent incidents given in Indian and cowboy plays under the pretense of picturing actual life is so repulsive in its low savagery, so beastly and unsavory, that it might be just as well to cut out such plays indiscriminately. When these plays are filled with murder, rapine, torture, and false sentiment, they are not only inartistic, but are ineffective save with a few low-brows who like them, and, besides, are turning millions away from the little theaters. They are repellent to the cultivated, and even cease in the course of time to stimulate the jaded appetites of the unwashed. (Kauffmann, Henstell, p. 48.)

The article concludes that the purpose of movie making should not be the "desire to stimulate what is low," but, rather, the intention to make the next generation "better than we are," to see that "their minds dominate their animal natures." From these articles and others like them, it is apparent that critics who were serious about film saw as their mission the raising of the cultural level of the audience. In this criticism, which is some of the earliest thoughtful discussion of the medium, Harrison can be seen as a precursor of many of the critics to follow. Being critical of Hollywood's genres was the writer's way of moving the audience beyond the appeal of genre to an appreciation of non-genre films, films usually produced outside of Hollywood, most often in Europe. For example, Stanley Kauffmann, writing in *American Film Criticism,* explains the beginning of this phenomenon: "The Films d'Art company was formed in France in 1907 to elevate the lowly, parvenu screen. This company produced potted versions of famous plays with famous actors, who were billed. As Arthur Knight says, 'people who would never have dreamed of going to the nickelodeons to see a cowboy picture, a tear-stained melodrama, or a slapstick comedy, somehow felt that movies must be all right, if they showed you the classics'" (Kauffmann, Henstell, p. 32).

Here, for example, is the summary review of the Italian film *Cabiria,* in the May 23, 1914, edition of *The Moving Picture World:* "It may well be said tht *Cabiria* ranks in the very first flight of the masterpieces of cinematographic art. Nor must I omit a tribute to Italy, the country which has given us all our greatest classics in films" (Kauffmann, Henstell, p. 32). High praise for foreign films by critics was nearly universal at this time.

There were, of course, exceptions to this critical perception, since critics did appreciate many American films and film artists. But on the whole, throughout the silent film period, critics had little interest in, or appreciation for, the popular Hollywood film genres—as genres.

With the advent of the talking film, critics turned their attention, and wrath, to the new invention as used/misused by Hollywood. For example, in a 1929 essay in *The Nation* entitled "The Talkies," Alexander Bakshy predicted that although talking pictures had tremendous potential, they might never reach that potential because of the "Hollywood robots" who "represent mechanized brains" unable to create and maintain a "genuine spirit of art" on film. He saw as the best hope for films "to counteract if not completely overcome the influence of Hollywood" and he applauded "the remarkable growth in volume and quality of amateur production together with the rapid spread of little cinema houses." Bakshy believed that these developments "will seize the artistic leadership in the movies and will force Hollywood to accept their superior standards" (Kauffmann, Henstell, p. 213). He was, of course, wrong.

This critical stance is similar to criticism of the silent period, except the amateur filmmaker had taken the place of the European director as the force for making film live up to its potential as an art form. In June 1934, Paul Goodman, in an article entitled "Faulty Cinematics in Hollywood," noted that

> the major causes for the corruption of the cinema at the present time leap to the eye and need not be described. On the one hand, the commercialism of Hollywood, "quickie" production and mass-distribution; on the other, the depravity of the public taste—each of these aggravating the other and driving it from bad to worse. (Kauffmann, Henstell, p. 306)

At about the same time, Otis Ferguson was lamenting the state of the Hollywood musical genre. He saw as the main trouble with the musical that it "rarely attempts to be more than a ragbag of various show tricks; and even when it does, there is no relation between its comedy, which is mostly wisecracks, and its songs, which are mostly sugar. As for possible plots, there are two in use: the Hymie-the-Hoofer type, where a boy makes the grade with his act; the My-Gal-Daisy-She-Drives-Me-Crazy type, where the boy makes the girl. These are naturally followed with no conviction, the chief problem in any given picture being how to bring in the first number" (Kauffmann, Henstell, p. 320)

During the early years of talking films, even when the critic was attempting to pay a compliment to the genre film, it usually was a kind of damning with faint praise. In writing about the Marx Brothers' musical *Animal Crackers* (1928). Bakshy notes, "musical comedy is not a subject to be taken lightly by a critic. He may be excused writing about it in the facetious tone characteristic of the genre itself, but may he be serious about it? At the risk of appearing a low-brow to some and a bore to others, I propose to be nothing but serious in discussing . . . *Animal Crackers*." Bakshy decides that the film is very good but not as good as it could be because of the "shortsightedness of Hollywood producers" who have not set a single director to explore to the full "the tremendous possibilities of this wonderful American genre" (Kauffmann, Henstell, pp. 236–37).

Similarly, Clifton Fadiman, discussing another Marx Brothers film, *A Night at the Opera* (1935), praises the film, but in an apologetic manner, with few references made to the musical comedy genre of which the film is a part. "The thesis of these comments is that the Marxes are now quite funny enough to be taken seriously. Suppose they were called Fratellini or Grock or any other name that did not exude a ready-to-wear atmosphere. And suppose these arrived here from Paris, all a-bulge with profound statements out of Bergson concerning the inner nature of comedy. Would there not be considerable genius-hailing and reverential analyses in alert periodicals . . . and comparisons with Mr. Chaplin etcetera?" (Kauffmann, Henstell, p. 323). To Fadiman, the film is a success, not because it is in the Hollywood genre tradition or because it may possess any interest on its own, but simply because it works as a vehicle to showcase the Marx Brothers' talent.

A more obvious attempt to ignore the genre and still praise a film can be seen in Welford Benton's critique of John Ford's *Stagecoach,* made in 1939. Although Benton's opening remarks acknowledge the film's parentage, "one of the greatest of all Westerns," the rest of the essay attempts to convince the viewer to ignore the fact that it is a western. Benton dismisses the story by saying that "it could be told comfortably between the two ends of one reel of film." But, according to Benton, *Stagecoach* puts to the test the theory that "the medium, not the story, is the thing." During the remainder of the essay, he explores the ways in which the medium serves to rescue the genre: "Only great screen craftsmanship could elongate so slim a story without stretching it too thin in spots. In Dudley Nichols, writer, and John Ford, director, [Walter] Wanger [the producer] had a team with many notable screen achievements to its credit, but no other I can recall matches *Stagecoach* as an example of cinematic skill." He praises the cinematography, the script, the actors and actresses, and sums it up by saying that the film is "one of the most brilliant exhibitions of sustained filmic motion the screen has given us in recent years of the talkie era" (Kauffmann, Henstell, pp. 367–68). Again, the genre is ignored.

The practice of critics ignoring the genres or harshly criticizing genre films continued, with few exceptions, until the late 1940s and early 1950s, when two landmark essays on genre films pioneered a way of looking at the American popular film that had important repercussions for the genre approach from then until now.

GENRE RESCUED: ROBERT WARSHOW'S APPROACH

Robert Warshow's seminal genre essays on the gangster film and the western film, collected in *The Immediate Experience* (1970), examine the genre as a way to better understand the American response to the experience of American life. Elevating the content of his essays from simple reviews of single films to a discussion of public attitudes and values provided Warshow the justification to write about movies, a subject he loved. He confesses, "I have gone to the movies constantly, and at times almost compulsively, for most of my life. I should be embarrassed to attempt an estimate of how many movies I have seen and how many hours they have consumed" (p. 27). Warshow's interest in film genres came, no doubt, from this obsession with American movies, and since most of the films he saw were made in Hollywood, it is easy to understand why the gangster and western genres had a particular appeal for him. Note, also, Warshow's apologetic tone—a reference to the common critical attitude toward Hollywood and its main product: genre films. Warshow's fluency in these film genres gave him the breadth and depth needed to write insightful genre essays, and his discussion brings new understanding to films long ignored by more sophisticated film critics, who, for the most part, were still ignoring the impact of Hollywood genres.

Warshow's essay "The Gangster as Tragic Hero" (*Partisan Review*, February 1948) is a groundbreaking example of genre criticism. Warshow emphasizes the historical importance of this genre to the audience and details the reasons for the genre's lasting popularity. The section quoted here defines precisely the nature of genre films in general and attempts to explain the important cultural values embedded in the gangster film in particular:

> In its initial character, the gangster film is simply one example of the movies' constant tendency to create fixed dramatic patterns that can be repeated indefinitely with a reasonable expectation of profit. One gangster film follows another as one musical or one western follows another. But this rigidity is not necessarily opposed to the requirements of art. There have been very successful types of art in the past which developed such specific and detailed conventions as almost to make individual examples of the type interchangeable. This is true, for example, of Elizabethan revenge tragedy and Restoration comedy.
>
> For such a type to be successful means that its conventions have imposed themselves upon the general consciousness and become the accepted vehicles of a particular set of attitudes and a particular aesthetic effect. One goes to any individual example of the type with very definite expectations, and originality is to be welcomed only in the degree that it intensifies the expected experience without fundamentally altering it. Moreover, the relationship between the conventions which go to make up such a type and the real experience of its audience or the real facts of whatever situation it pretends to describe is of only secondary importance and does not determine its aesthetic force. It is only in an ultimate sense that the type appeals to its audience's experience of reality; much more immediately, it appeals to previous experience of the type itself: it creates its own field of reference.
>
> Thus the importance of the gangster film, and the nature and intensity of its emotional and aesthetic impact, cannot be measured in terms of the place of the gangster himself or the importance of the problem of crime in American life. Those European movie-goers who think there is a gangster

on every corner in New York are certainly deceived, but defenders of the "positive" side of American Culture are equally deceived if they think it relevant to point out that most Americans have never seen a gangster. What matters is that the experience of the gangster *as an experience of art* is universal to Americans. There is almost nothing we understand better or react to more readily or with quicker intelligence. The western film, though it seems never to diminish in popularity, is for most of us no more than the folklore of the past, familiar and understandable only because it has been repeated so often. The gangster film comes much closer. In ways that we do not easily or willingly define, the gangster speaks for us, expressing that part of the American psyche which rejects the qualities and the demands of modern life, which rejects "Americanism" itself. (pp. 129–30)

Warshow's genre essay on the gangster film attempts to understand the dark side of the American dream by looking at those gritty films whose favorable audience response caused producers to make more of them. The examples he cites later in the essay from the films *Scarface* and *Little Caesar* (Mervin Leroy, 1930) bring out specific details of plot, imagery, and dialogue to support his definition of the genre and his acceptance of the genre as being worthy of serious critical attention.

Warshow's discussion of the western film in the essay "Movie Chronicle: The Westerner" (*Partisan Review,* March–April 1954) is less concerned with establishing the serious implications of the genre. The critic's attention here is directed toward the genre elements perceived in the western hero's attitude, in the elements of his world, and in his behavior patterns as they can be shown to operate in specific western films.

At the beginning of the essay Warshow compares the western hero with the gangster, noting that the gangster hero's life is lonely and melancholy because it has been his choice to live that kind of life. Such a career, according to Warshow, "is a nightmare inversion of the values of ambition and opportunity." In contrast, Warshow describes the western hero as a "figure of repose." He may be lonely and melancholy, but his feelings stem from the "recognition that life is unavoidably serious, not from the disproportions of his own temperament" (p. 137).

Warshow then describes other elements in the western hero's makeup and behavior. For one thing, women do not understand him. The woman in his life, who often comes from the East, is completely out of place in his West. Her failure to understand "represents a clash of cultures." Warshow says the western film shows the hero to have the deeper wisdom, while the woman from the East appears to be childish and inferior.

The western hero is a man of leisure, who need not be shown working to get ahead, for, as Warshow points out, "by the time we see him, he is already 'there': he can ride a horse faultlessly, keep his countenance in the face of death, and draw his gun a little faster and shoot it a little straighter than anyone he is likely to meet."

The images emphasized in the western film are vast expanses of land, horses galloping, backgrounds creating a sense of physical freedom; the central thematic meaning, according to Warshow, is violence. The western hero is not afraid to use a gun when the showdown comes. And it is Warshow's point that the showdown always comes, and the western hero is always forced to kill. Why does he do it? Warshow says he fights and kills to preserve the purity of his image: "He fights not for advantage and not for the right, but to state what he is, and he must live in a world which permits that statement." After describing the western hero's world, makeup, and behavior, Warshow explores the use of these elements as they operate in the film *The Virginian* (1929) which he discusses as an archetypal western film with an archetypal hero (pp. 139–41).

In the rest of the essay he explains how later western films either conform to or deviate from the archetypal pattern. For example, the film *The Gunfighter* (1951), which shows the western hero at the end of a long career of killing, "is done in cold, quiet tones of grey, and every object in it—faces, clothing, a table, the hero's heavy mustache—is given an air of uncompromising authenticity, suggesting those dim photographs of the nineteenth-century West." This, explains Warshow, is a change from the imagery that most western movies "have accustomed us to—harder, duller, less 'romantic'— and yet without forcing us outside the boundaries which give the western movie its validity" (pp. 144–45). Warshow's essay concludes, using *Shane, High Noon,* and *The Gunfighter* as other examples of how the western film, and specifically the western hero, fits into the genre tradition.

Warshow's genre essays analyzed both the western and gangster genres as reflections of American society and as unique artistic expression. Warshow was unique in his time. He willingly acknowledged that the man who watches the movie must be taken into consideration by the critic by confessing that he is "that man"—a man who admires Hollywood films. Warshow's approach to genre films was a distinguished beginning for genre criticism, but it was only the beginning.

GENRE CRITICISM AND THE POPULAR CULTURE MOVEMENT

The changes in cultural attitudes that took place in America during the 1960s produced a revolution in popular culture that extended from the town meeting hall in downtown middle America, to the lecture hall on the college campus. Where once only Shakespeare and the other classics were studied, now Mickey Spillane and pulp literature were taken seriously. Although many traditional critic/scholars were dismayed by this turn of events, others devoted their intellects to analyzing popular culture and began to explore, in depth, the field of film genre studies that Warshow first suggested as a potential area for scholarly interest. This revolution went hand in hand with the revolution in film criticism that was taking place, mainly in France and

Great Britian, where the critics, writing for journals such as *Cahiers du Cinéma* and *Sight and Sound,* had begun to praise the Hollywood auteurs who made the genre films they had grown up with as their main source of entertainment. The attention being focused on the American genres by British and French critics was, ironically, the reverse of what had happened in the early days of American film criticism, when American critics praised European film as the best possible cultural model to follow. The French and British critics of the early 1960s took the exact opposite approach, criticizing many of the more serious films of their countries as too pretentious and without personal style, preferring the quick, action-packed, movement-oriented genres of Hollywood.

As the popular culture movement grew on college campuses across the country, eventually leading to degree-granting departments of popular culture, so did the interest in the popular film—the Hollywood genre film. *The Journal of Popular Film* (now *The Journal of Popular Film and Television*) was founded in 1972 to provide an outlet for scholarship devoted to genres; it is still printing some of the best articles written from this critical approach.

CONTEMPORARY GENRE CRITICISM: GOALS AND METHODS

As we suggested earlier, genre criticism lies somewhere about midpoint on the spectrum bounded by contextual criticism at one end and textual criticism at the other. Both segments of the approach were first touched on by Warshow. On the one hand, genre criticism is intimately tied to a context of extra-filmic considerations of social institutions, social psychology, and history. On the other, the criticism is aimed at identifying formal and rhetorical patterns in films, discovering and describing cinematic elements and structures that are their own referents from film to film.

The critic can look at genres and their relationship to the culture in which they were made. For example, one might study the relationship between a western and the real West, the degree of prosperity in the society at the time the film was made, or the economic demands imposed by the system of production, distribution, and exhibition that made westerns a viable commodity. A critic can focus on a historical and evolutionary process whereby changes in the basic characteristics of a film genre reveal shifts in the attitudes and concerns of the genre's audience—or the critic can focus on the formal manifestations of genre, how filmic patterns repeat themselves and refer to one another and obey their own aesthetic laws. One emphasis focuses on change and the other focuses on repetition; one emphasizes how culture begets films and the other stresses how films beget films. Neither emphasis precludes the other, and the two are often combined in practice.

Most genre criticism seeks to identify, select, describe, and interpret the characteristics, history, and evolution of a group of films. Only a small amount of generic criticism has attempted the task of theorizing about the basic problem of defining the field of inquiry. Genres have often simply been assumed to exist. Essentially, the problem is the question of which came first, the chicken or the egg. One has to select a group of films prior to identifying them as a genre; however, the very selection is shaped by a definition of that genre supposedly not yet arrived at. What makes a critic talk about musicals as a group is some prior notion of what a musical is. The problem is serious, not a mere quibble, and deserves attention; nevertheless, a great deal of interesting and illuminating work has been accomplished by genre criticism in the last two decades.

Initial attempts to identify genres emphasized the obvious similarities among films: themes, configurations of action (the private-eye's pursuit of truth), subject matter (cowboys), objects and costumes (machine guns and dapper suits in films about the underworld). It is therefore not surprising that the largest body of generic criticism has been about film groups with the most viable characteristics: the western, the gangster film, the hard-boiled detective film, and the traditional horror film. These genres take place in specific settings and in certain time-frames, they have clearly identifiable plots, conventions and characters, and they are full of visually obvious and repeatedly used objects, the latter becoming iconic (the white hat on the good cowboy) in their ability to convey thematic and dramatic information beyond their material function and presence in a single film. Other genres have had less extensive treatment until recently, when critical attention has turned to issues of film structure and gone below the surface of film groups to identify and describe similarities in visual, aural, and narrative patterns. The new avenue of inquiry has turned attention to those previously neglected genres, like the musical, in which deep-seated psychoanalytic material can be located.

In addition to showing a critical preference for those film genres that are the easiest to discuss because they are the most repetitious and circumscribed in their surfaces and action, genre criticism is clearly biased in favor of popular films made for a mass audience, a complete reversal of early criticism, which often ignored or attacked genre films aimed at the masses. Genre critics seeking in films information about a culture often use the box office as a barometer of cultural approval and disapproval of a film's hidden messages and values. The genre critic concerned about the formal elements of film groups is fascinated by the variations on classic forms made by sequels and remakes and parodies; sequels and remakes are, of course, determined by the industry's estimation of popular demand based on box office success. Thus the generic approach places high value on popularity and on repetition and variation of a classic form rather than on novelty and invention.

This value system has recently moved genre criticism from merely cataloguing films chronologically and summarizing their plots to considering their historical evolution, their rise and decline in popularity, their phoenix-like cycles of birth, death, and rebirth. In doing so, genre critics have incorporated methods from literary scholarship, folklore, sociology, economics, and cultural anthropology, among other disciplines.

Structural Approaches to Genre

Although previously cited as an example of auteur criticism, Jim Kitses's *Horizons West* (1970) begins as a book on the western film. Before examining the work of three directors who made memorable westerns, Kitses describes the western genre as a group of films structured by a set of thematic oppositions. He was one of the first to apply the structuralist methodology of Claude Lévi-Strauss to popular film forms. Kitses's assumption is that genre films are like myths; important and often conflicting attitudes about culture and the individual's relationship to it are rehearsed and repeated in a ritualistic manner as each audience attempts to make sense out of opposing values. Feelings of belief and disbelief in the supernatural, for example, are played out in the horror film. Not only are general human values found in many genres, but historically and culturally specific ones are often embedded there.

The western film may carry out the task of retelling the age-old story of the hero and the community, but it also conveys specific concerns about the American past and the values associated with the frontier experience. The settling of the United States looms large in the rhetoric of the nation. We are reminded frequently of the "founding fathers," "manifest destiny," the virtues of "freedom," "democracy," and "capitalism." But we are also concerned about "social responsibility," "legalism," and "compromise." We want our freedoms to remain intact; we don't want people to abuse them. There is a continual problem of where to draw the line between the interests of the individual and the interests of the community. The frontier claims of unlimited freedom and social conformity are seen to be in conflict. Kitses finds the western the film form in which that conflict is most clearly reflected.

The major opposition conceptualized in the western is that between the wilderness and civilization. Depending on the specific film and its dramatic configurations, either one of these entities may be judged desirable or undesirable, good or bad. A particular film may suggest that the coming of civilization to the West brought with it all the corruption and greed associated with city life—bankers, clerks, crooked sheriffs—taking away the purity and innocence associated with the life lived closer to nature. On the other hand, civilization's creature comforts, law and order, and stability are just as easily praised in a western in which the decent, law-abiding, family-oriented farmers and merchants are seen as more valuable than the wild, crude, lawless ranchers.

Here is Kitses's table illustrating the deep ideological and psychic dialectic working in all westerns, which he identifies through a set of binary oppositions:

The Wilderness	*Civilization*
The Individual	The Community
freedom	restriction
honour	institutions
self-knowledge	illusion
integrity	compromise
self-interest	social responsibility
solipsism	democracy

Nature	*Culture*
purity	corruption
experience	knowledge
empiricism	legalism
pragmatism	idealism
brutalization	refinement
savagery	humanity

The West	*The East*
America	Europe
the frontier	America
equality	class
agrarianism	industrialism
tradition	change
the past	the future

Describing the tables, Kitses says,

> If we compare the tops and tails on each subsection, we can see the ambivalence at work in its outer limits: the West, for example, rapidly moves from being the spearhead of manifest destiny to the retreat of ritual. What we are dealing with here, of course, is no less than a national world-view: underlying the whole complex is the grave problem of identity that has special meaning for Americans. (pp. 11–12)

Thus Kitses points out that what lies beneath the surface of the western is our own ambivalence about these opposing sets of values. From moment to moment we find both good and bad aspects of the wilderness, hating its savagery but loving its purity. The same is true about the settled, conventional life of civilization. At any one moment Americans can champion the rights of individuals to fly in the face of all conformity, and, in the next, attempt to suppress any departure from the norm. We dislike European refinement and sophistication, on the one hand, but feel embarrassed about our provincialism, on the other. These conflicts are not really resolvable. In the western they can achieve, however, a dramatic resolution, one which is emotionally satisfying, so that the ambivalence, the paradoxes of our most cherished beliefs, need never actually be confronted. The schoolmarm from the East can marry the gunfighter at the end of the film, and we never have to worry about the conflict of values that such a marriage might entail. Or the gunfighter can move on to another town where his services will be needed and live happily ever after. For him there will always be another town overrun by baddies who will clearly need to be overcome. In this way, according to Kitses, the western serves to smooth over the cracks and breaks in our national self-image.

A More Interdisciplinary Approach to Genre

John G. Cawelti's monograph *The Six-Gun Mystique,* written in 1971, traces the history and development of the western genre in both literature and film. In *The Six-Gun Mystique,* Cawelti attempted, as he put it, "to canvass some of the central difficulties and possibilities in the interdisciplinary interpreta- tion of popular artistic forms, using the western as my primary example." Cawelti first surveyed the literature relating to the western genre, as well as other genres such as the gangster and detective. The works he examined included David Brian Davis's Marxist essay "Ten-gallon Hero"; Kenneth J. Munden's psychological study of the major figure of the western genre, "A Contribution to the Psychological Understanding of the Cowboy"; F. E. Emery's essay "Psychological Effects of the Western Film"; Sheldon Sacks's "The Psychological Implications of Generic Distinctions"; Peter Homans's "Puritanism Revisited: An Analysis of the Contemporary Screen-Image Western"; Northrop Frye's *Anatomy of Criticism;* and an essay by the child psychologist Jean Piaget, who examined genres in terms of play and game theory.

In explaining the complexity of genre study, Cawelti used what he described as "a large spectrum of disciplinary perspectives: history, literary criticism, various brands of psychology, sociology, journalism, mass com- munications and political science." In discussing the different genres from this variety of perspectives, Cawelti early in the essay explains how the function of theme in genres can be related to Freud's theory of "repetition compulsion," in which a man who has not worked through the psychological problems dealing with his sexual impulses for his mother "is doomed to constantly reexperience these impulses and the psychic conflict they gener- ate through various analogies and disguises." This idea Cawelti then inter- prets in terms of genres:

> The idea of repetition compulsion seems particularly germane to the analy- sis of [genres] such as the western and the detective story where certain character types and patterns of action are repeated in many different works.

Indeed, it is tempting to hypothesize that strongly conventionalized narrative types like adventure and mystery stories, situation comedies, and
sentimental romances are so widely appealing because they enable people
to reenact and temporarily resolve widely shared psychic conflicts. Fur-
thermore, this is an idea which can bring together social and psychological
conceptions of function, since it is quite likely that the child-rearing practices and ideologies of different social groups have created characteristic
psychic conflicts in various social groups or subcultures. These differences,
in turn, might help account for changing themes and conventions in popular
genres like the western. Similarly, the characteristic psychological syn-
dromes of different groups and periods may be partly responsible for the
evolution of a variety of popular story types like the classical detective
story, the hard-boiled detective story, the sentimental romance and the spy
story. (p. 12)

Cawelti defines genres as "structures of narrative conventions which
carry out a variety of cultural functions in a unified way." He sees these
unified conventions or genre formulas as "principles for the selection of
certain plots, characters, and settings, which possess in addition to their
basic narrative structure the dimensions of collective ritual, game and
dream." With this methodology as background, Cawelti analyzes the western
genre as it has appeared in the novel, on radio, and in film. In focusing
particularly on the western, Cawelti first discusses the "chief characteristics
of the western formula: a particular kind of setting, type of situation, and cast
of characters with a strong emphasis on a certain kind of hero." He then
explores the importance of ritual in the western, using the methodology of
Northrop Frye in *Anatomy of Criticism* (1957), in which Frye discusses the
"myths of romance," a narrative and dramatic structure of which "the
essential element of plot is adventure" and the major form is the "quest."
According to Cawelti, Frye's analysis of romance fits the western, since the
"central action of chase and pursuit dramatizes the quest." Of course,
Cawelti goes into much greater detail in explaining the similarities in the
characteristics of the western and those that Frye attributes to the romance:
"The struggle between hero and villain; the tendency to present both figures
as coming not from the town but from the surrounding landscape; the way in
which the hero's action is commonly associated with the establishment of law
and order" (pp. 30–31).

The upshot of the essay is that Cawelti analyzes the genre in detail using
a variety of critical methods that have come from other disciplines to, as he
explains, "accommodate many different kinds of meaning—the archetypal
pattern of heroic myth, the artistic imperatives of dramatic clarity and unity,
the influence of media, the tendency of popular forms to assume a game-like
structure, the need for social ritual and for the disguised expression of latent
motives and tensions—as well as its ability to respond to changing cultural
themes and concerns" (p. 31). The rigor of this critical method, although

dealing with a popular—some would say, frivolous—subject, demonstrated the need for further genre investigation.

The Western Genre as Social Myth

In Will Wright's *Six Guns and Society: A Structural Study of the Western* (1975), using the work of Kenneth Burke on the social structure of literature, Claude Lévi-Strauss on the conceptual structure of tribal myths, and folklorist Vladimir Propp's "morphology" of the folktale, the author attempts to point out important similarities between the structure of the western and the structure of myth as explained by Lévi-Strauss. Wright's reason for choosing myth as the key element in examining the western comes from the fact that, according to Lévi-Strauss, "myth depends on simple and recognizable meanings which reinforce and challenge social understanding." For this purpose, "a structure of oppositions is necessary." Lévi-Strauss saw myth as a "binary structure." He theorized that "when two characters are opposed in a binary structure, their symbolic meaning is virtually forced to be both general and easily accessible because of the simplicity of the differences between them" (pp. 16–17). According to Wright, "the western is structured this way, and . . . presents a symbolically simple but remarkably deep conceptualization of American social beliefs." Wright then goes into specific detail concerning the structure of the western, focusing mainly on the pairings as they can be seen to operate. For example, in the classical western, "a typical cast would include a wandering gunfighter, a group of homesteaders, and a rancher. Instead of representing equally valid, conflicting lifestyles, these characters would be presented as pairs of oppositions with each pair having a different meaning. The gunfighter is opposed to the homesteaders, a contrast representing individual independence versus social domesticity. The rancher, who is settled and domestic like the farmers, is opposed to them, but on another level or axis: the farmers represent progress and communal values in opposition to the rancher's selfish, monetary values—a contrast between good and bad. In this way, the generality of the binary structure is maintained, while the possibility for rather complicated action is created" (pp. 23–24).

After discussing the basic oppositions found in the western, Wright uncovers four basic plot narratives common to all western movies. He describes his method of narrative analysis as "a liberalized version of a method originated by Vladimir Propp for the analysis of Russian folk tales." Interpreting why certain of these plots were in vogue in certain decades and not in others, Wright comes to various conclusions about the western, its function, and the social psyche of the American audience who made the films box office successes. Before World War II, for instance, the most popular plot concerned the rugged and skilled individualist—the independent "loner"—who, motivated by personal and emotional reasons, successfully solves the problems of an entire community. In the late 1960s and early 1970s, the most popular western plot revolved around a group of professionals who solve problems of an organization like the railroad or the Mexican army rather than those of a community—their motives are financial gain; they are for hire.

The four basic plots Wright traces are the classical, the transition theme, the vengeance variation, and the professional. He attributes the shift in their popularity to a growing disbelief in the American economic myth of individual enterprise and an increasing faith in corporate power, a change in those American values that before World War II linked individual moral worth with successful independent business practice. Wright comments on the professional western plot, noting that the pattern of the classical western is changed and that

> a new pattern emerges in which men can work together for money yet through their work build a common bond of respect and affection that transcends any private desire for personal gain. The heroes not only form a group to do a job but find comradeship, a place to belong. This comradeship, while expressed in different ways, is revealed by systematic understatement—affectionate kidding or sarcastic remarks punctuated by demonstrations of sincere concern. . . . The major interest becomes the building and maintenance of the unity of the group, and the tension arises from the question: Can this unity survive, or will internal conflicts destroy it? (p. 104)

Films used as examples of the professional plot structure include *Rio Bravo* (Howard Hawks, 1959), *The Professionals* (Richard Brooks, 1966), *True Grit* (Henry Hathaway, 1969), *The Wild Bunch* (Sam Peckinpah, 1969), and *Butch Cassidy and the Sundance Kid* (George Roy Hill, 1969). In discussing the use of satire to create and maintain group bonding, Wright cites *Butch Cassidy and the Sundance Kid,* in which

> friendly irony abounds, dominating the relationship of Butch and Sundance and turning what would otherwise be a dull, almost plotless film into a moving portrayal of a warm, intelligent friendship. Butch and Sundance never say anything nice to each other, and Sundance never says anything nice to Etta (the love interest in the film), but somehow everyone knows that they are really very fond of each other." Wright makes the point when he acknowledges that "this is a very attractive idea of love and friendship, and while it is the basis of the group unity in all these films, it is perhaps most strongly expressed in Butch Cassidy (p. 109).

There are problems with Wright's conclusions—for films are as hard to compartmentalize neatly by decade as they are by generic characteristics. One of the quintessential classical westerns using Wright's prewar plot is *Shane* (George Stevens), which did not appear until 1953—eight years after the war. Despite the fact that one can always find significant exceptions to such arguments as Wright's, his study points to critical attempts to make genre study more than an exercise in cataloguing surface details.

Aesthetic Evaluation of Film Genres

In 1976, Stanley J. Solomon's *Beyond Formula* was published. The title alone gives an indication of the book's intent. In the Introduction, Solomon articulates the point:

> The theory I advocate in this Introduction and will be developing throughout the following chapters starts with the view that the truly typical elements of a genre, both visual and dramatic, are not necessarily the most obvious props and devices shared by bad films and television parodies. Secondly—and basic to the apprehension of qualitative variations within the genre—whatever these typical elements may be, they are not trite, repetitive patterns stored in film studio libraries or file cabinets, but artistic insights stored in the minds of such filmmakers as Alfred Hitchcock and John Ford. (pp. 1–2)

Solomon goes on to make a key point, one that would seem completely opposite of what earlier genre critics might contend: "From these premises evolves my belief that the most generic works—the most 'typical' works—of a significant genre are, artistically and intellectually, the best works of the genre" (pp. 1–2). Solomon attempts to prove this thesis in the remainder of his study, which examines the major genres, including the western, the musical, the horror film, the crime film, the detective film, and the war film.

Throughout the Introduction, Solomon takes great pains to emphasize the focus of his study, a focus that he believes to be different from other studies of genre films. He first distinguishes between a study of film genres and the study of film formulas. Formula studies are, according to Solomon, "the essence of almost all longer studies that purport to analyze and classify genres." Although he believes that it is in the area of formula "that genre and culture analysis may overlap, the latter expounding a view that the frequent reappearance of a formula in itself denotes sociological significance," Solomon insists that he is not concerned with the simple cataloguing that takes place in the standard study of film formulas. It is his contention that such film studies "usually convey no aesthetic quality, since the general formula itself attracts all the attention." Instead, Solomon sees genre study as a method of probing beneath surface details inherent in formula studies "for whatever dimensions of meaning adhere to the patterns manifest in the individual example."

In each chapter, Solomon begins by delineating the boundaries into which the genre fails. For example, in his chapter on the genre musical, "Singing and Dancing: The Sound of Metaphor," the introduction discusses musical films as capable of "certain strengths inherent in the genre that permit them to move back and forth between a realistic presentation and a metaphorical musical presentation. Within a metaphorical presentation, a song or dance becomes a symbolic revelation of an entire plot situation, or a disclosure of a character's inner feelings and deepest intentions. Aware of this double mode of presentation, audiences expect musical films to convey meaning in brief moments of song and dance, which, like Shakespearean soliloquies, are justified by convention and are supposed to be consistent with the realistic presentation that carries the story line forward" (p. 64). In explaining the way metaphor works in an actual musical, Solomon cites examples from a musical directed by George Stevens, *Swing Time* (1936). In one scene the lead character, Lucky, played by Fred Astaire, and Penny, played by Ginger Rogers, have decided to break up. All that remains is for them to say goodbye. They accomplish this, of course, in song and dance, which, according to Solomon, becomes a metaphor for a whole range of complex feelings that have to do with lovers parting. In Solomon's view, "the outstanding characteristic of the musical is its capacity to communicate different levels of meaning simultaneously; this may be so because the musical event derives its aesthetic appeal from its relationship to the classical standards for art and beauty—rhythm, harmony, proportion, and clarity" (p. 64).

Solomon goes on to discuss categories of the genre, including courtship-romance, musical biography, fantasy-romance, and parody, among others; he then lists some of the major filmmakers who collaborated on the most important musicals, and finishes the introductory discussion with an explanation of the theory of integration—that is, how the musical numbers are woven into the plot.

Solomon then provides an example of how some seemingly unintegrated musical numbers work on a deep metaphorical level. Embedded in the structure of the film but discoverable by the genre critic, such metaphorical patterns give the genre a degree of artistic credibility that normally would not be associated with a Hollywood musical. Here is Solomon's argument quoted at some length to show how this can be done:

> Sometimes the seemingly unintegrated musical number may actually give structural unity to a script that does not otherwise fully integrate its conception of character into the action of the plot. *An American in Paris* to a large extent overcomes some mishandling of its genre traits in the dialogue because the ideas successfully conveyed within the musical numbers compensate for deficiencies engendered by the script. For much of the film we perceive two conflicting characterizations of the hero Jerry (played by Gene Kelly)—one provided by the dialogue and the other by the musical numbers. As portrayed through the dialogue, Jerry is a man willing to accept sponsorship from Milo, a wealthy women who is sexually attracted to him, though he has moral qualms about what he is doing and even some doubt about his ability as a painter. He aggressively pursues Lise, a shop

girl he has fallen in love with, while at the same time acting thoroughly insensitive to the older woman. Jerry apparently is not a very attractive character. Yet for the sake of consistency the inner logic of the genre requires him to truly deserve our sympathy as well as the reward he achieves at the end, when Lise deserts her fiancé for him. The musical numbers collectively provide another level of characterization much more favorable than that of the script, and modify the negative traits Jerry exhibits in the story. . . . Relatively early in the film before his entanglements become complex, Jerry sings and dances the George Gershwin song, "I Got Rhythm." His performance is directed at the gamins of his Left Bank neighborhood, in what appears to be merely one of several musical numbers introduced for its own sake and readily separable from the rest of the film. However, this number actually serves to prepare us for understanding the real emotional identity of the hero as it is revealed later in the film. Among the children, Jerry is lavish with time and energy, teaching them not only bits of the English language but a philosophy of the simple life. As they chant, "I got . . ." he completes each line of the lyric "rhythm"—"music"—"my girl"—and the declarative emphasis of this recitation gives credence to a belief in the potential self-sufficiency of the marvelous performer who can assert these views with so much endearing vitality. Jerry's inner being shows, he "lets loose," and he convinces us of his talents. And in doing so he symbolically transforms the art of his performance into the potential art he must be capable of producing as a painter. (pp. 76–77)

Solomon sums up the case for the dance as crucial to the plot by pointing out that the "visual environment of the dance, a Left Bank street filled with children and Parisian shopkeepers, enhances Jerry's fundamental association with the community and fixes certain qualities of his character so that any future action that seems to be deviously motivated will be dismissed by us as a minor, temporary confusion. Jerry's openness and good nature, so firmly established by this number, subsequently supply an underlying unity to actions and statements not entirely assimilated into the later portions of the plot."

Solomon's analysis of the major genres in *Beyond Formula* attempts to redeem genre films as works of art, subject to the same critical scrutiny as any other artistic works judged by traditional aesthetic standards.

Genre Criticism as Social Reflection

Since genre films are viewed by large numbers of people in a given culture, critics have often suggested that recurrent themes, situations, and characters represent significant attitudes held by that culture; for example, feminists have pointed out the tendency for Hollywood films to stereotype male and female roles in society. For these writers, genre films depict the way people think about things already and reinforce the status quo. They simply hold a mirror up to society.

Nevertheless, some critics have made a case for the opposite view, pointing out ways that genre films may, in fact, be revolutionary, leading the audience in the direction of new attitudes and ideas. Stuart M. Kaminsky, in his book *American Film Genres* (1974), covers a wide range of genre topics, but in the chapter on the comedy film, he explains the genre's role in American history and its importance in reflecting and creating a climate for social change. Until this treatment of comedy films, the great comedies of the silent film stars, such as Keaton and Chaplin, were discussed primarily as works of individual comic genius that transcended the Hollywood formula to which they were attached. It is Kaminsky's contention that these films are great *because* of the genre patterns to which they conform, and that the patterns arise from the social conditions at the time the films were made. The genre, in other words, has been made manifest by the historical events and society's ways of adapting to those events.

Kaminsky begins by identifying the "dominant modes in the comedy genre": "the individual who is out of step with society mode" and "the man vs. woman mode." Kaminsky says both modes of comedy involve "serious aspects of societal existence: man and his struggle to attain a satisfying role in society, and the archetypal struggle for supremacy and status between men and women." In the remainder of the chapter, Kaminsky examines the "individual in society" portion of the genre, using the silent comedies of the 1920s as his primary focus. He suggests that the attempts of men and women to find their place in society is such a serious and threatening issue that the comedies become a vehicle used by the audience to face the problem, since "the only way many of us can deal with the subject is to remove ourselves from it by laughter" (p. 143). From this point of view, it is the societal pressure that becomes the impetus for the creation of and continuing audience response to the genre. The genre comedians chosen by Kaminsky include Chaplin, Keaton, Harry Langdon, and Harold Lloyd, who were all at the peak of their popularity in the 1920s. He then concludes with a brief analysis of Jerry Lewis's films of the 1960s as well as the films of the comedy teams Laurel and Hardy and the Marx Brothers. Kaminsky says he is attempting to examine "these individuals as genre figures, and not, as has so often been done, as comedians to be extolled or vilified, depending on one's contemporary response to their comedy" (p. 143).

He begins the analysis by describing the social history of the period from 1918 until 1927, viewing it as the major force in creating and sustaining the genre. It was a time of great cultural change that included a deep fear of Russia and the revolution, bringing with it a desire to retreat into isolationism, and the rise of the Ku Klux Klan, caused by the migration of blacks to urban areas. Also at this time came the myth of the self-made man in the person of Henry Ford, and the administration of Calvin Coolidge, who agreed with Ford that "the chief business of the American people is business." Along with this idea rose the myth that big business was the protector of the American worker. Other changes included the new morality, brought about partly by women's winning of suffrage in 1920, and partly by prohibition, which led to the excesses associated with bootlegging. These were some of the historical forces shaping American society and thought in this period.

Into this confusing and frightening time came the genre comedians of the golden era of silent film. These actors, according to Kaminsky, "reflected, in their film performances, the man alone—man against a chaotic, increasingly mass-oriented, mechanistic society. These were little men caught in the midst of baffling confusion, wanting to be a part of society, but unable to make it or live up to the myths of strength, the self-made man, and the sexual power that were at the core of their times" (p. 148).

Kaminsky then turns his attention to the individual films of the great silent comedians—none of whom better represents his point concerning man against society than Charlie Chaplin, whose humor was "thematic, relating closely to the history and myths of the 1920s." One of these myths deals with the self-made man as a person to emulate, on one hand, and as a cruel, power-mad capitalist, on the other. Kaminsky shows how Chaplin, in *City Lights* (1931), uses this dichotomy to point out the individual's confusion and frustration in dealing with this dilemma: "Chaplin has rescued an alcoholic millionaire, clearly a self-made man, a Henry Ford who hides from the rigidity of his real world in drink. When he is drunk, the millionaire takes Charlie to his bosom, and lavishes gifts and food on him. When he's sober, however, the man rejects Charlie and throws him out. Charlie quickly learns to accept defeat when he (the millionaire) is sober. The sober American 'success' is cruel, callous, inhuman; the released man is friendly." The interpretation of this relationship is made possible because of Kaminsky's use of the social history of the period: "The man embodies the two warring aspects of society in the 1920s: on one level, he represents callous industrial conservatism and business pragmatism; on the other level, the morally loose, free but erratic, middle-class American. The Tramp, like his contemporaries, is caught between these levels; somewhat at the mercy of both, he is unable to identify comfortably with either" (p. 152). In this analysis Kaminsky has used the genre figure of the individual in conflict with society, as he is depicted by Chaplin, to illustrate how that figure attempts to deal with the forces of American capitalist society, over which he has little or no control. The social aspect of genre has become for Kaminsky a pathway to illuminate an element of Chaplin's film, but it also throws light on the way genres respond to broad pressures of the social formation.

Where Kaminsky views a genre as promoting a climate for social change, other genre analysts have suggested just the opposite. For them, genres are not revolutionary but reactionary—they serve to reinforce the status quo. Feminist critics, for example, have written a great deal on the way musicals have used women as objects to be paraded for the male viewer's pleasure, thereby not only reflecting in a very public way the values held by the audience but indeed perpetuating them. In an article on the 1930s film *Dames* (1934), Lucy Fisher points to Busby Berkeley's use of women in his dance numbers to make this point. The women clearly become the director's material to be molded into spectacle, a set of images placed in an imaginary space, to be viewed not as individuals but as the epitome of attractive faces and bodies. "What happens in most Berkeley numbers (and quintessentially in *Dames*) is that the women lose their individuation in a more profound sense than through the similarity of their physical appearance. Rather, their identities are completely consumed in the creation of an overall abstract design" (Altman, p. 75).

Though women do play principal parts in the narrative sections of the film, Fisher shows how their depiction as totally dependent on men for approval and love ultimately transforms them into mere images of beauty without the capacity for self-determination, just like the women seen in the dance numbers. Feminists argue that this sort of portrayal of women is common not only to the musical but to all genres. Such stereotypes of women—the vamp, the schoolmarm, the blond bombshell, the faithful but long-suffering wife—presented consistently in the most popular films of any period are not images of women that might lead to a change in the way women are viewed and treated in the world outside the theater. Thus much criticism of genres today is based on the notion that they do not simply reflect social values but actually teach them. Since most genre films are produced for mass consumption, the values taught will invariably be those already in place, rather than those that seek to effect change.

Genre as Paradigm of the Hollywood System

Most recently, genre study has investigated the relationship of genres to the Hollywood film industry. In the early days of film, the recurrent theme of this type of criticism was that Hollywood coerced the entire filmmaking establishment into kowtowing to its business interests, by forcing unwatchable genre material on the filmmakers and on the public as well. But in 1981 a different response to the industry was articulated—Thomas Schatz's *Hollywood Genres*.

Early in the book, Schatz presents his contention that the "genre approach provides the most effective means for understanding, analyzing, and appreciating the Hollywood cinema." Schatz correctly points out that "individual movies may affect each one of us powerfully and somewhat differently, but essentially they are all generated by a collective production system which honors certain narrative traditions (or conventions) in designing for a mass market. As such, we cannot examine individual films without first establishing a critical and theoretical framework that recognizes the cinema's production-consumption process as well as the basic conventions of feature filmmaking." It is Schatz's belief that a crucial part of the artistic development of films during the studio system's classical era, from 1930 until 1960, was to be found in an ingenious system of film production, which emphasized the repetition of popular genres, created strictly for business reasons. In fact, the

beginning chapter of the text is entitled "The Genius of the System," referring to the Hollywood studio system, which had been, and continues to be,
the brunt of so much critical abuse. In summing up the importance of the
system, Schatz has this to say: "the studio system's role in the evolution of
narrative filmmaking was considerable, in terms of its national and international popularity and, more importantly, in its systematic honing of filmic
expression into effective narrative conventions. . . . The Hollywood imprint
generally involved not only isolated production techniques and narrative
devices, but established story types or 'genres' like the western or the
musical" (p. 26).

Another important contribution of the system was, according to Schatz,
the gathering together of a stable of technical wizards, superb artists—
including directors, writers, and camera operators—and a host of actors, all
working under contract with the studios, that were as brilliant as had ever
been assembled for a collaborative creative endeavor. Schatz discusses the
genre director, the narrative conventions of the genre, the genre as a social
force—all to demonstrate the impact of genre films and the Hollywood
system that produced those films. As with the other critics examined in this
chapter, Schatz pursues the sociological and mythical dimensions of the
genre approach, but he places the main responsibility for genre success on
Hollywood production practices.

For example, one can think of genre as a set of built-in satisfactions,
expectations of a certain kind of pleasure, shared by the audience and the
filmmakers. The star system developed by the studio is inseparable from the
idea of genre. A "Bette Davis film," a "John Wayne film," or a "Clark Gable
film" operates in the minds and imaginations of studio heads and viewers
exactly like a western, a science-fiction film, a swashbuckler. They are known
quantities, selected and refined from picture to picture, to ensure efficient
filming on the producer's side and a pleased patron on the consumer's side.
As Schatz suggests, it would be hard to conceive of John Wayne dancing with
Ginger Rogers, not so much because he couldn't have done it, but because it
wouldn't fit the persona Wayne and his producers had evolved over the years.
On those few occasions when Wayne did parts "out of character," the films
were not great successes. Audiences didn't buy such novelty. They wanted a
known quantity, the star image they had come to expect. Thus both the shape
and substance of genres, genre stars, and genre directors are an integral part
of an industrial process in which a product is manufactured to meet the needs
of both consumers and suppliers. That's the Hollywood system.

In the second part of the book, Schatz examines several individual
genres, using the methodology developed in the first part. He discusses not
only the genres but the great directors of the genre films, as Hollywood
auteurs who were able to thrive in the system, feed off it, and allow it to feed
off them, in a kind of symbiotic relationship, beneficial to both. Schatz points
out that "whether we discuss Griffith's melodramas, Keaton's slapstick
comedy, Ford's westerns, or Minnelli's musicals, we are treating Hollywood

directors whose reputations as artists, as creative filmmakers, are based upon their work within popular genres. As the studio era recedes into American film history, it becomes increasingly evident that most of the recognized American auteur directors did their most expressive and significant work within highly conventionalized forms" (p. 27).

Schatz's most interesting use of the Hollywood film industry as a catalyst for the creation of film art in the context of popular film genres comes in the chapter on the hard-boiled-detective film, the growth in popularity of which coincided with the emergence of the stylistic/thematic filmic technique known as *film noir*. Schatz suggests that certain directors, many of whom were brought to Hollywood from Europe by the studios, were responsible for the artistry of *film noir*. Influenced by the German expressionist film movement of the 1920s, by the rise in popularity of the gangster film as the Great Depression of the 1930s deepened, and by "a number of technological advancements," including faster film stock and camera lenses, these directors were able to create a world marked by visual contrast, with part of the screen lit while another part remained in darkness. It was a perfect form through which to capture the pessimism about the future held by many World War II veterans returning to civilian life in the late 1940s. According to Schatz, this artistic development, which reached its peak in the early 1950s, was the result of a "formal evolution" in Hollywood filmmaking, in which the "thematically naive, formally transparent linear narratives of the early sound era were steadily giving way to more complex, convoluted, and formally self-conscious films. Hollywood movies became visually and thematically more stylized, more opaque" (pp. 115–116).

This period of artistic growth in the Hollywood genre film Schatz calls "American Expressionism." And he finds it significant that what he sees as the ultimate artistic expression of American film could take place within the confines of the Hollywood genre system, in a creative atmosphere completely acceptable to the establishment figures who ran the system, as long as the films produced were profitable.

To sum up the period of American Expressionism, Schatz explains that

> three seemingly unrelated issues—noir techniques, a collective cultural angst, and the cinema's reconstituted and dwindling mass audience—coalesced after the war into a period of self-consciousness and self-criticism. This unprecedented formalism and aestheticism generally escaped American viewers because it evolved so naturally from Hollywood's formally transparent and prosocial narrative tradition. But consider how filmmakers from other cultures recognized and exploited the formal and aesthetic properties of American Expressionism—as in the French New Wave's obsession with the hardboiled detective, or the New German cinema's infatuation with '50s family melodrama. The ultimate irony is that the American mass audience, whose participation in the development of the Hollywood film industry had generated the world's foremost national

cinema, began leaving the theaters just when their economic and spiritual investment promised its greatest returns. (pp. 122–123)

Thus, for Schatz those *noir* films of the late 1940s and early 1950s have attained dual historical status: they represent the height of Hollywood's narrative sophistication and visual expression, but they also signal an era of formalism and self-indulgence, a confused social conscience, and a vanishing audience.

SUMMARY

The chief advantage of the genre approach is that it expands the boundaries of film criticism so that conventional, mainstream films, which in many cases would simply be ignored, become a fertile landscape to be explored and illuminated both as examples of film art and as reflections of the social matrix. The drawbacks of this approach must, however, be acknowledged. Simple counting of icons, endless cataloguing of differences, the defining and redefining of categories and subcategories of genres can become tedious exercises in scholarship. Nevertheless, the objections are minor when the achievements are examined. Genre criticism can be literate, innovative, and insightful in its ability to explain the form and function of the largest body of films ever produced, the films that affect more people than any other—the Hollywood genre film.

GUIDELINES FOR WRITING GENRE FILM CRITICISM

I. Sources
  A. Primary
     Most Hollywood-produced films have some connection to the genre tradition. With this in mind, begin to view films, both on television and in the theater, with the intent of finding genre characteristics. Look for films that (1) break out of the standard genre formula, (2) conform perfectly to a genre formula, (3) break new ground in an old genre, (4) satirize a genre, or (5) appear to be a member of a potentially new genre.
  B. Secondary
     Sample the genre film criticism in the bibliography of this text and review some films suggested by the writers and editors of that criticism. This will give you a feeling for what to look for in identifying or establishing a genre. Because genres appeal to the mass audience, often on a subconscious level, you may gain some insights

into the makeup and impact of a genre film by asking a friend or relative what he or she thinks and feels about it.

II. Method

Using the genre approach, examine the place of a contemporary film in well-established genre, or explore the ways that an established genre film deviates from consistent genre patterns. Try to establish a new genre, or examine a film that satirizes an established genre, such as the films of Robert Altman. Finally, explore your own responses to a film and explain how those responses are related to the nature of genre filmmaking, probing the psychological element of your response to genre.

III. Questions a Writer Using the Genre Approach Might Ask

1. Are there certain identifiable features repeated involving plot, character, theme, setting, and dialogue that can be classified?
2. Are any films in current release obvious examples of established genres?
3. Are any actors working in films today connected with certain genre traditions?
4. What hidden social attitudes or values are expressed in film genres?
5. Have any new genres been established in the last five years? If so, why? If not, why not?
6. What are the characteristics of the new genre or genres?
7. Is there a film that the audience would consider to be a part of a genre that, in reality, satirizes the genre or satirizes the audience's love of genres?
8. What has happened to different genres as they developed over the years—the western, for example?
9. Have any genres completely died out, or have any made a comeback (consider, for instance, the present popularity of *film noir* themes)?

PART III

Contextual Approaches: Examining Relations Between Films and the World Outside the Frame

Looking at film in a context involves seeing the effect film has on the world outside the movie house and the effect the world has on film. Both the auteur and genre approaches, though they may focus on individual films, also recognize the position of any single work within the context of other films. And indeed many such studies go further, placing genres within a historical, economic, or technological context. Musicals as a genre, for example, had to await the technology of sound, but they may also be seen as embodying certain attitudes related to Depression-era America. Filmmakers who work on contract for Hollywood studios have different restrictions on expression from those who are independent. And the possibilities for individual expression in films may be unique in a particular country in a particular historical period because of a whole host of reasons related to major events and developments in that nation at that time.

Dividing approaches into strict categories is somewhat arbitrary, of course, because any one approach to the analysis of a film may employ elements of other approaches. Nevertheless, it is useful to see some general tendencies that help to structure and define the various outlooks. We have called Robert Warshow's approach genre, yet Warshow wrote as a journalist, reviewing current films from a humanist viewpoint and at the same time placing the gangster and western film in social, historical, and mythic contexts.

But if there are no pure approaches, those listed under the heading *contextual* seem to be more specifically focused on the role films play in the world—how they reflect it, how they affect it—rather than on an interest in films as films. According to the contextual view, genres are worth discussing insofar as they intersect with the outer world; filmmakers merit study to the extent that they are determined by their sociocultural matrix. The *social science* approaches examine how movies exist within the context of human actions on either a sociological or a psychological level. The *historical* approaches consider how film exists as a historical entity, both as an aesthetic medium and as an economic fact. The *ideological* theoretical approaches explore how films generate meaning and whether those meanings are positive or negative as they influence their audiences.

And yet even here the approaches can be seen to overlap. Behavioral studies may focus on a past period and thus have a historical dimension. Ideological issues may be important to a historian looking at the development of some aspect of the relations between earlier films and later films. Ideological studies are grounded frequently in sociological and psychological precepts. Nevertheless, what distinguishes the contextual approaches is their insistence that films cannot be treated as ideal aesthetic entities abstracted from the world in which they were produced and viewed.

One can also safely say that contextual approaches are practiced primarily by academics writing for their peers and students. True, there are writers who may not have positions in colleges or universities who contribute to magazines like *Cahiers du Cinéma* in France and *Screen* in England; nevertheless, though their publications may be offered to the general public, they are directed to a specialist audience and not the average moviegoer. And it is also true that sociologists or historians may be asked to write an article for a magazine like the *New York Times Magazine* or *The New Republic* intended for a literate audience, but most of their work will be aimed at people in their own fields. As a student of film, however, you are part of that specialized audience and can be expected to dip into such works. The following sections should familiarize you with the directions being taken by these most recent developments in film criticism.

CHAPTER 5

The Social Science Approach: Films as Social Artifacts

Social Science Approaches Capsule

AUDIENCE: Social science scholars and film scholars.

FUNCTIONS: Identify the psychology of the film, the filmmaker, or the individual audience member; describe how the film reflects and affects society as an institution; examine the production of the film and the audience's relation to the product.

SUBJECTS: The institution of cinema as a whole; particular genres; the films of a period; audience's filmgoing habits; the production system; more examples of empirical studies than in other discourses.

WRITERS: Scholars in psychology, sociology, anthropology, economics, communications, and political science using the methods of analysis available to those disciplines.

PUBLICATIONS: Scholarly journals and books.

Far more than any of the other arts, movies have existed in a public context. By the end of the first decade of this century, everyone was aware of the motion picture as part of the social fabric of even the smallest community, catering to the public's desire for action, adventure, romance, comedy, and spectacle. From the earliest nickelodeons, through the sumptuous picture palaces of the studio years, to the multiscreen complexes of today's shopping malls, filmgoing has been a social phenomenon involving large numbers of people both at the production stage and at the point of consumption. Filmmaking and film viewing can be looked at as socially structured group behavior. At the same time, movies can be examined as a psychological phenomenon, affecting the conscious and unconscious states of the individual moviegoer. Movies appear to have a powerful and immediate effect on a viewer's emotions, but what are the long- and short-term effects on a person's psyche? Can watching film and television violence induce violence in the viewer? Does the violence have a particular impact on adults? on children? Almost from the beginning, society at large has expressed its concern about how the medium may affect a person's behavior for good or for ill, raising the issue of censorship. Social scientists have often been called upon to give analytical testimony on this point.

Over the years, general writers on film have often commented on either the social or the psychological implications of particular films or noted trends and cycles of films and tried to explain the connections between what was going on in the body politic and what was being presented at the movies, placing the movies in clearly defined social or psychological contexts. This chapter, however, will focus primarily on the work of professional sociologists, psychologists, anthropologists, and historians of culture who have applied their discipline's interests and methodologies to an analysis of film topics.

Though most students will not have the professional training to write social science film criticism, having an overview of the works described here should help clarify the kinds of questions asked and the kinds of methodologies employed by this field. And it should be noted that the social science point of view can be appropriated by the nonprofessional whenever the writer focuses on the relationships between films and their social and psychological contexts. Curiously enough, quantitative analysis, which is the basis for much social science research, has had relatively little impact on the study of film in this field. Statistics, questionnaires, audience surveys, and so forth have not been used as extensively by social scientists examining film material as one might expect. For the most part, intuitive, qualitative, and evaluative discourse—the kind students are already familiar with from the other approaches—has prevailed when films are the subject of discussion.

Each social science discipline regards films a bit differently. To a sociologist, individual films and groups of films can be thought of as both molding and reflecting a society's norms, values, ideals, myths, and particular structuring of experience, or world view:

> It is snobbish . . . to ignore mass cinema either as a sociological or as an aesthetic phenomenon. Going further, one can argue that the best *and* the worst films come from the same social structure of production, enter into the same mass market, present their particular views of the world, and have certain images in the public mind. Further: even a poor film may raise or explore an interesting social, moral, or personal problem. (Jarvie, p. XV)

To a psychologist, on the other hand, film is less influenced by the exterior and codified norms of social institutions and civilized interaction than by the interior forces of the individual and collective unconscious. Films are regarded as either individual dreams, which can be analyzed to reveal the psyche of the artist, or as shared and collective dreams, which play out certain disguised and unconscious dramas of fear and wish fulfillment that reveal the psyche of a culture. Walter Evans, writing in *The Journal of Popular Film* (Fall 1973), for instance, interprets the appeal that horror films have to the adolescent as sexually based and understandable as an example of Freudian sublimation:

> Many formulaic elements of the monster movies have affinities with two central features of adolescent sexuality, masturbation and menstruation. From time immemorial underground lore has asserted that masturbation leads to feeblemindedness or mental derangement: the monster's transformation is generally associated with madness; scientists are generally secretive recluses whose private experiments on the human body have driven them mad. . . . The vampire's bloodletting of women who suddenly enter into full sexuality, the werewolf's bloody attacks—which occur regularly every month—are certainly related to the menstrual cycle which suddenly and mysteriously commands the body of every adolescent girl. (pp. 356–57)

Social scientists in related disciplines, like anthropology, folklore, popular culture, and social psychology, all have their own emphases, but the sociologist and the psychologist share certain basic elements in their approach. Because they all believe that film is important more for its cultural and psychic revelations than for its aesthetic qualities, they generally treat popular films more often than esoteric ones. Their work rarely establishes hierarchies based on aesthetic tastes or moral responsibility. Instead, it usually records and describes, coolly avoiding judgment as to whether one film is better than another.

OVERVIEW OF SOCIAL SCIENCE ANALYSES OF FILM

As early as 1911, the impact of film on the audience was a major topic of discussion. Louis Reeves Harrison, writing in *The Moving Picture World,* comments on the violence and bloodshed in the "Indian and cowboy" films of the day. He points out that the films appeal only to a "few low-brows who like them." These "low-brows" are, according to Harrison, in danger when watching these films, which are "a deliberate attempt to awaken bestial desire, or feed blood to the coarser element of an audience by working up to a brutal scene for the mere sake of brutality." He implies that this type of film has a negative impact on all moviegoers and, through guilt by association, on all commercial films in general, so that this violence is turning many people away from the theaters. Implicit in this review is the unstated belief that films can stimulate antisocial behavior and the stated opinion that it is the film-maker's responsibility to enlighten and uplift the audience.

> We do not desire to stimulate what is low in our children, but to train them to exercise self-control, to let their minds dominate their animal natures. We hope to make them better than we are; millions of parents are giving the best part of their lives to that noble end. Moving pictures are now a factor in this evolution, and the best we can do—we who are interested in the business—is to treat the public with the same sort of decency and respect that we hope to receive. (Kauffmann, Henstell, p. 50)

Harrison, writing at the dawn of American filmmaking, raises the issue—impact of film on the audience—that has become central in social science-oriented film criticism.

Because of the nearly universal perception that movies have social and psychological effects on the viewer, political visionaries throughout the twentieth century have seen in film the means of influencing the mass audience for political ends. Lenin, for example, was quoted as saying, "The cinema is the most important of all the arts." He believed that film could be used as political propaganda to influence the masses. Influenced by Lenin's pronouncement, the Soviet filmmakers Sergei Eisenstein and V. I. Pudovkin patterned their theories of montage after the Marxist theory of the dialectic. Although these men made artistically important films that work on an aesthetic level, their films are, first of all, charged with political meaning. Documentary filmmakers, most notably John Grierson, Paul Rotha, and Leni Riefenstahl, admittedly used film as a podium from which to preach political dogma. In the area of fiction film, the French filmmaker Jean-Luc Godard abandoned commercial filmmaking for several years of his career in favor of political speechmaking on film.

In contemporary criticism, there are those who value film chiefly as they perceive it to influence the audience according to a particular social or political point of view. For example, a 1970s article in the liberal magazine *Ramparts* looks with favor on a return by Hollywood filmmakers to politically oriented films. While discussing the film *Executive Action* (David Miller, 1973), the article traces the demise of social protest in films following World War II and applauds its reappearance in this fictitious account of John F. Kennedy's assassination, which is portrayed as a right-wing conspiracy. Convinced of the power of film to influence the audience, the article praises this film because it supports the political position endorsed by the magazine.

Marshall McLuhan, concerned with defining types of media and examining the impact of media on the audience, devotes only one chapter of his well-known work *Understanding Media* (1964) primarily to film. Yet his description of film—its influence on the audience and its way of communicating with the audience—is obviously related to social science criticism. McLuhan's entire work explores how the media, including film, affect the audience to the extent of modifying ways of perception.

And, of course, film reviewers, writing for such diverse periodicals as *Commonweal* and *Good Housekeeping,* often concentrate on a film's redeeming social or religious value or stress a film's possible negative influence on a young audience. Though extremely general, such discussions of films show how nearly everyone recognizes the social and psychological dimension of the moving picture image.

Social Science Perspectives

Though any thoughtful consideration of a film is likely to raise questions about the intentions of the filmmaker and the impact of the film on the audience, explicit psychological and sociological criticism of film as it will be discussed in this chapter is a more exacting and narrowly defined form of analysis than found in other critical approaches. Critics using behavioral insights to help them interpret film are actual social scientists themselves, or follow the precedent set by behavioral scientists, political scientists, anthropologists, myth critics, and others who, in analyzing the world of filmmaking, attempt to gain insight into the filmmaker's subconscious motivation, the audience's unconscious motivation or the political and social impact of the film. In emphasizing these aspects, social science critics set aside consideration of the aesthetic or entertainment value of film; their writing has had a pervasive influence on film criticism in general in the past twenty years as the latest film theories have stressed the role of film in the social formation.

To the critic writing from the perspective of the social sciences, film is, indeed, *data*—and no less interesting as such than art. Just as an anthropologist is interested in the tools and clothing of tribal peoples, and a sociologist is interested in the games that children play, so a social science approach to film sees films as the artifacts or manifestations of a particular culture at a particular time; films have been used for various functions, been part of certain social rituals and institutions. Studied and described, they should yield information about, and insights into, the culture of which they are a part. The approaches of these behavioral critics have appreciably expanded both the boundaries of film criticism and scholarship and its methodology and language. That their work avoids setting up moral and aesthetic hierarchies but rather concentrates on observation and experiment in no way means it is necessarily cold or dull.

Indeed, the range of social science criticism is excitingly broad, often controversial. One study presents the results of a controlled survey of college students' attitudes toward movies, while another relates the findings of an experiment measuring the rise or fall in aggressive behavior following the viewing of a violent film. One article defines and categorizes the "basic" plots of pornographic movies and the composition of their audiences, while another identifies and examines the "nostalgia" film and relates it to those paradoxical values of American culture that revere both progress and the good old days. An anthropological "diary" contrasts two holy Zuni Indian kachina figures, or masks of ancestral spirits—one from 1890, which has its own cultural identity, and one from 1950, which has the head of Mickey Mouse. Federico Fellini's *8½* (1963) is analyzed as if it were the actual "dream" of its creator. The basic plot configurations and archetypal characters from the traditional sources catalogued by myth critics are located in films—our contemporary folktales and myths. Essays explore the creation and perpetuation of ethnic, racial, and sexual stereotypes in films. There are simple studies of how films influence dress codes (the undershirt business in 1934 suffered a sharp decline when Clark Gable exhibited a bare chest in Frank Capra's *It Happened One Night*) and studies as complex as a psychosocial investigation of how German cinema before World War II reflected and reinforced the desire of Germans for a paternal leader and their susceptibility to totalitarian rule.

Studies of the effects of film occasionally use quantitative research methods, and sometimes involve experimentation. They attempt to discover how film affects the formation of social attitudes (say, attitudes toward blacks) and actual social behavior in either a normal or a pathological sample of the population. Hypotheses can be formulated and then tested in controlled situations. Data can be amassed in quantity by sampling viewers through questionnaires, open-ended interviews, experimentation, and observation. While often fascinating and informative, conclusions drawn by these studies are frequently controversial.

Quantitative researchers have had difficulty in isolating the many variables inherent in the real film-viewing experience while retaining that situation intact enough to make their findings truly relevant to actual experience. For example, if Mr. X (a white) today sees a film that portrays blacks sympathetically and next month votes for a black candidate for office, can we be sure that the film played a role in determining his vote? He may have been influenced chiefly or entirely by a speech the candidate made, or he may always vote for the candidates of the party to whom the black belongs. Indeed, the wealth of variables makes interpretation of data quite inconsistent at times. Different studies by responsible social scientists have variously "proven" that film violence (1) provokes imitation in real life, (2) is cathartic and drains the viewer of antisocial hostility, and (3) has no direct relationship whatsoever to real life other than as an artificially constructed game with self-referential laws, rules, and values. Still, no matter how problematic such studies have been in the past, the application of quantitative research to film has the potential of contributing greatly to our understanding of exactly how movies affect human behavior. The controversial results, however, suggest the need for great care in the isolation of hypotheses, the identification of variables, and the rigor of controlled experimentation.

The books and articles examined in detail in the remainder of this chapter can give only a hint of the diversity of the published material using the social science approach to film. As noted earlier, it tends not to examine individual films, giving interpretations and evaluations, and thus may seem removed from the kind of criticism the student of film may be asked to write in most introductory courses. Yet a student can make the attempt to see films from this perspective in order to recognize the pressure the world outside the film exerts on the form and content of the films eventually released and the potential impact those films may have on reviewers.

You may have seen an article in your daily paper that remarked on the dramatic increase in enlistments in the Navy Air Corps after the film *Top Gun* (Tony Scott, 1986) became such a hit. If you were then to speculate about the relationship between the content of a film (this one in particular or others you may have seen), its popularity with the general public, and subsequent social activity, you would be employing the social science approach, albeit at the amateur, not the professional, level. Your familiarity with quantitative methods and procedures of research might be limited, but that doesn't have to stop you from conducting a random phone survey or making up a questionnaire to hand out on campus to attempt to find out something about people's moviegoing habits or preferences. Any time you look at movies as a reflection or molder of social values, you are, indeed, seeing them from the same perspective as a social scientist.

Thus, paying close attention to the works cited here will not only give you a sense of what social science perspectives lead to, how such research is conducted, what questions are asked, and how they are formulated; but it may also suggest possible avenues for your own thinking about film which may then structure your criticism of a particular film or group of films or your thinking about the relationship of film and society.

Though the social science approach to film is broad, we can identify three major areas of concern. Most social science writers' work will fall under one of the following categories: (1) the effects of film on viewer behavior and attitude, (2) film as a reflection of psychic and cultural identity, (3) the production, distribution, and exhibition of film as a social structure, organization, and institution.

THE EFFECTS OF FILM ON VIEWER BEHAVIOR AND ATTITUDE

Early cultures used storytelling as part of religious ritual. Its aims were seen as pure and good, its effects on the participant uplifting and noble. But somewhere along the way, storytelling entered secular life. Storytelling became entertainment. And at least as far back as ancient Greece, concerns were raised about the possible deleterious effects of listening to tales of war, adventure, and romance. Would listening to descriptions of antisocial behavior motivate people to act in harmful ways? Everyone seems to recognize the power of stories to affect our emotions, but how does that translate into social activity or psychic health? Depending upon the answers to such inquiries, societies have promoted some kinds of stories and banished others.

Stories told in movies seem to many observers to be an even more powerful stimulus than those told in other mediums. For this reason, social scientists continue to debate the extent of that power and what its effects might be. Though from the earliest days of the nickelodeons, there had been many attacks on the movies by Christian moralists for depicting naughty behavior, concerted efforts to curb movies' licentiousness did not arise until the 1920s. Late in the decade, shocked either by what was perceived as the loose morals of the flapper generation or the depiction of the fast life in the films of the period, the moral majority of the community called out for action. Something had to be done to stem the tide of immorality. One result was a massive investigation of the movies by social scientists who were given grants to find out just how bad the effect of movie viewing could be on innocent minds.

In 1928 the Reverend William H. Short, executive director of the Motion Picture Research Council, a group organized to promote research on the influence of film on human behavior, applied for, and received, a $200,000 grant from a private charitable organization called the Payne Fund to support an investigation of, according to Short, "what effect motion pictures have on children." Working with Short were a group of prominent educators as well as university sociologists and psychologists. When Short received the grant, he organized this group of experts into the Committee on Educational Research of the Payne Fund to lead the investigation, which extended from 1929 until 1932 and produced a series of twelve studies on all aspects of film, including attendance, content, the relation of behavior shown in films to normal social behavior, the effects on sleep and health, the emotional effects, the relationship between films and delinquency, and methods of teaching children to distinguish between good and bad films. The study was conducted, according to Short, in order to "develop a national policy concerning motion pictures."

The studies, which focused on children and young adults as subjects, used four basic research methods: (1) psychological experimental procedure, (2) question-answer testing, (3) rating scales, and (4) questionnaire, life story, and interview techniques (Jowett, p. 221). Of all the methods, perhaps the most important—and clearly the most controversial—was that used by Herbert Blumer, a highly respected sociologist at the University of Chicago. Blumer attempted to provide an understanding of film's effect on conduct, based mainly on written autobiographies, supplemented in some cases with interviews, conversations, and questionnaires written in response to the experience of watching films. The respondents ranged in age from high school student to adult, including 634 students in two universities, 481 college and junior college students in four schools, 583 high school students, 67 office workers, and 58 factory workers. From these autobiographies, which were gained with what Blumer calls "the utmost care and attention" in verifying the accuracy, reliability, and sincerity of the responses, he theorized that films were more than entertainment to many young people but

> were authentic portrayals of life, from which they draw patterns of behavior, stimulation to overt conduct, content for a vigorous life of the imagination, and ideas of reality. (Jowett, p. 225)

He goes on to add that

> because motion pictures are educational . . . they may conflict with other educational institutions. They may challenge what other institutions take for granted. The schemes of conduct which they present may not only fill gaps left by the school, by the home, and by the church, but they may also cut athwart the standards and values which these latter institutions seek to inculcate. (Blumer, p. 197)

As a specific example of this influence, Blumer cites the ways films affect the young audience's feelings toward what he calls "passionate love." He first describes the end results of a survey of students who witnessed passionate love scenes on film, including the finding that 30 percent "showed either admission or evidence that the writer had been made more receptive to love by love pictures." Autobiographical examples from the respondents of the arousal of passion are presented at some length, and include the following excerpt:

> *Female, 19, Scottish parentage, high-school junior.*—I have always been very emotional over love scenes or anything like a love scene. I usually clench my fists, or if sitting next to anyone whom I know very well I will squeeze their hand. Sometimes if a scene is very "mushy" the cold chills run up and down my back. When I see such pictures I often feel that I would like to have someone make violent love to me. (Blumer, p. 110)

After citing many other examples of this kind, Blumer sums up the study of the impact of films on a viewer's feelings of passion as follows:

> These accounts reveal, again, a picture of emotional dominance—the effect to which we have referred as emotional possession. . . . There may emerge from this "molten state" a new stable organization directed towards a different line of conduct. The individual, as a result of witnessing a particularly emotional picture, may come to a decision to have certain kinds of experiences and to live a kind of life different from his prior career. . . . In this sense, without attempting to evaluate the matter, it seems that emotional possession induced by passionate love pictures represents an attack on the mores of our contemporary life. (Blumer, p. 115–16)

The conclusion is as obvious as it is flawed. Despite the admission that only 30 percent were affected, film is seen as the catalyst capable of producing irresponsible emotional behavior. The researcher makes no mention of the possibility that the respondents may have used film as the excuse for passionate thoughts already in place. The results of studies like this appear predetermined by the mind set of the researchers. Since the release of these early biased studies, however, behavioral scientists have tried to be more objective in probing the connection between film and audience behavior. With the advent of television, this inquiry was expanded to include that medium. Most studies produced after the 1940s, although they do acknowledge film, focus primarily on the impact of the ubiquitous small screen.

Post–TV-Era Studies of the Film's Effect on Viewers

In 1966, when Andre Glucksmann examined the available research on violence shown on television and in the motion pictures for his editorial survey *Violence on the Screen,* he reported finding 2500 titles on the subject worldwide. He divided these into the following categories: (1) "General Opinion," (2) "The Impact of Cinema and Television," (3) "Sociological Study of Effects," (4) "Study of the Psychological Mechanisms Involved," (5) "Laboratory Studies," (6) Cultural Studies. Major studies in each area were assessed to determine if concrete conclusions could be drawn from the data pointing to the effects of screen violence on young people. In each of the areas, conclusions were contradictory. For example, in terms of sociological effects, Glucksmann found after reviewing the research that "no precise relationship can be established by the use of statistics between the influence of cinema and television, and deviant behavior." Even though, he acknowledges, some researchers have suggested the opposite, the overwhelming emphasis of the findings would seem to refute this viewpoint. Although many people believe that there is a firm connection between film violence and behavior, no hard evidence has been produced to support that claim. Six years after the Glucksmann study was published, it was updated and reprinted with an afterword by researcher Dennis Howitt in which he notes: "There is no doubt that to draw any firm conclusions on the basis of the available evidence about the effects of television and film violence is a risky occupation. The reasons for this are obvious enough. The empirical research available says nothing which is reliable and specific enough to allow decisions to be made" (p. 466).

Confirming Glucksmann's findings, the comprehensive report on the influence of the media—film, television, and print—on the morals of American society, the *1970 Presidential Commission's Report on Obscenity and Pornography,* concluded that "empirical research designed to clarify the question has found no evidence to date that exposure to explicit sexual materials plays a significant role in the causation of delinquent or criminal behavior among youth or adults." The simplicity of both statements masks the vast number of reports, studies, and other research findings that were drawn on to reach these conclusions. The commission's conclusions, however, did not put the questions to rest. In fact, the result of this report was an outpouring of studies and "minority reports" intended to disprove Glucksmann's and the commission's findings. One of these reports was the body of evidence collected and summarized in 1974 by Victor Cline, clinical psychologist at the University of Utah. His anthology of scientific studies and personal opinion essays by respected behavioral scientists and educators is titled *Where Do You Draw the Line?* and advances the hypothesis that, indeed, viewing indecent and violent scenes, whether in magazines, on television, or in films, is a definite cause of deviant behavior. In summation, Cline, after compiling and reviewing the material, determines that the evidence suggests

> the possibility of harms associated with exposure of humans to significant amounts of media violence as well as to certain kinds of pornography. Indeed, on the basis of a great deal of scientific evidence presented here, it would be difficult to deny such an assertion. (p. 358)

With Cline's study as a backdrop, the *Meese Commission's Report on Pornography* (1986), using experts of its own, reversed the findings of the 1970 commission, stating that there was a causal link between the viewing of antisocial material on the screen and the acting out of antisocial behavior. As a result of the findings, two members of the commission resigned, with the intent of issuing a minority report. The findings had produced another controversy and an outpouring of support on both sides of the issue.

The lesson to the student is obvious. Social science is not an exact science, and human response to a source of stimulation, whether it be film or some other form of media, is very difficult to predict or to quantify. However, these studies do delineate an area of research that has continued non-stop since the Payne Fund studies and, at the least, provide food for thought and create incentive for social scientists to continue exploring the relation of images and audiences.

Although determining the impact of the media on the audience through research data has been the method most favored by social scientists because of its seeming objectivity, many books have been published that look at film's effect on the mass audience but adopt a less quantitative, more intuitive methodology. Daniel Boorstin, in *The Image, or What Happened to the American Dream* (1961), relies, for evidence, primarily on personal observations gained over his years of experience as a cultural historian. The method of research is not scientific but personal, and Boorstin makes the point that the approach is intentionally personal for the reason that he is "suspicious of all mass medicines for national malaise and national purposelessness. The bigger the committee, the more 'representative' its membership, the more collaborative its work, the less the chance that it will do more than ease or disguise our symptoms." He is arguing against the type of committees, such as the presidential commission mentioned earlier, that often come to contradictory conclusions. Boorstin sees the impact of media in general and of film specifically as directed at the individual and, therefore, he feels qualified to draw on personal experience that he "shares with all Americans."

In describing film's influence on the audience, Boorstin prophesies the decline of America's value system partly because of film's tendency to turn reality into an empty image. Boorstin says his purpose is to "describe the world of our making, how we have used our wealth, our literacy, our technology, and our progress, to create the thicket of unreality which stands between us and the facts of life." The writer points to film as one example of that unreality which leads to what he calls a "dissolution of literary forms." He argues that because literature can be so easily translated into film, the audience may forget the literary original and substitute as a completely adequate translation the film adaptation. He describes film as a "more vivid, more universal medium" which has done much to "dissolve the very concept of literary form." Boorstin is aware of the film industry's early and continuing inclination to adapt novels to the screen. He describes the result of these adaptations:

> The most vivid form in which important literary happenings now reached people was no longer direct. The novelist's product was his novel: a pattern of words with a form all its own. The larger audience, however, now experienced not the novel but a motion picture adaptation of the novel. Of course it was only the printed page that could offer the authentic "original" version of the author's creation. The movie, at best, was an image of it. (p.145)

Boorstin argues that because most people find film "more vivid and more impressive than the spontaneous original," the literary form becomes only a "secondhand account" disregarded by the audience. Boorstin accepts film's power to influence the audience, but he sees this power as harmful to the masses. This negative view of film's power is similar to that of the previously cited behavioral scientists, but it is written by a historian, with the stated purpose of ignoring data that can often be contradictory. But it should be clear that this method does not solve the problem. One could argue that Boorstin's subjective approach undermines his conclusions just as much as the contradictory results of a variety of quantitative studies on audiences' response to film undermine their conclusions.

Many social critics, such as Boorstin, Cline, Glucksmann, and the authors from the Payne Fund studies, seem to be interested in only one thing: film's impact on the audience. In these cases, the impact is shown to be at worst harmful, at best only neutral. Very few studies have hypothesized that film could be used as a positive influence. There are those studies, however, that examine films not primarily as a force that changes audience behavior, but as a reflector and reinforcer of that behavior on an unconscious level. These determinants are studied principally not by examining an audience's responses, but by looking at the films themselves to explain what they reveal of the audience's psyche. This approach provides students with the fascinating opportunity to consider a film in relationship to his or her own hidden world of dream and fantasy as well as those more public dreams and fantasies shared with fellow students.

FILM AS A REFLECTION OF PSYCHIC AND CULTURAL IDENTITY

A critic studying film as a clue to audience identity is less influenced by the surface layer of content than by the interior forces of the individual and collective unconscious. Films are regarded as either shared and collective "dreams" that play out certain disguised and unconscious dramas of fear and wish fulfillment revealing the psyche of a culture, or as individual dreams that can be analyzed to reveal the psyche of the individual viewer or of the artist who made the film.

The first attempt—and still one of the most fascinating—to understand a society by discovering its unconscious desires played out on the screen is Siegfried Kracauer's study of German film, *From Caligari to Hitler* (1957). The forces analyzed at work in German films of the 1920s and 1930s are reflective of the German psyche and can help explain Hitler's rise to power. The analysis begins with an artistically and culturally important film of the silent era, *The Cabinet of Dr. Caligari,* released in 1920, shortly after Germany's defeat in World War I, and ends with Hitler's ascension to power in the mid-1930s. Kracauer's thesis is that "through an analysis of the German films deep psychological dispositions predominant in Germany from 1918 to 1933 can be exposed—dispositions which influenced the course of events during that time and which will have to be reckoned with in the post-Hitler era."

Kracauer's goal was to psychoanalyze the German collective unconscious by finding the hidden significance in Germany's popular films. He believed that films are a valid medium to study, since they are "never the product of an individual" but are, rather, a collaborative effort of expression, which are not as prone as other arts to the "arbitrary handling" of content and style, "suppressing individual peculiarities in favor of traits common to many people." He also believed that because films are made for a mass audience, they most often attempt to "satisfy existing mass desires." Kracauer, however, did not consider all films equally important as reflections of the collective unconscious. He concluded that isolated box office hits did not necessarily guarantee that the films had tapped the German unconscious; the vital element was the repetition of popular, important motifs that reoccurred in many films. As he explained:

a hit may cater only to one of many coexisting demands, and not even to a very specific one. . . . What counts is not so much the statistically measurable popularity of films as the popularity of their pictorial and narrative motifs. Persistent reiteration of these motifs marks them as outward projections of inner urges. (pp. 7–9)

He also had to account for the fact that the audiences for these films were predominately middle class, not a cross section of society that the idea of "collective unconscious" would seem to suggest. He solved this dilemma by determining that "middle-class penchants penetrated all strata," exerting a "unifying influence in the depths of collective life." In other words, the middle classes were, in his view, representative of the German psyche in general.

It is interesting to look at the way Kracauer supports his thesis through examination of a specific film, in this case one of the most important and popular German films made during the silent era, *The Cabinet of Dr. Caligari*. Students of film might do the same thing by looking closely at a film like *Rambo III* (George Cosmatos, 1988) and speculating about what the popularity of such a film tells us about the American psyche, what desires and fantasies are being expressed by such a film. Kracauer begins by describing the plot of *Caligari* as it was first realized in the original script by Hans Janowitz and Carl Mayer. The story deals with a psychiatrist/entertainer, Dr. Caligari, who has under his power a somnambulist named Cesare, a frightening figure with the ability, while under Caligari's hypnotic power, to predict the future. The somnambulist performs with Caligari in a traveling circus. At one of the circus's stops, Caligari is mistreated by a government official in the town. As a result, Caligari commands Cesare to kill the official, which he does. Cesare is also instructed to kidnap and kill a beautiful girl named Jane, but he is so taken with her beauty and innocence that he lets her escape. The protagonist, a young man named Francis, along with Jane and her father, a physician, attempt to solve the murder of the government official, as well as other crimes committed by Cesare. They eventually unmask Caligari as the power-mad brains behind the killings.

Kracauer points out that in the original script, the character of Caligari "stands for an unlimited authority that idolizes power as such, and, to satisfy its lust for domination, ruthlessly violates all human rights and values." But the final version of the script was drastically changed by the film's director, Robert Wiene. In this version, the protagonist, Francis, is a mental patient in an institution, who tells the original story (it then appears on the screen as a flashback) to a fellow mental patient. The details of Francis's story are the same as in the original, with Cesare, who resembles a Frankenstein monster and lies in a coffin-like container, rising up at Caligari's command to do his bidding. At the end of the story, the director of the mental hospital, who turns out to be Caligari and who Francis thinks is evil and out to kill him, is transformed from the power-mad monster of the original script to the good doctor in the film. The film ends with the doctor indicating that he believes he can "cure" Francis of his psychosis.

According to Kracauer, while "the original story exposed the madness inherent in authority, Wiene's *Caligari* glorified authority and convicted its antagonist of madness. A revolutionary film was thus turned into a conformist one." But Kracauer also recognizes that the film's message reflects a "double aspect of German life by coupling a reality in which Caligari's authority triumphs with a hallucination in which the same authority is overthrown." He suggests the same thing occurred when Hitler came to power. Many believed the Natzi movement was anti-authority and refused to recognize the opposite truth until it was too late. The study goes on to look at other important German films made following *Caligari,* with the same result: those films are seen as a reflection of unconscious thought patterns that would obviously favor what was to become the Nazi world view.

Following in the footsteps of Kracauer's study came George A. Huaco's *The Sociology of Film Art,* written in 1965. In the foreword, Leo Lowenthal notes that "with the exception of *From Caligari to Hitler* . . . the cupboard of significant sociological work on the film has remained rather bare—at least in terms of the sort of rigorous scientific and conceptually clean work now presented by Mr. Huaco." Huaco examines three crucial periods of film history—the German expressionist film from 1920 to 1931; the Soviet expressive-realist film from 1925 to 1930; and the Italian Neorealist film from 1945 to 1955—with the expressed purpose of describing the reasons for the rise and fall of the three stylistic periods and finding out why these periods "develop precisely these filmic possibilities, and why at this particular time." To do this, Huaco examined "the cultural context within a socioeconomic and political system" as determined by the "presence or absence of four structural factors: a cadre of film technicians, the required industrial plant, a favorable mode of organization of the industry, and a favorable political climate." As can be seen, the focus of the study has shifted from the film's reflection of the audience's predisposition toward certain filmic motifs, to the film's style as determined by subtle and obvious societal influences, both inside and outside the industry.

This attempt was much less ambitious than Kracauer's, but it also was less prone to what Paul Monaco, in his *Cinema and Society,* describes as the *post hoc, ergo propter hoc* fallacy, reading "too much out of the films through hindsight" by tacking "a number of filmic themes together" and finding them "all pointing to Hitler's ascension to power in 1933." Huaco states, for example, that "it is questionable whether '*Caligari* symbolized society.'" But Huaco did believe that it is possible to study the formal attributes of German-made film, such as *Caligari,* which he calls the "first fully expressionistic film," to discover what sociologically observable determinants came together in the making of the film. One of the major cultural structures examined by Huaco, and one that Kracauer ignored, centers on the analysis of the cadre of film technicians who created the expressionist film. Of those technicians, the director receives special attention.

As we noted earlier, the auteur theory had not gained currency in 1947, when Kracauer's study was published. However, by the 1960s, the theory was at the peak of critical fashion. Therefore, it is not surprising that Huaco examines "the common social characteristics" of the expressionist directors with the conviction that "the examination will provide an . . . explanation for the distinctive conservative ideology of the expressionist film." He then provides biographical information concerning each director, including Robert Wiene, director of *Caligari*. Included in the survey is place of birth, formal education, and previous occupation of several of the most important German expressionist directors. In summarizing these biographical statistics, Huaco points out that these directors, including the director of *Caligari*, were

> largely middle class or upper middle class, well educated, with a common background in painting and theater, and of romantic-conservative political orientation. This orientation, in turn, seems to be congruent with the more pragmatic conservatism of the UFA [Germany's major film studio] film production and distribution empire. We suggest that the convergence of these two structural factors provided the necessary (and perhaps sufficient) conditions for the conservative ideology of German film expressionism. (p. 80)

The biographical study of the film directors, the identification of their social class using Huaco's analysis, has led to a better understanding of the influences that resulted in the particular aesthetic and ideological structures that identify this film movement.

A landmark book describing the formation of an American social identity by examining how media reflects and subtly influences that identity is Harvard sociologist David Riesman's *The Lonely Crowd* (1950). Riesman labels three distinctive American character types: "tradition-directed," "inner-directed," and "other-directed." His main concern is with the other-directed type, which he finds dominant in twentieth-century American urban society. The common trait of an other-directed individual, as described by Riesman, is the psychological need to trust and depend on contemporaries as the main source of self-identity and motivation. These contemporaries include friends, acquaintances, and, curiously enough, the mass media. Riesman postulates that through signals from these outside sources, other-directed personalities choose their modes of behavior. As a result, the individual becomes extremely sensitive to the actions and wishes of others. Riesman cites examples from film to reinforce this thesis. For instance, the gangster film as a genre can be interpreted by the other-directed audience "as a cautionary tale as to what happens if one goes off on one's own pursuits. Success is fatal. According to the code of the movies one is not permitted to identify with the lonely escapist; his lot is pictured . . . as a set of miseries and penances." The success of the genre film could be attributable, as Warshow surmised, to the fact that it strikes a responsive chord in the subconscious of the audience—an other-directed audience, as Riesman defined it, so characteristic of mass America.

Riesman also looks at films that directly reflect the character traits of the other-directed members of society. For example, he discusses the film *Body and Soul* (Robert Rossen, 1947), which can be seen from the sociologist's point of view as a paradigm for other-directed character behavior:

> The hero (John Garfield) is a Jewish boy from the East Side who gets to be boxing champion and proceeds to alienate all surrounding groups: his family circle and faithful girl; his unambitious, devoted retinue; the East Side Jews who see him as a hero. He agrees for a large sum to throw his last fight and bets against himself, which would have brought him wealth—and utter alienation from these groups. En route to the fight he is told that the Jews see him as a hero, a champion in the fight against Hitler. Recalled to "himself" he double-crosses his gangster backers by winning the fight; and, poor again, he is restored to the primary group of family, girl, and Jews. (p. 168)

Here, the other-directed nature of society determines the resolution of the film's plot. Riesman comments: "There was no way for this winner to take all; had he thrown the fight, he would by the movie code have had to meet disaster, but he is saved by his financial reversal" (p. 168). This filmed view of an urban society reflects the other-directed character of the hero and the peer social group. Riesman believes that a film of this type trains the other-directed character in group adjustment.

The final book in our discussion of film as a reflection of cultural identity, Martha Wolfenstein and Nathan Leites's *Movies: A Psychological Study* (1950), examines film as a representation of the audience's fantasies. The authors look at movie plots and then try to determine what fantasies these plots gratify. Student writers can avail themselves of this approach, since everyone participates in common fantasies. Wolfenstein and Leites theorize that art, and especially a mass art such as film, serves as a substitute for daydreams. This holds true, they found, primarily in American culture, where daydreaming itself is frowned upon as impractical. Americans, under the pressure exerted by the commonsense ethic, find imaginative release in a novel, radio program (television had not made its impact when this study was written), or film. For Americans these forms serve as daydreams for otherwise frowned upon, make-believe experience. In analyzing films, the authors are interested in themes that have gained common acceptance. They believe that these themes have in some manner tapped the reservoir of common daydreams.

The book examines the themes, or patterns, that occur in film after film because, in the authors' opinion, these films are windows into this secret world. The book also discusses foreign films, but only to distinguish those characteristic elements of American films. For example, the authors point out that

> in both French and American films the police are apt to be incompetent, and innocent characters are suspected. But the consequences of such a situation are markedly different in the French and American treatments. In American films, for the most part, the falsely accused is intensely energetic on his own behalf, carries on his own investigations, which are much more efficient than those of the police, and succeeds in clearing himself. . . . In the French film, the falsely accused may attempt suicide or allow himself to be captured without a struggle. (p. 15)

The theme of the innocent man who appears guilty is one that recurs in American film. The authors first list a number of films in which the theme is present in some form and then analyze the reasons for its recurring presence. For example, the film *Fallen Angel* (Otto Preminger, 1945) fits perfectly into the pattern. The hero is suspected of murdering a beautiful waitress. Although he has been unfaithful to his wife, whom he married for money, she still stands by him even after he has panicked and fled. Then, according to the authors, "Suddenly she becomes important to him and the other women unimportant. Moved by her poetic (For love alone can make the fallen angel rise) and practical (Don't run away, go back) inspiration, he returns to the place of the crime and discovers the real murderer." One analysis offered by the authors to indicate the value of this plot as material for daydreams is interesting because it supports Riesman's exploration of the character of the individual in an other-directed society:

> This recurrent pattern in which the main characters know they are innocent (except where they have amnesia), but are accused by a leering or ostracizing or punishing world with which they struggle to clear themselves, may be related to various factors in American life. The older drama of conscience, where the conflict was internal and the individual suffered from feelings of guilt, has been transformed into a conflict between the individual and the world around him. Self-accusations have become accusations of others, directed against the self from outside. In the upbringing of Americans today there is a particularly mixed ethic. A great many standards have to do with how things are going to look to the neighbors, with what will impress other people. These standards are probably the more explicit. Along with this external ethic, there continues an often less articulate code incorporating convictions that certain things are right and others wrong. This inner ethic occasions self-accusations which tend to be perceived as accusations coming from outside. (p. 189)

The main difference between Riesman and Wolfenstein and Leites is the point of view from which the films are analyzed. Riesman uses film as an example to reinforce his description of certain types of behavior patterns common to a specific society. Wolfenstein and Leites, on the other hand, see in film evidence of individual daydreams that have become manifest in the collective unconscious.

Film as Myth

One can pursue this method of viewing film as a reflection of cultural identity further by examining the film's deep structure as a part of the collective unconscious that reoccurs as myth. A myth is a concrete expression of something found in our collective unconscious that has universal significance to an entire culture. That concrete expression is often in the form of an anonymous story or stories that cluster around similar groups of motifs, characters, and actions. This approach can be found in the myth criticism of Parker Tyler and Yvette Biro.

Parker Tyler's books on myth in movies, *The Hollywood Hallucination* (1944) and *Myth and Magic in the Movies* (1967), are early works on the subject. Tyler describes film as "a free, unharnessed fiction, a basic prototypic pattern capable of many variations and distortions, many betrayals and disguises, even though it remains imaginative truth." Film, Tyler believes, is as powerful as or more powerful than the other arts in capturing the subconscious patterns of human experience that surface in every age as myth. He bases his analysis on Freud's theory of the subconscious, which, according to Tyler, states "that beneath the upper levels of the mind lies a vast human capacity to think in terms of frantic passions and above all in terms of symbols." These symbolic patterns appear, says Tyler, in all art, but he has no interest in explaining how film compares with other art forms. Rather, he analyzes film as an embodiment of myth. Typical of Tyler's method, as illustrated in *Myth and Magic in the Movies,* is his use of myth criticism to uncover archetypal elements, in this case the main characters, in the popular American silent film *City Lights* (Charlie Chaplin, 1931). Charlie, as the archetypal fool, shows

> the state to which the king, his ancient patron, has come in the person of the modern capitalist—vulgar, materialistic, and perverted, the apotheosis of Sancho Panza himself. The comedy of affection and enmity staged between Charlie and his fickle patron is essentially the comedy of the king and his fool, at one moment the consoler and friend of the king's bosom, at another the object of his good-natured cuffs. The modern element in the tramp-capitalist relationship is its sinister intimation of the split personality in the capitalist, induced by dipsomania, which may lead to dementia praecox and the impulse to kill. (p. 80)

Tyler is obviously not interested in the immediate aesthetic effect of watching a film or in discovering and proving its artistic worth. He sees in film evidence of the mythic imagination at work, and he describes film as a system of mythical elements forming archetypal patterns. Although Tyler broke ground in using myth criticism in *Hollywood Hallucination* and *Myth and Magic in the Movies,* it wasn't until 1982 that a thoroughgoing critical treatment of myth in film was published.

The main question asked by Yvette Biro in *Profane Mythology* (1982) is, simply, "Why should we consider film-thought as a branch of the tree of mythical thinking?" Her answer to this question is that in the concrete world of film images can be discovered a type of thought that Biro believes is closely related to, on the one hand, the "malleability of time-space, freedom to transgress the natural boundaries of reality" found in dreams, and, on the other, to what Biro calls "child-thought or magical thought" where "events follow not only logic but also passionate motivations and driving emotions." The upshot of the argument is that thought itself may be "embodied in ways other than the royal road of discursive logic, making use of different means and thereby, of course, acquiring a different character." That "different character," it turns out, is that film is a mythic art form, the collective unconscious brought to the screen in the form of "image events" that through visualization take on significance. According to Biro, "image events are culturally determined; they transform the 'sign universe' of action to suit the 'concrete logic' of the film. What happens, essentially, is that allusion, by means of sketchy presentation and powerful emotional emphasis, ritualizes simple actions," which gives those actions mythical significance. As Siegfried Kracauer has pointed out in another context: "Film is the discovery of the miraculous in everyday life"—for "the miraculous" read "the mythical."

The ability of film and other media to create modern myth, almost without knowing it, from the stuff of everyday life, was not lost on the critic Roland Barthes, who, according to Biro, "does not consider myth-making an innocent or neutral activity." Instead, according to Barthes, film awards the "status of mythical absolute to the unwhole and the ephemeral, shamelessly attributing eternal life to transitory and therefore questionable truths." It is from this negative explanation of film as creator of myth that the title *Profane Mythology* arises. Barthes's negative view of film as a creator and perpetuator of valueless, meaningless myth is, however, turned to a positive value by Biro, who asserts that on the screen the trivial has become "the cinema's true, very own territory." She believes that with enough repetitions as they constantly appear on the screen, the everyday becomes ritualized and gains great significance, which is obviously one of the valuable characteristics of myth.

At this point, one of Biro's examples needs to be cited to show how she transforms a specific film's images into the stuff myths are made of. The film she chooses, Karel Reisz's *Every Day Except Christmas* (1957), is one she calls "modest." It is the simple story of a big city waking up to begin the commercial workday, and the frustrations of that day, which happen "every day except Christmas." In twenty minutes of film time, all the labor that takes place in the hours between dawn and the close of the day are compressed, so that the events assume the characteristics of a ritual. Events as simple as piling produce into display cases become, according to Biro, metaphors for the human struggle that are almost as obvious and poignant as the Sisyphus legend. Thus the ancient myth becomes embodied on film, and so becomes an "archetypal situation," since, as Biro points out, "in the cinema the most profane human activities and everyday misery appear as extraordinary and comprehensive experiences, which, charged with the emotional content of ceremonies, present to us the malevolence as well as the benevolent pathos of labor."

She adds that it is the "compelling mythicizing nature of the film, the ambiguity of presenting banality containing the metaphor" that she is attempting to illuminate in the example taken from Reisz's film. She also uses this example to "verify film's ability to lend a challenging quality to everyday phenomena with its raw emphasis and articulation of recurring rhythms, to address us both emotionally and intellectually" (p. 80).

Myth critics, like Biro and Tyler, perform an important function, since they uncover in film a medium for tapping and sorting the myths of modern life. Unlike the other behavioral critics discussed in this chapter, however, myth critics do not ignore aesthetics when analyzing film. In fact, Biro contends that only the great films can tap the collective unconscious in ways that can have truly lasting impact. But in the final analysis, myth critics are most concerned with film in its context: the society and the individual psyche of those viewing and creating films.

THE PRODUCTION, DISTRIBUTION, AND EXHIBITION OF FILM AS A SOCIAL STRUCTURE

Social scientists frequently analyze film as an institution that reflects the structure of the society in which it is made. They also attempt to find out how this institution influences the broader society at large, which then, in turn, influences the production of films. Studying patterns of production, distribution, and exhibition can illuminate not only films and the film industry but also the connection of the film industry to social institutions beyond the scope of the industry. Recent investigations have attempted to describe and relate the microcosmic social structure of the Hollywood production system, with its studio pecking orders and its functional roles, to both the films produced by that system and to the culture in which that system flourished. Studies can also look at the society at large to determine its impact on the industry and, therefore, on the films created in that society. Hortense Powdermaker's anthropological study, *Hollywood the Dream Factory* (1950), and the monumental study of the film industry's place in American society, written by Garth Jowett as a project for the American Film Institute, *Film: The Democratic Art* (1976), show the possible range of this method.

Hortense Powdermaker approaches film from the point of view of a social anthropologist. From July 1946 to August 1947, she lived in Hollywood to study the behavior of the movers and shakers in the film industry. Her study is one of the earliest examples of a close scholarly analysis of the industry.

Although the film industry has undergone change in the last quarter of a century, her excellent insights still prove valuable in describing a closed, powerful society at the height of its influence. The thesis of her book is that the social system in which films are made influences significantly the content and meaning of those films. She describes that system and draws the conclusion that because of the conditions under which films are produced, films seldom reach a level higher than the lowest forms of mass amusement. She finds the industry governed by the philosophy of "give the audience what it wants"; the filmmaker, however, never can be sure what that mysterious something is until box office receipts are tallied. The confusion leads to a system in which money and the belief in luck become the key ingredients to success. Picking winners in film scripts takes on the same mystique as picking winners at the racetrack. The atmosphere surrounding this organized irrationality Powdermaker depicts as one of constant crisis combined with a definite strain of anti-intellectualism.

Under the uncomfortable, repressive, pressure-packed working conditions of the studio system in its heyday, she finds little evidence of creativity. As in any industry, film is seen as a product to be mass-produced and sold for profit. The industry set-up reflects these conditions. The executives at the top are not the creative geniuses but the wheeler-dealers who set themselves up as gods and who, according to Powdermaker, enjoy the role. They thrill in exploiting and manipulating other human beings, while in reality they are nothing more than high rollers who gamble completely on instinct. Their view of life that luck—or, as it is commonly called in film, "the big break"— determines the outcome is reflected in films in which, according to Powdermaker, artistic consideration is meaningless:

> Life, success or misfortune is usually portrayed as caused by luck or an accident. Only rarely does a movie show the process of becoming successful or the process of disintegration. Either one is treated as a *fait accompli* in the beginning of the picture or as caused by accidents during the course of the movie. Most movie characters, whether hero or villain, heroine or jade, are passive beings to whom things happen accidentally. Rarely do they even try to think through the situation in which they find themselves. They are buffeted about and defeated; or Fate smiles on them and almost magically they are successful. (p. 328–29)

The belief in luck combines with the belief that everyone has a price. In the minds of these "men who play god" it is the profit motive, not the artistic motive, that acts as the major moving force.

Powdermaker's findings concerning Hollywood filmmaking in the late 1940s and early 1950s have been substantiated by other insiders writing in later years about the Hollywood studio system. Except in the form of trashy novels, publicity releases, or films like *The Stunt Man* (Richard Rush, 1980), which seek to expose the workings of the film industry, the possibility of learning firsthand about the system is limited for most students. Through social science studies, however, they can gain a wider understanding of filmmaking practices and the way films are ultimately produced.

Even though the film factories, the back lots, the movie moguls, and the mobs of contract players are gone, the same mentality seems to haunt today's supposedly more independent (and thus possibly more creative) productions. In his book *Final Cut (1985)*, Steven Bach, a former senior vice president and head of worldwide production for a major Hollywood studio, chronicled the making of the disastrous film *Heaven's Gate;* and David McClintick, a reporter for the *Wall Street Journal,* in his investigation of power in Hollywood, *Indecent Exposure* (1982), explored the irrational, sometimes illegal, methods executives use to run the Hollywood film industry. Both books are of the opinion, here articulated by McClintick, that little has changed in Hollywood since the days of Hortense Powdermaker's study:

> Even with a more diverse group of power seekers, even with all the changes wrought by television in the fifties when it became a mass medium competing for audiences with movies, even with all the impending changes posed by new forms of home entertainment, the institution of Hollywood has changed far less than is conventionally believed. More than a place, Hollywood is a state of mind. And the same elemental forces that drove it in the twenties and thirties still drive it today. In addition to the pleasures of power, there are money, fame, sex, a stake in creating American popular culture, and an opportunity to have a great deal of fun in the pursuit of these pleasures. (pp. 53–54)

Although this material is not film criticism per se, it can shed much light on the reasons films are made. Knowledge of this kind is useful when trying to understand a subject in order to write about it with more authority.

Film: The Democratic Art (1976) is Garth Jowett's exhaustive historical study of the motion picture industry's attempt "to gain social and cultural acceptance, and the problems encountered in the accommodation process." In chronicling the impact of American society on the film industry, as well as the impact of the film industry on society, Jowett raises several key questions concerning the importance of American film as a communication medium: "What social, cultural, economic and political adjustments are necessary to accommodate this new force? What institutional changes will have to be made, and what are the long-term psychological effects on the population? In a more abstract vein, what changes occur in the collective sharing of symbols in that society?" (p. 18). The study traces the social history of the film industry with the intent of answering those questions.

Jowett's study is incredibly comprehensive. A glance at the table of contents gives a sense of the scope of the work. From chapters on the development of the industry, to those on the meaning of Hollywood, from an examination of the first attempts at film censorship, to a description of the overt control of motion pictures, from a discussion of the decline of the Hollywood institution in the 1950s because of the influence of television, to an analysis of the uncertain future of the industry, Jowett explores every conceivable way in which the creation of the new industry, based on mass communication, affected American society and was in turn affected by American society. Although it is impossible to provide a complete in-depth analysis of this work, the section of the book dealing with censorship shows clearly the interface between society and film, the area of special interest to social scientists. Jowett makes evident that society's demand for censorship came about in response to films that were, because of their unprecedented popularity, having a tremendous impact on the society. By examining the history of censorship, Jowett illuminates the ways the industry was influencing society, while at the same time illuminating the ways in which the society attempted to influence the industry. Although the industry fought censorship, it was a losing battle, since, as Jowett makes clear, producers opted from the beginning of commercial film production to handle film as a commodity to be consumed and regulated by the marketplace, instead of as an art form to be treated as a facet of the artistic community. This is not to say that Jowett does not consider film to be an art form; rather it indicates that, industrywide, the profit motive was central, and when censorship became an issue, the powers caved in to the demands of the censors rather than risk profits.

To trace the rise of censorship, Jowett begins by examining those decisions, whether consciously made or not, that led to the star system, the creation of the feature film, and the motion picture palace—decisions that helped to identify film in the public's mind as a commodity. He makes clear, however, that these choices were pragmatic, a response to the success that films encountered among the mass audience, and were, therefore, lucrative. At the time that these decisions were being made, the first responses to the industry from thoughtful, diverse elements of society were being heard, including William Dean Howells's 1911 editorial in the pages of *Harper's*, suggesting that film could have a positive influence and would become even more valuable when the content of the pictures matured, and a graduate thesis written in 1916 called "A Social Study of the Motion Picture," which acknowledged the tremendous popularity of film and suggested that it must "be considered a potent factor in molding the minds and morals of the nation."

Leading to his discussion of the beginnings of actual censorship of the motion pictures, Jowett develops the issue historically to illustrate the earliest attempts to control film to "make it more responsive to local standards of morality." Efforts first made in 1897 to censor prizefight films eventually led to federal legislation to "prevent interstate transportation of such films." But other films, regardless of content, were also considered morally offensive, especially when shown to children, and attempts were made to ban them and to close the movie houses for good. Because of the popularity of the films, however, and the public's constant support of the distributors, no serious attempts were made after 1909 to restrict motion pictures entirely. Jowett, in painstaking detail, describes the methods used to censor films that, from 1907 on, came mainly in the form of city ordinances and rulings by state censorship boards. The methods were quickly tested in the courts and found legal. The most important case, according to Jowett, was the one brought by an Ohio film company against Ohio's state censorship board. The Supreme Court's unanimous decision in favor of the state of Ohio encouraged the censors to continue their efforts.

As a result of this pressure, the National Board of Review, or NBR, was established, with the blessings of the industry, to screen all films before they were shown in New York theaters. Shortly thereafter, the power of the NBR was broadened to include films distributed throughout the United States. According to Jowett, the board "represented a compromise between complete freedom from legal censorship, and the various forms of local, state or possible federal censorship by politically appointed boards." The board's main function, which it accomplished, was to help the industry police itself and serve as a shield in its fight against national censorship; however, since the board's financial situation was always in doubt, and because compliance by the industry was always voluntary, in the end the NBR failed.

Jowett outlines society's continued problems in trying to determine the proper moral content of films, and illustrates the sometimes antagonistic relationship between elements of American society and the film industry. Clearly, the industry often made decisions concerning subject matter strictly on the basis of pressure brought to bear by society (box office success or failure, moral outrage by religious groups). But Jowett just as clearly describes the pressure brought to bear by the movie industry, simply on the basis of its unique position as a medium of communication enjoyed by overwhelming numbers of people, on society. Because of the mass appeal of motion pictures, the industry proved to be vulnerable to the pressures of censorship.

In the chapter "The Motion Picture Controlled," Jowett details the struggle of the industry and society to deal with the issue of censorship in the 1920s and 1930s, beginning with the establishment of the Hays office and ending with the takeover of that office by the powerful Catholic Legion of Decency. According to Jowett, the value of the Hays office, which was actually a part of the industry, paid for by the industry, was that it defused, as had the NBR before it, some of the harshest calls for the nationwide censorship of film. Nevertheless, after eight years of the Hays office, there had been "no noticeable improvement in the moral standards of the movies." The industry, by allowing the Hays office to be used as a scapegoat, was shirking responsibility in the face of mounting public criticism. When it became clear that the Hays office was ineffective, religious groups, headed by the Catholic Church, attempted to persuade its members, as individual citizens, to pressure filmmakers and distributors to clean up their act. But the public failed to respond. The attack against movies started in earnest in 1933, when church authorities began making speeches to the effect that American films were destroying the moral fabric of the country, primarily the youth. They pointed to the fact that the Hays office was powerless and that something else needed to be done. That "something" was the newly formed Catholic Legion of Decency. Jowett's description of the methods backed by the Legion to bring pressure to bear is a masterful explanation of the inner workings of a portion of society—the religious community led by the Catholic Church—in its battle against a powerful industry, but an industry, nevertheless, dependent on the society for its survival. Pressure was exerted through letter-writing campaigns, church sermons, speeches at Catholic conventions, newspaper editorials, pastoral letters, some boycotting of all films, and a concerted effort of the Catholic clergy to persuade members and nonmembers alike to join the Legion and to take the Legion oath, pledging to carry out the fight against immoral films. Many organizations, including the National Education Association, joined with several fraternal groups, such as the Elks and the Masons, in assisting the Legion in promoting the pledge program (p. 252).

A motion picture rating system was set up and its standards became common knowledge to every local Catholic parish in America, so that eventually twenty million Americans received the church's film recommendations each week. As a result, according to Jowett, "the Catholic Church was able to accomplish by 'institutional force' what other groups such as the National Board of Review had been unable to achieve."

The film industry responded to the Legion by complying with its wishes. What in the other arts might have seemed unthinkable seemed the only possible choice for the film industry. It followed this course by establishing the Production Code Administration Office (PCA), with Joseph I. Breen, a prominent Catholic, as its head. It was agreed that no major Hollywood company "would distribute or release or exhibit any film unless it received a certificate of approval signed by the PCA."

In the face of censorship, as Jowett makes clear, national film critics at first attacked but later supported the Legion of Decency. Those who didn't were accused by powerful members of the Legion of being "unreligious," and an example was made of them. In the end, both industry and critics accepted the limitations of the Production Code as enforced by Breen's office. Writers and directors often tried to slip one past the censors, but producers of the 1930s and 1940s invariably altered scripts according to the suggestions made by Breen and his readers. Until the 1950s, married couples in the movies, for example, always slept in twin beds, no matter what married couples did in the world outside the theater. Vice was always punished. One cannot view the films of the 1930s or 1940s without seeing the image of the industry coated with the veneer of religious morality. Exhaustive and thorough studies like these provide the student critic with a clearer understanding of the relationship between American film and American life.

SUMMARY

The works chosen for discussion in this chapter were mainly written about film in the studio years before television changed the complexion of our life style. To a large extent, the TV image has replaced the film image as the main area of interest for social science critics. As Jarvie points out, "among the mass media, cinema is neglected as against television. . . . Indeed almost anything under the heading 'mass media' by a sociologist or a social psychologist will be about television, with glancing references to radio, newspapers, and films, in that order." Nevertheless, studies that can be considered landmark works on film and the film industry offer important documentation of film's influence on society at crucial periods in its development. In looking at any large body of film criticism, moreover, it is not hard to find numerous essays that are in some way indebted to the social science approaches. Humanists, film historians, ideological critics, and general reviewers are all aware these days that films do not exist in an aesthetic vacuum. Film continues to be analyzed for its sociological content, for the impact it makes upon society, and for what it may tell us about the individuals in that society. Film critics psychoanalyze characters' behavior in films and speculate about film's effect on members of the audience. For film seems to be both preeminently social and private. As it has developed in technology, it has expanded its capacity to explore both social and psychological worlds. Filmgoers can hardly escape the socialization that takes place through film. But at the same time, in the darkened privacy of the film theater, they are free to let the film reach into their own personal psyche. No wonder the social science approach has attracted so many critics of film. For the student writing about film, this knowledge can lead to some of the most stimulating criticism of the movies.

GUIDELINES FOR WRITING SOCIAL SCIENCE FILM CRITICISM

I. Sources
A. Primary
For the student film critic, this approach is difficult to use, since the primary materials are difficult to gather. For example, primary materials include both individual and group responses from the audience, and information concerning the thinking processes and group functioning of the filmmakers themselves. Although you may not have the

background, educational training, or resources to use all the techniques discussed in this chapter, you can use your own insights and experiences as well as limited social science methodology as the basis on which to write a critical analysis using the social science approach.

B. Secondary

Preview films that seem to have caught the audience's imagination by becoming huge box office hits. A film phenomenon such as *Fatal Attraction* (Adrian Lyne, 1987) would be a good possibility. Then see if other films have been made as spinoffs of the original film. A film like *Black Widow* (Bob Rafelson, 1987) comes to mind. Seeing these films might lead you to discover their psychological underpinning. Study the works cited in this chapter or other social science works in the library to determine if you can model your approach after any of them. Look at journals, such as *Psychology Today,* that occasionally examine films from a social science approach. Discuss the approach with members of the psychology and sociology departments in your school.

II. Method

Use one of the examples in this chapter as a takeoff point for your critical analysis. For instance, you could write a paper using Daniel Boorstin's approach—personal insights based on his own responses to the impact of film on behavior. You can rely to some extent on your own thinking and behavioral response to a film to write a paper about the social context of films. Be objective. See the films as part of your culture, not merely as personal experience. Don't be afraid to conduct your own mini-sample of an audience attending a film, make up a questionnaire to survey members of your class concerning a film being discussed, or conduct a random phone survey to determine people's response to current films. Use your own experience, the experience of your peers, and your reading to support your position.

III. Questions a Writer Using the Social Science Approach Might Ask

1. Why is a certain film so popular?
2. What are the underlying reasons—mythic, sociological, psychological—for a film's success with the public?
3. How is the community affected by a certain film?
4. Are there any documented social responses to current films, such as the Navy's report that enlistment jumped after *Top Gun* was released?
5. What does the rating system have to do with the psychology of film viewing?
6. How does moviegoing play a part in the social life of the audience?
7. Has the advent of cable TV and videocassettes changed the impact of film on the mass audience?

8. Are films like dreams? like fairy tales? like religious rituals? Is this good or bad?
9. What can films tell us about the audience?
10. How are ethnic minorities and women treated in film? stereotyped? handled realistically?

CHAPTER 6

The Historical Approach: Viewing the Past

Historical Approach Capsule

AUDIENCE: Historians; film scholars; students.

FUNCTIONS: Describe and analyze film in its historical context; examine changes over time in aesthetics, economics, social impact; judge films for their historical impact.

SUBJECTS: The total field of cinema: films, filmmakers, production practices, technological development, social attitudes, and so forth.

WRITERS: Historians; film scholars.

PUBLICATIONS: Film journals; scholarly books.

Compared to other arts with their centuries of history, the motion picture has a relatively short past. Yet it has a clear-cut historical framework. From the efforts of the early pioneers at the end of the nineteenth century, who sought to invent a way to expand the ability of the photographic apparatus to capture and preserve an image of the world as it exists in motion, through the rise of the story film and the business of mass entertainment around World War I, the addition of sound and color by World War II, to the demise of the studio system and the advent of television in the 1960s, the various stages of development are apparent. The changes in the medium and its presentation can be traced. The difference between the silent, black and white one-reelers at the turn of the century and the modern wide-screen color films with multiple sound tracks and convincing special effects is noticeable even to the casual observer. Simply enough, there are the films to be seen as evidence of these changes. Although the movie industry seldom saved prints or negatives for posterity, copies of films from all eras have survived. Everyone is familiar with some form of silent film even if may be only a couple of Chaplin's early shorts; sound films from the studio years appear on cable TV; current films screen in theaters and make their way to the local video store. And there are museums and archives dedicated to preserving the film remnants from the past. A find of silent films long thought lost makes the evening news. At some level of understanding we all know what film history is—all those films produced from 1895 right up to the latest highly acclaimed blockbuster.

And yet film history involves more than simply viewing the films of the past and cataloguing their prominent characteristics. The historian today asks many different questions about the relationship of those films to their times and what they have to say to us in our own time. Nevertheless, the historical approach to film criticism is always marked by the context of history—both the general history of the world from the time the first films were made until now, and also the specific history of the movies as a business, as technological achievement, as artistic artifact. Those using a historical approach when assessing films attempt to understand how films have happened in time. As Robert C. Allen and Douglas Gomery point out in their seminal work *Film History: Theory and Practice* (1985): "The entire project of film historical research—what topics receive scrutiny, which questions get asked, which approaches are taken—is conditioned by (1) the history of film history and film studies as an academic discipline, (2) the perceived cultural status of film as an art form and industry, and (3) the particular research problems presented by the nature of film technology and economics" (p. 25). Most of the previously discussed approaches have a historical dimension as well. An auteur study of John Ford is in many ways historical because the films were made in the past. The changes in his work can be examined as they took place over time. The same can be said about the humanist, genre, and social science approaches. In this chapter, however, we will examine primarily the scope of historical studies as they apply to film history in general.

Historical scholarship and criticism is the most research-oriented of approaches. One cannot begin to interpret facts until they are gathered. That gathering may consist of taping oral histories from people with long years of involvement in the film industry; of locating and poring over books, newspapers, personal papers and documents, and studio files; and of the long-winded process of collecting, sifting, and verifying all manner of conflicting information. Often such work is tedious, lonely, and unheralded when its findings are published, but it needs to be pursued as the foundation upon which any sort of interpretive criticism can be based.

Initially most film historians were chroniclers rather than interpreters; facts were gathered and presented in chronological sequence about the development of the technology of the cinematic apparatus, the birth of the industry, the transition from silent to sound films, the emergence of the acknowledged "masterpieces," and the facts behind their production. Some studies were surveys of historical development; others limited their attention to particular film studios, filmmakers, film stars, or national cinemas. Currently, however, historians are interpreting their factual data more overtly, not only recording what happened when, but also suggesting why it happened and the significance of the event. Instead of simply cataloguing the various designs of movie palaces built in the 1920s, for example, a recent study draws the conclusion that the ornate Middle Eastern decor of the period reflected the public's desire for submersion in "Arabian Nights" fantasies on a gigantic scale. Interpretation of the past has become a common strategy in historical studies of film today. It is within this broader context that we will examine the historical approach to film criticism, as practiced chiefly by professionals. For the most part the student critic will not have access to a significant amount of primary historical material, though he or she may be able to see a number of films from the past and attempt to make a judgment about them. The bulk of a student's involvement with the historical approach will usually be through the reading of film histories and the writing of research papers based on secondary sources.

HISTORY OF HISTORICAL STUDIES

Film history as an academic discipline is barely two decades old. Though one can recognize the historical impulse in such work as Robert Grau's *Theatre of Science* (1914), Terry Ramsaye's *A Million and One Nights* (1926), Benjamin Hampton's *A History of the Movies* (1931), and Lewis Jacobs's *The Rise of the American Film* (1939), it wasn't until the 1960s and the rise of film studies as an acceptable academic discipline that serious scholars with a historical bent began to examine film's past. There are many reasons for this lack of interest in the motion picture as an object of historical study. From the beginning, the movies, especially in America, were considered unworthy of investigation because the academic establishment viewed them as popular (which they were) and hence not a part of high culture. Most scholars believed that the function of the academy was to preserve and present to current generations only the best and highest examples of artistic achievements from the past. But this idea gradually changed by the midpoint of the twentieth century. Culture was no longer defined as simply that body of material selected for the education and pleasure of a sophisticated elite (a "cultured" person was familiar with that body of material—the great paintings, literature, and music of the ages, the classics), but came to include any aspect of life that represented the values and attitudes of a people at a given time and place. Originally a concept fostered by anthropologists studying tribal societies, it soon became associated with the study of developed societies, including the anthropologists' own. Many academics in fields other than anthropology became interested in studying popular culture of all kinds. The movies were just one of those areas of interest.

From the mid-1960s to the late 1970s, the discipline of film studies expanded on campuses all across the country. One of the most prevalent introductory courses was historical; it was usually called "A History of the Movies" or "American Film History" or simply "Film History." The popularity of this course created a demand for film history textbooks that would survey the entire spectrum of films from the beginnings to the present. In other academic disciplines, introductory textbooks are usually based on specialized studies carried on by scholars in the field published over the course of many years. These introductory texts (like the one you are now reading) frequently present a consensus of informed opinion, a set of accounts and hypotheses generally accepted by practitioners of the discipline. Many film histories could not do this, because, literally, there was no basic research of an organized kind anywhere to be found. And since the writers of such books were not in a position to conduct basic research—for example, going through the trade papers of 1903 to find out what anyone at the time might have written about Edwin S. Porter's *The Great Train Robbery*—they simply based their work on Grau's, Ramsaye's, Hampton's, and Jacobs's books without closely examining these writers' sources. Though all four of these books contain some accurate material, their authors were not trained historians who followed rigorous research methods. In fact, much of what they wrote is anecdotal, based on memory, hearsay, and personal opinion. Nevertheless, the demand for film history books as texts for the burgeoning history classes was so great that three of these books were reprinted between 1965 and 1970 and used as texts in film classes, joining the other texts in the perpetuation of certain myths about the early days of cinema.

THE CREDIBILITY OF FILM HISTORY: A PROBLEM OF ACCURACY

The reason these few early historical film surveys, beginning with Grau in 1914, take on such importance is that they have been used by critics and scholars as raw material—the building blocks upon which later historical and, in the final analysis, critical judgments were made. Therefore, in order to use these historical accounts to aid in the process of criticism and scholarship, the student/critic must first be aware of the problems inherent in relying on these surveys as a basis for critical judgment in historical matters and the general problems inherent in all historical studies.

Most readers of general film criticism automatically recognize that the writer is arguing for a point of view, trying to establish, through example and rhetoric, a logical basis for the particular position being presented. There are no "facts" to be discovered which will prove that a certain film is good or bad, part of a genre, or created by a genius. The reader simply must ask that a writer define the terms of the argument, must be on guard against shaky reasoning and sweeping generalizations, must try to spot the biases and assumptions that may lie hidden behind the fancy prose, and must insist on substantial evidence before accepting the critic's conclusions. Skepticism, disagreement, and a contrary opinion seem normal responses to nearly all critical approaches—except the historical. Most of us have grown up with the notion that history is "what happened" and that the historian's job is to find out the facts and present them in the order in which they occurred.

Modern thinking about history, however, has changed. Today, historians are more inclined to suggest that all histories are interpretations, even if only by omission. If history is everything that happened, no one can grasp "everything" in any meaningful way; all events cannot be enumerated. Thus a history of a period, of a movement, of a nation, must be someone's view of it, what the particular historian has decided to emphasize, include, pay attention to, present as important. It is even clearer that the raw material of history is being interpreted when the historian begins to draw conclusions, show how one thing led to another, demonstrate what influenced what. If this is true of histories in general, it is certainly true of film histories. Thus the reader of film histories, especially historical surveys, who plans to use historical material in his or her criticism, must be on guard and not take everything the writer says at face value.

Just as with other forms of literature about film, the reader should be skeptical and ask questions: Does the writer give sufficient evidence to support a hypothesis? Is the writer drawing information from primary or from secondary sources—primary sources include such material as trade journals, studio records, interviews with participants, and the films under consideration (if authentic versions are available), whereas secondary sources are books and articles written by those who presumably had access to primary sources. Even those writers who were around at the time in question may have a particular view of things that slants information. Do the writer's conclusions seem to be based on the evidence presented? Are the writer's biases visible? For example, a history of American film written by an American in America might be very different from one written by a French writer in France.

For the beginning student of film criticism, it may be impossible to answer all these questions. Survey film histories that you are most likely to read may not make clear the writer's assumptions. The sources of evidence are seldom listed: footnotes presumably slow down the reading process. Nevertheless, the best advice is not to believe everything you read as if the information and conclusions were unarguable fact. The following examples of the inaccuracies that weaken historical film studies are included to give you a brief overview of the problems you are likely to encounter when attempting to analyze historical works about film's past. For instance, both Ramsaye and Grau suggest that though popular with vaudeville audiences when first introduced as part of the program in 1896, the movies were so simplistic in their subject matter and treatment that, by the turn of the century, they had devolved to the level of "chaser," an act so boring that it was placed at the end of the program in order to drive audiences out of the theater. Many film history surveys repeat this point. Recent scholarly studies, however, have not found this to be true. Examinations of playbills for vaudeville programs of the period indicate that the films were not inevitably at the end and that they indeed were often highly promoted as "feature attractions."

To further illustrate the problem of depending on the early works, we can note that nearly every survey film history cites Edwin S. Porter's *Life of an American Fireman* (1903) as the first film to use cross-cutting between two sets of simultaneous actions. This view was based on a version of the film shown around 1914, a copy of which is still available from the Museum of Modern Art in New York. In the 1970s, researchers found evidence in the paper print collection of the Library of Congress that the original version of the film may not have cross-cut between the fireman outside the burning house and the trapped victims within, but rather that both these sequences were shown in their entirety one after the other. We may never know exactly which of these two versions of the film was intended by Porter in 1903. The object here is not to diminish Porter's role in the evolution of cinematic art but simply to remind ourselves that every conclusion drawn about "what really happened" is subject to further scrutiny. We need to realize that the development of any technique, particularly in film history, may have had a number of causes, not simply a single one.

Another problem with historical accuracy is the traditional conception of history as a narrative. One can imagine a metaphorical root for the word *history:* it can be read as "his (mankind's) story." Rather than simply presenting us with the evidence of actions and counteractions, lists of films, their casts and crews, release dates, descriptions of plots, box office receipts, publicity material, and so forth in a dry and routine manner, most film histories do tell a story of the growth and development of an art, the writers pointing out links and influences and key films, focusing on the way people have come to do what they did. And like most narratives, historical narrative tends to have its heroes and heroines, its fools and villains.

Grau and Ramsaye, for example, write film history as a narrative depicting great individuals overcoming material and aesthetic obstacles in order to give the public a new form of art far superior to any other, capable of appealing to millions. In fact, for both authors, high box office figures are synonymous with aesthetic accomplishment. For them the public knows what art is: the movies are truly a democratic art. And this audience deserves to know the story of the many individuals—producers, inventors, and filmmakers—who have persevered to move film from a primitive state to the comprehensive maturity of its present form. Thus Grau and Ramsaye mix aesthetic criteria and economic criteria with the nineteenth century's adulation of romantic individualist heroes. Looking back at the first projected films of the Lumiere Brothers and early Edison material from a decade or two later they find their heroes in the men who transformed the movies into something "cinematic." After Edison's beginnings, they see Melies as the first story-teller, the first to use editing to create narratives which could not be done on stage. Then Porter is acclaimed as an innovator because he developed cross-cutting, or parallel editing. And these innovations set the stage for Griffith, who, according to the theory, put all the innovations together, to create the film masterpiece. The progress is electric, dynamic, and aesthetic, moving ever onward and upward, waiting only for the next technological or aesthetic breakthrough in the eternal progress toward cinematic perfection. Ramsaye, in particular, articulates the "great man" concept of film history, praising these cinematic pioneers for discovering that the camera could be an ex-pressive and not merely a recording device. For him, the history of the movies is the history of individual artists struggling with their medium and yet being lofted skyward by its potentialities.

Not satisfied with the discovery of heroic possibilities, writers of film history, like documentary filmmakers, are always on the lookout for dramatic action, such as the battles among the new titans. Erich von Stroheim's importance to the growth and development of film may be argued, but he certainly was a colorful figure whose notorious fights with his studio were legend. And it is, indeed, the legend of von Stroheim that gets repeated in most histories. Once again, the reader should be aware if the film history sounds like a narrative. It may be good reading, but is it good history? The answer to this question may depend on what the reader demands of a history, what the reader's perceptions are, what kinds of questions the reader wants a history to answer.

VARIOUS FUNCTIONS OF HISTORICAL MATERIAL

There are a number of ways the film critic/historian uses historical material in his or her approach. The most popular, judging by the amount of critical material using this approach, is to ascertain and validate the movies of the past as aesthetic objects. One may argue about the value of a contemporary film according to some aesthetic criteria, but extant films from the past sometimes may automatically be considered "classics" because they have stood the test of time. The aesthetic film historian will challenge or reaffirm such assumptions regarding a film's worth. A second reason to look at the history of film is to examine the changes that have occurred in the technology of film. This approach suggests that the early days of film were primitive and that modern films, because of their greater technical proficiency, contain the possibility of a more complete and complex fulfillment of the potential inherent in the medium. The third area of investigation concerns the nature of the institution of film as a business and a social fact. How did the film reflect its times both ideologically and economically and what kinds of influences did it have on the community?

Aesthetic Historical Film Criticism

Though originally invented as a scientific curiosity designed to make the movement of the world available for closer and repeated inspection, movies rapidly became a storytelling medium. Like other forms of storytelling—the short story, the novel, the play, the opera—the movies could be judged on the basis of how well they told a story. At first the criteria were adapted from the other forms of storytelling art, but eventually the movies established their own premises for excellence. It is hard to say which came first, the ability to tell a story well in the way only film could, or the conception that there were cinematic ways in which to tell the story. In any case, early films show very little use of those devices peculiar to cinema but not found in literature or drama—editing, framing, camera movement, camera angle, or camera distance—to tell the tale, while later films use such techniques extremely well. By 1914, the idea that going to the movies meant seeing a feature-length fiction film which audiences viewed in a theater in order to be emotionally stimulated was clear to all. The extent to which that expectation was fulfilled constituted for a major portion of the audience the aesthetic criteria for film both then and now. If it made you laugh or cry, feel fear or joy, hang on to every action until it was over, then it was a good movie.

As with the other storytelling arts, however, some viewers invoked traditional aesthetic criteria of a higher sort. Did the form and content of the movies rise to the level of great literature? Did spectators respond to movies the way they responded to Shakespeare or Melville or Hardy? Did the film have important themes revealed in a masterful manipulation of the medium? Were films, in short, high-culture art? This question was asked regularly from the earliest days right through the studio years, and usually the films were found wanting—at least in their own times. There were exceptions, of course: *The Birth of a Nation* (D. W. Griffith, 1915) was treated as a "serious," "uplifting," artistic experience, a genuine "masterpiece." But for the most part, films appeared to be simply entertaining, their primary aesthetic function to provoke an emotional response in the average filmgoer the first time the film was placed in release. Unlike great books, which often yield deeper insights on second reading, films were not thought to be worth more than one viewing.

At the movie theater, everyone who buys a ticket is a critic. The immediate sense of a film's quality, how it strikes the contemporary audience—"Gee, that was a great picture. You oughta see it!"—a kind of word-of-mouth criticism, often determines whether or not a film remains popular after its first screenings or whether it is forgotten totally. But what then of the scholar, the serious viewer, the critic, the historian viewing the film many years after its original release? How does critical consensus about a film's aesthetic value arise? Why, for example, in the 1920s was Chaplin famous and popular because everyone thought him the funniest comedian around, while in the 1960s, film historians pronounced him an artist, a master filmmaker whose work has enduring value? Why has Harold Lloyd, perhaps even more popular in the 1920s because he was perceived as even funnier than Chaplin by his contemporaries, not been accorded the same high standing in film history today? The notion that film history is a series of masterpieces that it is the historian's job to locate, identify, and preserve for subsequent generations, simply suggests that many, if not most, film historians see themselves as humanist aestheticians. It is the historian as critic, as judge of aesthetic value, an operative concept similar to practices elsewhere in the academic world of literature, music, and fine-art histories.

These were well-established paths for film historians to follow. One aesthetician who pursued that path, by using history to validate film as a serious art form, was Erwin Panofsky. In Panofsky's work, aesthetics and history complement each other to clarify what Panofsky believed to be the true nature of film art. His influential essay "Style and Medium in the Moving Pictures" ties aesthetic theory so closely to the beginnings and growth of the medium that the essay stands not only as perceptive theoretical speculation but also as an example of aesthetic film history. The essay was written in 1934 and revised in 1945, and Panofsky never felt the need to alter its general tenets. Today, it still reads as one of the brightest, most reasonable descriptions of how film history can be used to shape a theory of film aesthetics. Panofsky does not trace the growth of film for its own sake; rather he attempts to place film in relation to the older arts in order to discover what it is in the nature of the medium that is unique, and to suggest critical standards for future film critics and filmmakers.

To begin, Panofsky describes the way in which film's initial development deviated completely from the development of the older theatrical forms. He claims that the first films were popular, not for their specific subject matter but because things appeared to move no matter what they were. This emphasis on movement as inherently important can be seen in Panofsky's reference to films as "moving pictures." He traces the birth of the film narrative to similar narrative forms in other types of folk and popular art, thereby contradicting those who saw film as an outgrowth of the legitimate theater. When early films had a narrative element, according to Panofsky, it was borrowed not from theater adpatations but from pictorial images and simple subject matter found in popular art forms. As Panofsky describes it, "The earliest movies were indeed pictures: bad nineteenth-century paintings and postcards . . . supplemented by the comic strips—a most important root of cinematic art—and the subject matter of popular songs, pulp magazines and dime novels" (Talbot, p. 17). These early films were a curiosity or regarded as lowbrow entertainment, which led to the highbrow audience's belief that filmgoing was a type of slumming. However, these early films were extremely important to the development of film art because they established "that dynamic contact between art production and art consumption which . . . is sorely attenuated, if not entirely interrupted, in many other fields of artistic endeavor."

In tracing the development of film in the early days, Panofsky notes that the first conscious attempts to transpose folk art to serious art took place in 1905 in a film adaptation of *Faust*. This influence by legitimate theater on film subject matter and productions was the filmmaker's attempt to graft film to art. But these serious film performances were stiff, stilted, and, in general, not suited to the film medium. The opposition between film as film and film as art still can be felt today any time a classic drama or a hit play is made into a film without attempting to find cinematic equivalents for the original verbal structure. In summarizing the historical rise of film, Panofsky argues that the "legitimate paths of evolution were opened, not by running away from the folk art character of the primitive film but by developing it within the limits of its own possibilities."

In setting the boundaries of film's subject matter and technique, Panofsky's position is clear: if a film tries to go beyond the cinematic limits that have been historically demonstrated to work to the medium's best advantage, the resulting film will, to some degree, fail. The possibilities of film are not the same as those of the theater or of any other art form. In Panofsky's view, a film succeeds to the extent that it exploits its unique and vital techniques, techniques that have been discovered through analysis of the historical development of the medium. Specifically, he mentions films as different in theme and subject matter as *Topper* (Norman Z. McLeod, 1937), *The Man Who Could Work Miracles* (Lothar Mendes, 1937), *Lost Weekend* (Billy Wilder, 1945), and *Madame Curie* (Mervyn LeRoy, 1943), which all employ techniques uniquely tied to the nature of film. These techniques include embodying disembodied figures, performing miracles, conjuring up hallucinations, creating full-scale battle scenes, shifting scenes by movement within the frame (such as following an automobile across town in heavy traffic), creating elemental phenomena, performing surgical operations and experiments, and creating scenes of general havoc and destruction. According to Panofsky, these techniques "not only always retain their primitive cinematic appeal but also remain enormously effective as means of stirring the emotions and creating suspense." Along with the ability to create marvelous visual happenings, film also has the power to place the eye of the spectator in the consciousness of the character by portraying psychological experiences on the screen so that the imaginings of the character appear as stark realities instead of as written descriptions. In Panofsky's view, "any attempt to convey thought and feelings exclusively, or even primarily, by speech leaves us with a feeling of embarrassment, boredom, or both."

Panofsky makes the point by discussing the use of sound in films from the historical perspective, coming to the conclusion that when film learned to talk, it still remained "a picture that moves" and did not become "a piece of writing that is enacted." Panofsky accurately recalls the fact that the silent film was never silent but, like the ballet, demanded accompaniment. The transition to talking film simply meant that the accompaniment shifted from music to words and music combined. Panofsky's point is that the visual should always reign supreme. He says that in film, sound is subject to "the principle of co-expressibility." By this he means that the importance of the film script "depends not only upon its quality as a piece of literature but also, or even more so, upon its integrability with the events on the screen." As an example of different uses of dialogue on the stage and screen, he describes two short scenes from the filmed version of Shaw's *Pygmalion* (Anthony Asquith, 1938), which were completely omitted from the stage version. The scenes involve Eliza's phonetic education and triumph. According to Panofsky these two scenes in the film

> are not only supplied but also strongly emphasized; we witness the fascinating activities in the laboratory with its array of spinning disks and mirrors, organ pipes and dancing flames, and we participate in the ambassadorial party, with many moments of impending catastrophe and a little counterintrigue thrown in for suspense. Unquestionably these two scenes, entirely absent from the play, and indeed unachievable upon the stage, were the highlights of the film; whereas the Shavian dialogue, however severely cut, turned out to fall a little flat in certain moments. And wherever, as in so many other films a poetic emotion, a musical outburst, or a literary conceit (even, I am grieved to say, some of the wisecracks of Groucho Marx) entirely lose contact with visible movement, they strike the sensitive spectator as, literally, out of place. (Talbot, p. 21–22)

Throughout the essay Panofsky's theory of film art can be traced to the early developments of film history. He sees in these developments an analogy between film and literature. He argues that as "the writings of Conan Doyle potentially contain all modern mystery stories (except for the tough specimens of the Dashiell Hammett school), so do the films produced between 1900 and 1910 preestablish the subject matter and methods of the moving picture as we know it." His examples of films from this crucial period include Porter's *The Great Train Robbery,* the films of Melies, the comedy of Max Linder, the early animated cartoons of Walt Disney, and, of course, the early films of D. W. Griffith. Panofsky finds in Griffith's films of this period "not only remarkable attempts at psychological analysis (*Edgar Allan Poe*) and social criticism (*A Corner in Wheat*) but also such basic technical innovations as the long shot, the flashback and the close-up."

To Panofsky the success or failure of a film depends on the filmmaker's understanding of and respect for the integrity of the film medium. He says that although films have become more sophisticated, the best are still those that, like the early films of Porter, Disney, and Griffith, express themselves in terms that are compatible with those subjects and techniques developed in the early days of film history. Panofksy's theory, unlike others that try to impose limits on the possibilities of film arbitrarily, sets only the limits that were historically based and that were modified and perfected later on. Panofsky traces the evolution of films from the jerky beginnings to what was at the time the culmination of the sound film—the animated films of Walt

Disney. He describes this evolution as a "fascinating spectacle of a new artistic medium gradually becoming conscious of its legitimate, that is, exclusive, possibilities and limitations." In Panofsky's hands, film history comes alive as a fascinating subject in its own right, even as it is being used to define and elaborate an aesthetic critical theory.

The student, however, must be aware of the shortcomings of this approach. Panofsky, for example, considers Walt Disney's films the ultimate triumph of the film medium—based on his aesthetic historical guidelines. Such an opinion has little critical support today, when examined in the light of four and a half decades of additional film history. Film's range of aesthetic experience may include *Snow White* (1937), but it appears to us far wider than Panofsky would have it. But the point is that historical criticism dealing in aesthetic judgments often applies subjective standards rather than objective ones. And if instead of Disney, Orson Welles were Panofsky's ideal film artist, we might be more likely to agree, yet the critique of this method would be the same.

When academics became interested in the movies as an object of aesthetic scrutiny during the 1960s, however, it seemed natural to use the model already applied to art or literary history as pioneered by Panofsky and others. So until very recently, film history has been primarily aesthetic history. Nearly all the film history surveys, for example, adopt this perspective. Gerald Mast, in his introduction to *A Short History of the Movies* (1986), says, "The history of the movies is, first of all, the history of a new art" (p. 2). Jack Ellis states that his *A History of Film* (1979) explores the idea that "certain countries at particular times have contributed most interestingly and importantly to the evolution of the art form" (p. ix). Though these histories mention technical developments and industrial problems, their primary focus is on the film as an art. The films, filmmakers, and events they elect to describe are those that seem to show evidence of film art. In general they see the outline of film history as a developmental process moving toward greater and greater artistic achievement, and at the same time suggest that certain films from the past were so expertly crafted that they can be enjoyed as masterpieces of film art that do not suffer from the ravages of time.

These two views may seem at first paradoxical, and yet they seem to accommodate each other easily. A certain level of accomplishment is posed as an ideal in a given period—let's say before World War I. Thus one can admire the work of Melies and Porter in making artistic breakthroughs in the technique of cinematic storytelling, but not until *The Birth of a Nation* (1915) do we have a great masterpiece. Griffith's film, using all that was available to him in the way of content and technique, surpasses by a wide margin what other filmmakers produced and approaches the ideal possible under the limitations of his time and place. Hence that film can be seen as both a stepping stone in the movement toward greatness for film art, with Griffith as the master artist, and a masterpiece worth experiencing in its own right because it has a lofty subject matter—and it utilizes the medium to its fullest.

If *The Birth of a Nation* does not seem to have the immediate appeal that, say, a *Citizen Kane* (Orson Welles, 1941) might, it is the job of the film historian and the class in film history to prepare the student in such a way as to make that film the rewarding aesthetic experience it is for the film historian.

Most film history surveys are organized by ticking off the years in such chapters as "The 1920s," "The Coming of Sound," "The Studio Years," and so on, showing the development of film art and identifying the films and filmmakers that have contributed significantly to the process. In each period, certain films are designated as masterpieces. These are the films that are most likely to be shown in a film history class because, like certain plays by Shakespeare, Shaw, and Ibsen in a drama survey course, they are considered important for students to experience, both as examples of their period and valuable in their own right, judged by traditional standards of artistic achievement. In one sense this is applying the humanist approach (see Chapter 2) to films from the past.

Limitations to this method, however, cause some modern film historians to question the approach. For one thing, though there seems to be some consensus about which filmmakers and which films are important, the criteria for selection are often inconsistent, seemingly based on the tastes of the historian rather than on more objective grounds. Erwin Panofsky, though arguing objectively, may actually be rationalizing his tastes in film. Arthur Knight, in his work *The Liveliest Art* (1957), thought Orson Welles's *The Magnificent Ambersons* (1942) a better film than *Citizen Kane* and gave it greater coverage. He faulted *Kane* as suffering "from an excess of experimentation." His analysis of the film is fascinating, but his contention that one film is "better" than the other is simply argumentative.

Another problem facing the aesthetic approach to film history based on the "masterpiece" standard is the availability of the primary sources, the opportunity actually to see the films of the past. Surely there have been other great films that have been lost or destroyed, and there may be some films available for viewing that have been overlooked. If nothing else, this approach needs to acknowledge this fact. For years, many modern historians suggested, on hearsay evidence from those who had seen it in their youths and some available fragments, that Able Gance's film *Napoleon* (1926) was one of the great masterpieces of the silent era. Not until the early 1980s could this hypothesis be tested, when a fully restored version of the film was released for public viewing. Though some scholars have agreed with the earlier opinion, others have not, finding the film repetitive and dull (it is four hours long!). Even the claim made by most film surveys that Griffith was the architect of modern cinematic narrative conventions can only be fully argued if the historian has actually seen most of the hundreds of short films made before World War I, not only by Griffith but also by his contemporaries in America and around the world. The film history survey writer, however, may not have the time or the funds to do this kind of basic research; only a small number of the best-known and easily available rentable films may be personally viewed. Thus the claims and judgments made about the aesthetic importance of a filmmaker or of certain films need to be viewed with a questioning attitude. The beginning student, of course, may also not have the resources to challenge the content of a film history survey, but should keep in mind the possibility that the writer may simply be repeating what earlier writers have stated, without ever doing any basic research of his or her own.

This is not to suggest that arguing about the relative merits of films from the past is not an appropriate intellectual activity. In fact, students should take heart from the current controversy over the status of the masterpieces of the past and realize that their views on the experience of watching such films are as valid as any that have been published. You can make aesthetic judgments and define your views in a thoughtful, logical, well-organized essay and make a contribution to the ongoing debate.

Film History and the Impact of Technology

Film history has an aspect that has never been carefully considered in the older, more established arts: the impact of technology on the artistic process. Because filmmaking is such a mechanical operation, most film history surveys have had to pay attention to the changes in technological improvements in the cinematographic process. In fact, one school of thought, evident in some of the earliest writers on cinema like Grau and Ramsaye but continuing up to the present, suggests that advances in technology made greater achievements in the art of film possible. It may have been an engineer who figured out a way to increase the illuminating power of incandescent bulbs or increase the resolution of lenses or diminish the hiss and background noise picked up on sound recorders, but once these improvements in the apparatuses were available, filmmakers of vision presumably used such inventions to further the expressiveness of the motion picture. In other words, many aesthetic innovations appear as a function of technological ones.

Thus, for example, most survey histories of film spend some time discussing the coming of sound. First they describe the expressive powers of the moving camera brought to a high degree of artistic perfection by the end of the silent era and explain that, between 1927 and 1930, since early, bulky sound equipment did not allow much camera movement during a shot, the expressiveness was initially destroyed. By 1930, however, the sound on film system became the industry standard and editing could return to the flexibility it had enjoyed during the silent era. And when technicians had made it possible both to record sound and move the camera again, directors like René Clair in France and Rouben Mamoulian in America became artistic pioneers in their creative use of sound. Clair, for example, post-dubbed the sounds of a soccer match over the image of two men fighting over a coat backstage in a theater, rather than using the "natural" sounds of the fight. For most aesthetic historians, the real interest lies not in technological improvements but in the creative uses of those innovations that enlarged the artist's toolbox. There is seldom any discussion of why certain advances came about in the first place, how they fit into the general history of technology, or what significance they may have had for the economic patterns of film production as an industry, one among many competing for the audience's leisure dollar.

Frequently such histories make claims about technological improvements unsubstantiated in any way by basic research. For example, aesthetic film historians have consistently asserted that with the introduction of the optical printer and edge numbering of film stock in the early 1930s, the average length of a shot in movies decreased. In other words, films used more shots and the editing rhythm was quickened—the pace of 1930s films was heightened. In a series of articles in *Film Quarterly,* however, Barry Salt, who actually took a representative sampling of films from that decade and used a stop watch to time the lengths of the shots, suggests otherwise. He did the same for films made before and after the optical printer's introduction into the filmmaking process, and came up with the astonishing conclusion that the average shot length had not decreased at all in the 1930s and, if anything, had increased slightly. This points to the perennial problem of film history surveys—the repetition of earlier writers' impressions rather than some solid empirical investigations.

An analysis of technical change in the film industry that took into account a larger view of the relationship between Hollywood and the world around it, backed by detailed investigation of studio records, trade papers, and other hard evidence, would help to place the aesthetic, or "great man," view of film history in a wider context. Clearly, there were inventors and studio executives who played a part in, let's say, the coming of sound to the movies. And there were screenwriters and directors who were quick to exploit sound's artistic as well as commercial potential. Yet the whole sense of what happened and why will be enlarged when more detailed studies are done. Conclusions about how the shape and form of films changed and how precisely this process is influenced by the technology will be on firmer ground. For now, Raymond Fielding's anthology *A Technological History of Motion Pictures and Television* (1967) provides a wealth of informative articles on a variety of technological innovations culled from the journals of the Society of Motion Picture and Television Engineers. There are other books and articles specifically devoted to the histories of particular technologies, such as color, cinematography, and sound, which have laid important groundwork in this area.

Economic and Sociological Perspectives on Film History

As has been noted earlier in this book, the word *film* almost always conjures up the image of the feature-length narrative movie, a form which has affinities with traditional drama and literature. The study of the classical arts seldom involves an examination of the business end of things (though a more than casual interest in Shakespeare's work will reveal the way the drama of the time was related to the monarchy and its position granted by royal license and sponsorship). It is the aesthetics of the form, the values of a period, or the careers and works of specific artists that attract our critical concern. Applying the same pattern to film study, seeing films as isolated artistic objects experienced subjectively by individuals, has simply been taken for granted. Even at a glance, however, one conspicuous difference between the traditional arts and the art of the movies is obvious: movies have a very well-defined industrial context. Everyone has some awareness that "Hollywood" is more than just a geographical place. It is an institution, a state of mind, and big business. From World War I on, the movies have required large amounts of capital, a huge labor force, and a mass audience in order to be produced. Looking at the methodology of promotion and marketing of novels and poetry may seem to yield little of importance about what the nature of literature is, whereas a study of the promotion and marketing of movies appears to be of far greater importance in explaining what happened over a period of time in the movies. Film art is more dependent on the structure of the filmmaking business as an institution interrelating with other institutions in the social fabric of the community than any of the traditional arts. Film historians have seen the value of approaching film from both economic and sociological perspectives as well as from the aesthetic perspective.

Several anthologies present good descritpions of the influence of film's development as a business: Tino Balio in *the American Film Industry* (1976) and Gorham Kindem in *The American Movie Industry: The Business of Motion Pictures* (1982) have selected a number of informative articles that deal with the growth and development of the economic structures of Hollywood. Clearly the early days of cottage industry competition, when a three-minute film could be made for the cost of the film stock and anyone could buy a projector for $150 and begin exhibition in a storefront, changed markedly into a complicated, expensive corporate structure by the time of the First World War. What had started out as a minor entertainment for working-class audiences, produced, distributed, and exhibited by a host of small, individual entrepreneurs, became a big business. As the product grew longer, stories required the services of writers, stock company actors and actresses became highly paid stars, studios were built to house the "factory" of technicians needed, distribution networks were developed, and picture palaces, some incredibly ornate, became commonplace as the site where the product and the eventual consumer met.

The kinds of films made, their themes, their subject matter, and their style of narrative construction became standardized in order to use this "plant" most efficiently and thus reap the highest profits. By the middle of the 1920s, the film industry was dominated by a handful of "majors"—corporations with enough financial strength to weather the ups and downs of economic cycles and limit the entry of new faces into the business. With the advent of sound, their position was strengthened, for they had the capital to retool successfully for the new process. By the early 1930s, Loew's, Warner Brothers, RKO, Fox, and Paramount were referred to as the "Big Five." These firms owned production facilities, their own distribution companies, and their own chains of theaters. The "Little Three," Columbia, Universal, and United Artists, produced their own films but owned few theaters. Any analysis of the aesthetic properties of the films made during the studio years surely must take into consideration this powerful institution and how it operated. Even as late as the 1960s, a case can be made for the domination of world markets by this Hollywood oligopoly. Thomas Guback suggests in his *International Film Industry: Western Europe and America Since 1945* (1969) that the exploitation of European markets by American films led to a deterioration in the quality of the films made on both sides of the Atlantic. He argues that the mainstream commercial narrative films of the period were bland, unrealistic, full of cardboard characters, and permeated by a slick style that kept viewers' minds away from the real world's problems. Thus the content and style of motion pictures may have sources other than simply the skill and creativity of the artists engaged in the filmmaking process. The industrial organization itself may set the terms within which films, and only certain kinds of films, can be produced.

With this sort of knowledge in hand, of course, it becomes easier to estimate the value of alternative cinemas, to understand the difficulties involved in the creation of different kinds of films for different kinds of audiences. The achievement of third world cinema, movies made in the underdeveloped nations of the world primarily as political protest, can be recognized and interpreted more clearly when we know something about how the Hollywood system as an economic entity has dominated the world marketplace for movies, and about how public expectations of what a narrative film should be have been created by that system to ensure an ongoing and receptive audience. Third world films very frequently appear either obscure or poorly crafted to spectators accustomed to the Hollywood style of swift-paced narratives designed to show characters ultimately resolving conventional conflicts. Knowledge of how such audience expectations are created by the market system goes a long way toward explaining why African and South American filmmakers frequently violate those conventions purposely, in order to make their anti-exploitation views more noticeable. What appears as "poor" filmmaking technique is, in fact, a way of undermining the audience's dependency on the fantasies of the Hollywood style. It forces the audience to think about the relationship between the purveyors of film and the intended audience.

The relationship between the movie industry and the audience is a matter pertinent to sociological inquiry. In Chapter 5 we discussed this as an approach to film criticism. The questions "Who makes movies?" and "How and why?" can be rephrased to add the historical dimension. In reference to a given historical period, "Who made movies?" "How and why?" and "What effect did they have on the audiences?" are valid questions. To be sure, the sociological investigator of today can sample the current audience through questionnaires and do a content analysis of all the contemporary films relevant to the questions being asked. The sociological historian comes up against all the problems attendant on any other historical research—not only are many of the films unavailable for viewing, but the audiences are gone, too.

In one sense we will never know what it was that 1930s audiences found so appealing in gangster films and musicals. Andrew Bergman in *We're in the Money* (1970) does a good job of positing what those attractions might have been, but he explicitly states that his conclusions are based on a comparison between the history of the Great Depression period and the films he was able to see. We will never be able to poll the thoughts and feelings of the producers and directors of the 1930s, to find out what they thought they were doing when they built their industry, never know precisely who made up the movie audience or the extent of the impact of the movies on people's lives. Was it true, for example, that sales of men's undershirts dipped drastically after *It Happened One Night* (Frank Capra) was released in 1934, supposedly because Clark Gable didn't wear one in a famous scene? This may seem like a frivolous question, but it does suggest that audiences in the past had a strong relationship with the events and the stars viewed in the movies. Such questions are intriguing and worthy of investigation, though the methodology can never be as precise as most social scientists would like.

For example, Siegfried Kracauer's pioneering work *From Caligari to Hitler* (discussed in Chapter 5) makes the case that the films produced in 1920s Germany contain a set of themes and relationships that reflect the country's great fear of social chaos and the desire for a strong leader who would put things to rights. Written in 1947, after the full extent of Hitler's infamy was common knowledge, the book describes a certain group of well-known German expressionist films from the 1920s, like *Caligari* (Robert Wiene, 1919), *The Last Laugh* (F. W. Marnau, 1924), and *Metropolis* (Fritz Lang, 1926), which in fact do seem to have the themes Kracauer says they do. He takes as his basic assumption the notion that movies are something like public dreams, made for the mass audience by people who are in tune with that audience, the films reflecting the psychological yearnings of their viewers. Thus an investigation of the films can tell us what the people's deepest desires are, what unconscious problems they are obsessed with. This is not an uncommon assumption about films, and we will take it up again in Chapter 7 in regard to modern Freudian theory. Kracauer's critics have pointed out, however, that he is not a trained psychoanalyst, and that the basic assumption about the way audiences relate to films has never been proven. They have also suggested that he has, looking back in perfect hindsight, selected the films that fit his hypothesis and thus has made the evidence fit the conclusion instead of coming up with a conclusion after examining the evidence. Psychoanalyzing the past is a difficult proposition, full of potential pitfalls. Yet the effort is a valid one, for insight into the relationship of audiences to movies in the past can clearly help us understand the relationship of audiences to film in the present.

PROBLEMS INVOLVED IN CONTEMPORARY
FILM HISTORY

The difficulty in accepting the statements of early film historians has been documented in this chapter. And the problem is broader than has been suggested so far. Contemporary scholars of history in general are involved in a debate over the nature of their enterprise. *Historiography* is the term used to identify this new concern about the approaches used in investigating the past. At first thought there doesn't seem to be a problem. We have all grown up with the idea that history is a study of what happened in the past. We presume there are certain facts that are unarguable—the Pilgrims landed at Plymouth Rock in 1620, the U.S. Constitution was hammered out in 1787— and it is simply the historians' job to locate the facts, to weed out the truth from the fancy, to find out what George Washington really did in his life as opposed to the elementary school stories about the cherry tree incident.

But historians today are inclined to question this basic assumption. They prefer to make a distinction between *history*—that which happened, the mere facts, many of which are unobtainable—and *histories*—what people wrote about history, how people perceived what happened, how events are interpreted, not only by contemporaries of the events but also by those writing afterwards. The latest thinking on the matter argues that what is written as a history of some event or occurrence is different from the event or occurrence simply because it is written by someone for some purpose, even if that purpose is ostensibly to record "exactly what happened." Every history of anything, then, is seen as an interpretation of the events and activities under discussion. At its extreme position, some historians argue that we can never know the past at all, only the filtered vision of those who decided to record some things as important and to forget others. In other words, the past, as we know it, is a kind of fiction. At the other end of the argumentative spectrum are those who say that, even given the limitations of the all-too-human observers, a historian can, by dint of great effort and much basic research, come up with a pretty close approximation of what really happened. The historical reality is potentially perceivable, even if exact causes and effects are subject to argument.

This explanation of the problems of historical research and what, in fact, can be achieved by it, applies to film history as well. Despite the fact that film projected on screens is not even quite a hundred years old, and that the history of film has taken place in an era of great documentation—newspapers, magazines, photographs, and the extant films provide a remarkable resource—the basic difficulties of historical research are not much different from those that confront historians of the Punic Wars of Rome. Human beings write about what interests them. They save what seems important at the time. And what seems of importance to one person may seem insignificant to another. Thus even the physical evidence available in trade papers concerning the early days of film in the United States is only the record of what certain editors, reporters, and columnists thought was of interest to their particular readers at the time. They were journalists serving the film business community, not intellectuals probing the art of the movies.

And yet trade papers are an important source for the film historian. They supply us with something that is better than nothing at all. The pages of *The Moving Picture World* (begun in 1907) can at least tell us what writers at the time thought was significant. Even what they don't mention may be important. For example, the first Biograph film in which D. W. Griffith appeared as an actor, *Out of an Eagle's Nest,* was reviewed in *The Moving Picture World* in 1908, but, as was common until many years later, the performers' names are not mentioned. The movies were packaged stories being sold on the strength of their ability to interest an audience in action, spectacle, and sentiment.

Besides this basic problem of historiography in general—the idea that documentation from the past is random and subjective—the pursuit of film history suffers from certain gross physical limitations. The prevailing conception the film industry had of itself, that it was (and is) selling a first-run, essentially one-time-only experience, meant that prints of films had no value after the first year or so of their release. Hence many were destroyed, to avoid having to pay storage costs or to recover the silver in the emulsion. Cellulose nitrate, the material out of which film stock was made until the 1950s, decomposes over time, so that even when prints were spared and stored, they were often lost to the ravages of chemical breakdown. Thus thousands upon thousands of films that might have provided insight into the filmic past have been lost forever.

In addition to the films, movie companies often threw out their corporate records when they seemed of little use, records that could have given researchers valuable information about business practices, marketing publicity strategies, and so on. Only recently have some of the studios become aware of the scholarly uses for their materials (and the tax advantages); the last decade has seen several collections from Warner Brothers and MGM, for example, find their way into university libraries.

The other pressing dilemma facing modern film historians, in addition to the paucity of original material, is the lack of basic research itself. World history is a large field in which many people have been engaged for many years. Investigations of detailed and specific subjects are conducted routinely and the published results are available in libraries everywhere. In the twenty years or so in which it can be said that film history has become an academic pursuit, not enough people have written specialized studies about small areas of interest. Survey texts of British or American political history, for example, are summaries of intense concentrated research on smaller topics by armies of scholars. There are books written about single battles in the War for Independence, for example, or biographies of minor politicians in the Continental Congress. Film historians, on the other hand, have for the most part taken on the entire field of American film or Hollywood, whereas what is needed is a closer look at narrower topics. A book like John Fell's *The American Film Before D. W. Griffith* (1986) or the seven volumes in the *History of British Film* (1946–50) series by Rachel Low, which covers that country's output only up to the 1930s, are steps in the right direction. To be sure, poring over corporate records or investigating early exhibition patterns in a single town by reading through city records for deed transactions may not be very glamorous. But the need for basic information about every aspect of film over the years is an essential ingredient in making film history a richer and more complete view of the past.

The problems of writing accurate film history are excellently sorted out in Allen and Gomery's *Film History: Theory and Practice* (1985) previously mentioned. They discuss historiography in general and then apply the latest thinking to a variety of approaches available to the film historian. Specific case studies in such areas as aesthetic history, economic history, social history, and so forth show by abundant examples how newer methods and current ideas can expand our knowledge of the past and change our views of some of the previously accepted "truths" about the history of the movies. In their conclusion the authors call for an increase in historical investigation conducted in a far more rigorous manner than has been common in this area.

THE FILM STUDENT AND FILM HISTORY

As has been noted earlier, recent work in film research has uncovered many facets of the past that were unknown or overlooked by writers like Grau, Ramsaye, and Jacobs when they wrote those first "histories" of film. Even beginning students of film history today are getting a clearer picture of what we want out of a history of any subject: as close an impression of what really went on as possible. The latest film history survey texts have incorporated much of the new information. At least we now believe that the history of film is a much more complicated set of circumstances than ever before. The "great man" or the "masterpiece" approaches simply do not go far enough and in fact may present a distorted view. But there is a great deal more information out there yet to be found, and diligent scholars are needed to track it down.

Indeed, there is room here for the beginning student of film to make a contribution. No matter where you live, the movies probably came to your area around the first decades of this century. Perhaps it was in the nickelodeon era or in the 1920s. Perhaps someone years ago went to Hollywood and worked in the business and then retired in your hometown. That person might still be alive and available for interviews. A search through the daily newspapers of an earlier day, for notices of theater openings, attendance figures, special premieres, unique marketing strategies like "dish night" and reduced admissions on certain days might yield information not only for an original class paper but possibly for an article that might be publishable.

"The History of Motion Picture Activity in Saint George, Utah, 1919–1927" may not seem like an exciting topic at first, but if enough information of this sort was uncovered in enough small towns, who knows what kinds of conclusions one could arrive at about the nature of film and of filmgoing in America? Many of the generalizations made in a number of books are based only on evidence of film in the larger metropolitan areas. Perhaps our view of the role of the movies in American life would be changed if we had more information about what really went on in the hinterlands. So, go to it. Be encouraged. Try your hand at writing film history. Do some research of your own out in the field and see if you can turn up something, something new and interesting in the ongoing search for the history of film.

The only alternative for a student who has an interest in film history is to do a research paper from secondary sources—reading the books that have already been written and distilling some conclusions from them. This, too, might be valuable as you approach the texts with a fresh eye, trying to see if the writers are making sense, if they have done basic research, if their arguments are based on some hard evidence or whether they are just rationalizing their opinions and tastes.

Clearly the best evidence for a paper about the films of the past would come from viewing the films themselves. If your school has a collection of old films to which you have access or if you are in the proximity of an archive, take advantage of such opportunities. Even if the very oldest films, those from the silent period, are not available, many of the films from the studio years are on videocassette. Sometimes close viewing of such films may reveal something that other writers haven't noticed, or your reactions may corroborate conclusions drawn by previous writers. Either way there is a chance to respond to the films and to make observations that might prove very valuable, indeed. Looking at a number of John Wayne films from early in his career to the very end, for example, may point up aspects of the star system and how it worked. Your observations, combined with readings about the star system, can produce a good essay in film history. Just remember that your conclusions, adequately supported, are as important as anyone else's. There is always the possibility of making a significant contribution to the ongoing process of defining film history.

GUIDELINES FOR WRITING HISTORICAL FILM CRITICISM

I. **Sources**
   A. Primary
      1. Local newspaper files deserve a try. Most newspapers have a "morgue" of back issues that contain articles and reviews about film events of the day.
      2. It may be difficult to trace people who have had some connection

with movies in your area (for instance, former owners or operators of movie houses). You can make inquiries of current theater owners who may know their predecessors personally or may know how to locate them.

3. Nearly every town has a historical society. Often it will have material on residents who went off to Hollywood to work.

4. Some universities have original studio documents in their libraries. Trips to famous archives where collections of both films and documents are stored, such as Eastman House in Rochester, New York, or the Library of Congress in Washington, D.C., may be feasible.

5. Films from the past, of course, are randomly available on videocassette at stores. Some university libraries have collections of prints or tapes for student use.

B. Secondary

Head for the library. Use the card catalogue both under subject (film, cinema, movies, motion pictures) and author (filmmakers, producers, critics). Read everything you can get your hands on about your subject, including books and articles. Use indexes to periodicals and books in the reference section of the library to find material—*The International Index to Film Periodicals,* for example.

II. Method

The historical attitude requires researchers to digest a great deal of material found in books, archives, or interviews in order to discover patterns of development that take place over time. Film history is too broad a subject, so the writer must narrow the search to smaller areas such as aesthetics, technology, social impact, or economics. Student writers, especially, need to focus on the topic that can be treated thoroughly in the length of the assigned paper. All of the other approaches, of course, can be given a historical dimension as well. Examining the films of an auteur from the silent period, for example, is essentially a historical study guided by the principles of the auteur approach. The main interest in historical criticism, however, will be in finding out the relations between various elements in the past and/or how the elements of the past lead to the present.

III. Questions the writer of historical criticism might ask

1. What is a well-made film? What elements of theme, composition, lighting, camera movement, acting, and so on, make films of the past worth reseeing?

2. How do the artistic conventions of one kind of film differ from those of an earlier or later period?

3. How do certain aesthetic elements coalesce to become a film movement like Italian Neorealism? What are the properties of such a movement and how do they influence subsequent filmmaking?

4. How do genres originate? change over time?

5. When did sound, optical printing, the zoom lens, color, or other device enter motion picture making and what were the effects of these latest technologies?
6. Who watched film in the early days? Why? Who made films and under what conditions in the past?
7. What effect did movies have on a particular era like the Great Depression? How did films reflect or influence the social life of the audience in a given time?
8. What were the organizational structures of the movie world, both of the industry and the audience?
9. How did movies take part in the economic structure of a period? How were they financed, distributed, and exhibited before World War I, during the studio years?
10. How do economic patterns affect the social and aesthetic aspects of a time frame? Were there differences between European and Hollywood business practices? Was the star system an aesthetic, social, or economic system?

CHAPTER 7

The Ideological/Theoretical Approach: Using Basic Principles to Uncover Deeper Meanings

Ideological/Theoretical Approach Capsule

Audience: Film scholars; students.

Functions: Describe and analyze film's properties; attempt to find the essential aspects of the medium and its relation to the culture; seek answer to the basic question: What is Cinema?

Subjects: Film in general; film as a field of activity, a signifying system that has aesthetic, economic, social, and historical dimensions.

Writers: Film scholars.

Publications: Film journals; scholarly books.

Undoubtedly some kind of theory underlies any critical response to the movies. The humanist who feels movies should reveal something about human nature as it is lived—the human condition—discounts films like genre films that romanticize human relationships. The humanist thus holds some basic assumptions about narrative and its purpose in the scheme of things, and these assumptions can be called a *theory* even if it is a general theory about the function of narrative covering all fictions and not simply film. Hence it is not a film theory per se but one that the humanist applies to all forms of narrative, including film. There are other theories, however—drawn from an examination of film and specifically about the nature of film narrative, what it is, how it functions, what its purposes are—that apply only to film. Film scholars and students of film rely mainly on these more specific theories to support their critical approaches to particular films, groups of films, and film in general.

Sometimes critiques of films or books about film subjects will not spell out the theory underlying the writer's views. Some writers are not aware that they have a theory to stand on; they have never articulated their basic assumptions to themselves. Pauline Kael, writing film reviews for *The New Yorker,* on the other hand, has some kind of basic notion of what films are about which guides her response to films, but this basic notion appears in writing only here and there in her long career. Her basic slant on movies is not evident in each and every review she writes. Many film writers committed to a particular theory of film, however, make their guiding principles absolutely clear. Bill Nichols, the author of *Ideology and the Image* (1981), for example, states early in the book that he is a Marxist. For the most part, the critical approaches dealt with in this chapter will be those that are spelled out, not hidden. These are self-conscious, fully articulated theories of film enunciated by particular writers over the years and recognized as the most influential on film scholars and critics today.

Some of the most difficult and abstract theories to be discussed are part of the contemporary discourse taking place in all the arts, in which the primary definitions of the nature of art and how it produces meaning, why it produces meaning, and for whom it produces meaning are being rethought and reargued in the light of modern theories about language, culture, and psychology. Without question, the particular works of criticism that stem from the ideological/theoretical approaches are written for specialists and not the casual viewer of movies. But these approaches are becoming the most influential in both American and European journals today. Anyone seriously interested in the study of film needs to grasp what the terms are and what the first principles assume. This is not always easy, because the concepts are difficult to explain and frequently the explanations are written in a specialized vocabulary understood only by those already committed to the particular approach. We shall attempt to guide you through the forest and shed some light on what is going on in film criticism today, but it will be a quick trip. These views require time and energy to digest. We can only open the door a little bit here in this introductory book. For those who have the desire to pursue these matters further, check the bibliography.

THE FUNCTION OF THEORY

One could suggest that a discussion of film theory is inappropriate for inclusion in a book about *critical* approaches to film. In general we think of film criticism concerning itself with describing and illuminating the practices of specific films, whereas film theory, although derived from the practices of specific films, tends to generalize its conclusions and make them applicable to all films. And film theory moves even further away from the criticism of specific works when it concerns itself with the ideal and potential practice of films, those made and those yet to be made. Nevertheless, film theory lays the groundwork for understanding individual films, film movements, film styles, and the relationship of films to their contexts. Systematic in its methods and comprehensive in its analysis, film theory makes possible the understanding of the ways in which all films work.

The basic function of film theory is to organize and logically arrive at a systematic formulation of the nature of film. Indeed, the key questions posed by all theoretical writing about film are: What is cinema? And, conversely, what isn't cinema? These questions are further refined and more narrowly phrased: What is it that all films have in common? What are the unique properties of the medium? What does film have in common with literature, music, dance, and the plastic arts? Is film primarily a narrative form or is it a visual and plastic art? Does film mirror the everyday world, create its own world, or dictate its visions of a world to the audience? Is the medium's uniqueness in its representational properties or in its power to create illusions? What *should* films do and what do they do *best* to make the most of the medium's capacities? Are films instruments of ideology and, if so, how does that affect the audience?

These are some of the sweeping questions posed by film theory in its attempt to organize and understand the medium. No matter how they are phrased, though, the questions can be reduced to four basic avenues of inquiry: (1) the relationship of the medium to its raw materials, the technological aspects of cinema; (2) the relationship to its subject matter, the aesthetic considerations; (3) the relationship to its mode of production, the economic matrix; and (4) the relationship to the social and political context, the ideological elements. Usually most theories have to deal with all of these elements, but some may not. More recent theories tend to be less interested in aesthetic questions than earlier theories. But whatever the concerns, a film theory will be both descriptive and analytic, and either implicitly or explicitly judgmental about what film is and should be.

There is no one theory of film, no single system that comprehensively answers the basic questions about the medium to unanimous critical and scholarly satisfaction. Just as there are many critical approaches, there are also numerous conflicting theories of film existing side by side—although shifts in the aesthetic and philosophical currents of any given historical period have tended to favor one set of theories over another. The first film theories were formalist, perhaps in response to both the limitations of silent film in reproducing a total representation of the everyday world (no color, no sound) and the obvious power of cinematography and editing to manipulate the images on the screen and meanings in the minds of the viewers. After World War II, realist film theory came into being partly in response to the growth of documentary art and the popularity of Italian Neorealist films. More recently, phenomenological film theory has attempted to reconcile the expressive and mimetic capacities of film by shifting attention from the supposed split between montage (juxtaposition of images through editing) and *mise-en-scène* (long shots and long takes) to the notion of film as a fluid and eclectic medium that always uses both devices. Currently, semiotic, Marxist, feminist, and psychoanalytic theories dominate the primary channels of cinematic discourse, finding in both film's materials and subject matter elements of ideological communication between the dominant value system of a community and its members at large. Tracing the growth and development of these various approaches as they attempt to define the nature of film will reveal not only the variety of theoretical positions but also the intellectual underpinning for those positions.

THE HISTORICAL PERSPECTIVE OF THEORETICAL DISCUSSION

A number of commentators have suggested that all thinking about the cinema is determined by its ability to reproduce lifelike images of nature. No one argues about this basic property of the movies, the fact that, except for some rare experimental films in which designs are painted on the raw film stock and then projected, something must exist in front of the camera in order for a film to come into existence. This prime factor, however, has been seen in either a positive or a negative light. Theorists feel that cinema should, by virtue of its manipulative properties (editing, lighting, framing, and so on), create something within its own terms that is very far removed from the everyday world, or they believe that movies should emphasize this recording capacity to the highest degree—that is, they should represent on the screen as close an approximation of the everyday world as possible—not only in documentary but in fiction also. The two views are identified as the formalist school of thought and the realist school of thought.

Formalist Discussions

From 1895 to the end of the silent period, most theorists were formalists. Despite the fact that some of the pioneer filmmakers, like the Lumiere Brothers, basically saw in their invention an opportunity to capture the movement of reality, by the First World War it was the fiction film that had captured the imagination of the populace. Story film as opposed to documentary is essentially formalist even if it purports to tell what real life is all about: it's still a made-up story. To be sure, the activities of people before the camera have to be actual or they couldn't be filmed, but those activities and those people are structured by the conventions of fictional narrative and dramatic acting. Even in saying this, however, we recognize that made-up stories can be presented two ways, either realistically or expressionistically. Most mainstream films abide by certain conventions of realism—characters behave physically and psychologically like normal humans, time and space are presented as if they were similar to the time and space the audience inhabits, and the viewing position of the audience is limited to a very restricted range: we are nearly always at eye level with the characters, as if we were in their physical space, always ready to see dramatically significant activities, to hear important dialogue. On the other hand, time and space can be chopped up and rearranged through conspicuous editing. Simple linear cause and effect may be brushed aside in order to express themes or concepts or to produce emotional responses in the audience. Characters can be fantastic in their appearances or behavior, or they may exist as allegorical representations of attitudes or ideas. Lighting, costumes, and sets may be exaggerated in order to convey special meanings. Unusual camera angles or distorting lenses can change the viewer's perspective, bringing to mind the discrepancy between everyday life and what is presented on the screen.

The split over these two tendencies was resolved in the silent era by most critics taking the side of the formalist, or expressionist, view. Nearly all the first writers on film argued that the mere reproduction of pre-camera events wasn't art. And it was an art they desired. As early as 1916, Vachel Lindsay, an American poet, saw poetic qualities in the cinema. It was these he praised in his book *The Art of the Moving Picture*. Hugo Münsterberg, though a psychologist, also saw film's ability to stimulate the mind and heart of the viewer deriving from film's formal qualities. When movies imitate the illogical connections of a dream, he argued in *The Photoplay: A Psychological Study* (1916), that's when they are most powerful. Both men praised the cinema's ability to change and restructure the normal and lived flow of everyday life into something new and artificial—that is, artful. They saw film's essential quality released when viewers recognized the formal construction, became aware that what they saw on the screen was material shaped by an artist's guiding hand, knew that the frame was an artificial space divorced from real space; it was more like a mirror of inner space, the workings of the psyche.

In the 1920s, the praise of film's artifice continued. Though there are considerable differences between the views of V. I. Pudovkin and Sergei Eisenstein, both agreed that editing, the ability to fragment time and space and rearrange them for the filmmaker's purpose, was the key to film's special nature. The medium was made to be manipulated, and the more you did it, the more artistic you were. If a film used strange lighting, or rapidly cut from one shot to another, or jumped from place to place without letting the audience know what the relationship was between places, the viewer could tell something was being done by someone to produce those images and their order on the screen. There must be an artist doing it and therefore it was more "artful" than the other kinds of films, in which it seemed as if the screen were simply a window on a world very much like the one the viewer occupied, a window through which one simply watched characters act out a story as if no one were manipulating anything at all, as if the filmmaker had nothing more to do than turn on the camera and keep it pointed at the action.

Certainly most viewers, somewhere in their minds, are aware that a good deal of manipulation is going on in a standard narrative film, but most films try to hide that manipulation from the consciousness of the viewer during the screening of the film. Pudovkin and Eisenstein, however, wanted the work of the artist to be visible on the screen. In 1926 Pudovkin published *Film Technique*. In the book he argued that narrative construction in film was created by the linking of shots with other shots to create connections and continuities which were not there in the pre-camera reality. He emphasized the artistic control of cinematic devices and techniques by the filmmaker, but suggested that meaning arose from separate images by a kind of accumulation forced by the contiguity and the logic of the narrative. When a character looks off screen and then we cut to something, the contiguity between the shots suggests that the second shot is what the character sees even if the two shots were taken in different places by different cameras. Though Eisenstein believed that the shot was the cornerstone of film construction, he disagreed with Pudovkin on the necessity of letting the narrative dictate the editing. Published essays during the 1920s and 1930s, but not collected in volumes until later—*The Film Sense* (1942), *Film Form* (1949)—his ideas emphasized the collision of images rather than the linking of images. Eisenstein believed that film meaning was created by a dialectical process in which the conflict between the meaning of image A and the meaning of image B (one appearing consecutively after the other) was synthesized by the spectator into meaning C. For example, juxtaposing an image of a man (A) followed by the image of a peacock (B) would produce the idea (C) of a vain man in the viewer's mind. Clearly Eisenstein saw film as a set of materials that could be manipulated by the filmmaker to produce the desired intellectual as well as emotional effect in the audience.

The final summation of the formalist position was produced by Rudolf Arnheim in his book *Film as Art* (1933). Writing just after the sound film had gone through its growing pains and had virtually banished the silent film from the screens of the world, Arnheim argued that the art of film was finished. Since sound film demanded an aural fidelity to nature—when a person's lips moved in a sound film, you had to have the words on the sound track, too— one could no longer freely play with the visual dimension. And for Arnheim film was a visual art whose basic property was not the ability to capture nature's image but to rearrange those images into new and affective patterns.

It was not that Arnheim was asking for an abstract film. He, in fact, praises film for revealing the secrets of the human heart, but he was convinced that the only way the medium could substantially affect the viewer was through artistic manipulation. Metaphoric inserts invented by the film artist and placed within the context of a given action to reveal a character's feelings were no longer possible in the sound film. Such creative substitutions for expression of feelings were taken over in the sound film by dialogue. For Arnheim this reduced the film artist to something as mechanical as the apparatus itself: the art of the movies became the art of filming verbal dramas. And since the stage had the vitality and immediacy of live performance, film appeared to be nothing but a pale copy of an original. Arnheim's book, which codifies the formalist position, was widely read for years. In the late 1950s, it was reprinted and used as a text in college film studies classes. Arnheim's influence can still be seen today in nearly all the manifestoes relating to experimental and avant-garde filmmaking which state that film art exists only when a filmmaker manipulates the elements of the cinematic process and does not simply imitate or re-present nature.

Realist Discussions

The transition to sound at the end of the 1920s did appear to make film more literal, emphasizing its closeness to the world off screen. When later, in the 1930s, color cinematography became possible, the ability of the film to capture nature, to produce an image that truly looked and sounded like what most people perceive as the real thing, was overpowering. Technology had changed the appearance of the movies; now theory had to take this new ability to provide greater visual and auditory fidelity into consideration.

During the war years, however, little was done in this direction, perhaps because narrative films, particularly in America, still tended to romanticize their subjects. In the aftermath of World War II, Italian Neorealist films—with their themes and stories taken from street life, shot on locations in war-torn rubble, acted by nonprofessionals—captured the attention of the filmgoing world. Here, it appeared, were real stories about real people caught in the moment of real suffering or joy. Though recognizing that the Italian films were still fictional films, critics saw an incredible power emanating from film's ability to record something as vital and alive as these stories. They were powerfully moving, and gave rise to a new interest in praising film's recording ability, the ability to catch life on the run and present it to the spectator.

Spurred by his excitement over the new developments in film, André Bazin founded a critical journal in Paris, *Cahiers du Cinéma*. In a series of articles from the late 1940s through the 1950s (later collected in two volumes, *What Is Cinema?* I and II), Bazin articulated the realist position with style and authority. He argued again and again that the prime function of film was to authenticate the world it created, a world intimately connected to the pre-camera world. The best way to do this was to use the long take and the long shot and the moving camera. Long takes give the impression of real time; long shots allow us to see complete figures in relation to their milieu; the moving camera knits time and space together in a contiguous whole so that events can appear to be actual. Bazin praised Orson Welles's films, for example, because they used deep focus (extended depth of field where foreground and far distant background planes are all in focus), which gave the viewer the freedom to create the relationships between character and character, between character and context, a process similar to what the spectator does in the world outside of the theater. Bazin disliked excessive editing, or *montage* (Eisenstein's term), which forced the viewer to see only what the filmmaker allowed, made the connections absolute, without ambiguity. He wanted the presence of the filmmaker to be unnoticed by the viewer. Noticeable visual flourishes by the film artist were to be avoided.

Surprisingly enough, Bazin liked Hollywood genre films: he wrote positively about the western, for example. Even if their stories were fantasies, the standard technique of invisible editing (the classical style) aimed to authenticate that world. On the other hand, Siegfried Kracauer, an equally powerful spokesman for the realist aesthetic, was suspicious of certain kinds of fictitious content. In his book *Theory of Film: The Redemption of Physical Reality* (1960), Kracauer assumes the existence of an objective, external, real world and asserts the notion that film must conform as closely as possible to that world. This does not mean he favors documentary film over all other modes, but he does find that certain subjects common in narrative films are less acceptable because they are further from the truth of the physical existence experienced by the spectator. Thus musicals (particularly of the integrated kind, in which characters who are not performers in the diegesis, or narrative, break out into song and dance), westerns, and other costume dramas are downgraded for their lack of allegiance to the fundamentals of everyday life. For Kracauer the best narrative films are of the Neorealist type—shot on locations, not in a studio, using amateur actors instead of professionals, and telling stories about everyday events, rather than those that exaggerate suspense, drama, or humor. Kracauer agrees with Bazin that the traces of the filmmaker's artistry should not show on the screen. The story should unfold smoothly and naturally. Montage violates this smoothness and thus is to be avoided.

For both Bazin and Kracauer modern technology—the advent of color, sound, and wide-screen processes—allow a closer representation of the world that exists in front of the camera before it is filmed. For them the frame is to be considered a window on the world; editing is something that merely joins scenes together. The meaning of a film should arise from the relationships within the content of the images, not from an artist's manipulation of the images. The formalists, like Arnheim and Eisenstein, however, looked back to the silent film, in which the absence of sound and the use of black and white film were patently not reproducing a likeness or a facsimile of the everyday world, and in which it was necessary for the filmmaker to emphasize and express a world, states of emotion, and characters' feelings through formal means—editing, lighting, camera angle, and stylized acting. Although Eisenstein eventually came to realize he could still deploy formalist strategies in sound films—one does not have to slavishly imitate the external world on the sound track—Arnheim never changed his mind. He wrote a preface to the reissue of his book in the 1950s insisting that over twenty years of sound film had not proved him wrong. Formalists today (generally avant-garde and experimental filmmakers) continue to denounce the standard, mainstream narrative film in which the illusion of reality dominates all other considerations.

Until very recently the opposition between formalists and realists—between those who saw the frame as a space to be filled with art and those who saw the frame as a window on the world, between those who wanted to be aware of the artist's handiwork and those who didn't—occupied the center stage of theoretical discouse about film. In the 1960s, a French critic and aesthetician, Jean Mitry, influenced by the contemporary philosophy of phenomenology, attempted a synthesis of the two views. Phenomenology itself suggests that all perception of the world is a relation between a subject's inner consciousness of an outside world and the outside world. That is, the world is neither entirely objective nor entirely subjective. We cannot totally invent the world. Though a sound is only ever heard in our interior ear, it does not exist only in our minds, but in other minds as well. Thus a particular sound must have a certain objective quality to it, though we cannot prove it by literally going into the mind of another and hearing it from that perspective. But there are times when we clearly will ignore a sound or interpret it in such a way as to suggest that we have within ourselves the ability to negate or alter, for all intents and purposes, an absolute external objectivity. Thus the world as we perceive it, as we know it, is neither totally subjective nor totally objective. It is rather a shifting set of operations between the inner self, which we can only validate subjectively through intuitive sensation, and an external objectivity, which we can only validate through intellectual abstraction.

The key point here for film theory is that film is perceived the same way as anything else: it is neither entirely one thing nor the other, but a relation between opposites. The nature of film is neither montage nor *mise-en-scène,* neither formalist nor realist. Every film is an image and therefore never "real," always mediated. This applies to documentary footage as well as to fictional material. And yet the images in every film have an actuality in the time–space continuum of the world before being transferred to the film stock, their pre-camera reality. Thus Mitry, in a two-volume work called *Esthétique et Psychologie du Cinéma,* argued that the previous opposition between the proponents of realism and the proponents of formalism was misplaced. The nature of film, he believed, embraces both aspects and does so all the time. Even when Eisenstein was using his montage of collision to produce new meanings, he had to use images of actual people and places and objects, all of which maintained their recognizability as images of people, places, and objects in the external world. The image is always an analogue of its original, pre-camera reality. But at the same time the film frame organizes the material and changes its meanings. Even when Jean Renoir was using his long shot and long-take style to portray a real world, he was changing that world in the process. Of necessity, it was a fictional world created as much by editing as by simple recording. Thus, seeing images of objects on the screen, we are aware of a double message. The frame is a window on a world, but also a space to be filled by composition, editing, and lighting. The images make us think of the objects they represent, but also remind us of their status as images in a system of images.

No matter how altered or distorted the images of the external world, they are still objects to be perceived as imitations, or representations, of the world outside the film. At the same time, the status we accord to the objects that are representations of objects is fundamentally different from the status we accord to the objects themselves. In recognizing that they are *like* the objects represented, we also know they are *not* the objects. Thus all films are confluences of the expressive element—someone manipulating materials for a purpose—and the realist element—the objects represented asserting their claim as objects in the world. Mitry suggests that each film, whether documentary, narrative, or poetic, combines the expressive and the realist elements in one proportion or another, depending on the film's intention. Italian Neorealist films, for example, emphasized a close relation with reality, while Disney animated films stress the disparity. Mitry's main object in his work was to synthesize the claims made by the two disputing camps, to bring Eisenstein and Arnheim into a truce with Kracauer and Bazin. Mitry saw that both camps were right—that film was not either/or, but both/and. Every film is shot and edited, but it also shows pictures of the world and its motion.

MODERNIST CRITICAL STRATEGIES

It is significant that Mitry wrote in the 1960s. At that moment he seemed to have put an end to further theoretical speculation. The two possible ways of seeing film's primary nature had been married, never more to be divorced. Nevertheless, the critical activity of a theoretical nature that was accelerating in other fields would soon spill over into film theory. The fields of semiology and structuralism came into full flower; Marxism and psychoanalysis were revitalized. Feminism became a worldwide movement that found an intellectual footing in these burgeoning disciplines. Starting in France, the discourse in the new analysis of language, politics, and culture spread to England and then to America. After André Bazin's death, in 1958, *Cahiers du Cinéma's* editors promoted a Marxist editorial policy. *Screen,* a British film magazine, adopted the same principles in the 1960s. Throughout the 1970s, the British translated a host of material from French cultural critics who wrote film criticism grounded in semiology, structuralism, Marxism, feminism, and the new Freudianism. Once translated into English, the new criticism—sometimes called "post-modernist"—caught on in American academic circles and has become the primary discourse in such film journals as *Wide Angle, Film Quarterly, The Velvet Light Trap* and *Quarterly Review of Film Studies.*

Though we will separate each of these areas of inquiry to outline their basic tenets, modernist film critics do not usually keep them apart. Umberto Eco, for example, was originally a semiologist writing and investigating languages as sign systems, trying to find out how meanings are generated linguistically. But once having ascertained that language is culture-bound and that culture is the interface between individual psychology and group politics, Eco began to use Marxist and neo-Freudian principles in his work. He applied these elements to motion pictures as well because, for him, a movie is simply another example of a meaning-generating set of signs. Similarly, contemporary feminist film critics combine elements of psychoanalysis and Marxist anticapitalist assumptions in their discussion of films, not only because films are produced in a male-dominated industry in a capitalist economy, but also because these feminist critics see mainstream films as representing the male's fear of and desire for women. The writers of modernist film criticism take for granted that their readers will have a general knowledge of all these new areas of discourse.

Semiological Practices

Semiology is the study of sign systems. Language is the most important of these, but the semiologist may examine gesture, fashions, table manners, business etiquette, or narrative in order to see how these constructs work to generate meaning. The influence that semiology has had on modern thought is extensive, primarily because of its basic assumptions about the relationship between reality and the linguistic sign. Ferdinand de Saussure, a Swiss linguist writing at the beginning of this century, came to the conclusion that the sign that represents an object, place, or person in the world is arbitrary. He also reasoned that if the sign (a word like "apple") was arbitrary, a person's knowledge of the thing (an actual apple) was extremely tenuous, if not impossible. Earlier discussions of language assumed that an empirical reality existed and that words represented the various objects of that reality so that our minds could handle them with economy.

Semiology suggests that we cannot actually *know* anything about the world, that we can only *know* the signs. We know the world only through signs, but signs are not the world. So we can understand only a conventional, abstract accumulation of qualities that are associated with the sign "apple," but never know the apple itself. Of course we can eat an apple, see an apple, feel one if it falls on our heads. Sensuous, immediate experience takes place. But knowledge about that apple, when we think of it as "a-p-p-l-e," is generated by the relationship of the sign "apple" to other signs and not the relationship that this arbitrary set of sounds (and corresponding letters) has with any actual apple. Saussure said our understanding of meanings about the world are forever lodged in a system of arbitrary signs. All our thinking, naming, and speaking, whether to ourselves or to others, must perforce take place within the dimensions of the language we know. As soon as we say to ourselves, "There's an apple," or "This apple tastes good," we have moved out of the realm of immediate experience into one of mediated experience, once removed from the actual physical relations implied by the statements.

Any word, "cat" for example, takes on its meaning by convention and not by any connection with the physical thing. And the word "cat" doesn't mean "this cat" or "that cat": it means all that we associate with cats. It is a concept, not a percept. And all that we associate with "čat" is arbitrary, because, depending on our culture, we might never think of eating one, whereas for other cultures, "cat" might include the quality of becoming Saturday night's dinner. "Cat" means whatever it does because it is part of a system of relationship among other verbal signs. It is distinguishable from other "signs"—"cot," "sat," "bat," and so on—because of minute but perceptible differences in phonemes (sounds), and its precise meaning is fully clarified only by its position in a string of signs—"my cat," "the big, white cat," "She shrieked like a cat." When you "understand" the string "my cat" in the previous sentence, you do not have an actual referent to put there, for you have never seen or petted my cat. But you have no difficulty in understanding what the concept of "my cat" means in the spoken or written context—hence the conclusion that we deal exclusively with these conventional concepts when we understand anything, but never deal with an objective reality, for who can say what that objective reality is, when the only way we can define it is by the tokens, the signs, the counters, the words we have been given? Saussure claimed that all meaning comes from within the system of the particular language and that there is no meaning outside of it.

It follows, then, that we are determined by our language, limited by the range of possibilities articulated for us by the culture we enter. We can learn different languages, but this doesn't change the basic proposition. We can know only what language allows us to know, only imagine what language allows us to imagine. And since the language is created by the culture and not by any one of us, we are determined to enter the place in culture that has been reserved for us. Even if a person invents a new word for something, it will have no communicative value unless others (the culture) agree to use it. This important idea informs all the other ideas of all the other modernist critical systems. It is this seminal idea of semiology that serves as the backbone, the underpinning, of all the other moderist theories.

The notion that people are determined by their culture is the mainstay of modern ideological critical strategies, but this idea is not without its paradoxical quality. If we are determined by the culture and cannot change it, we might ask, What is the point of criticism? Perhaps it is simply to make this fact clear and known. In a sense, that was all Saussure intended semiology to do, merely to describe the mechanisms whereby meaning is generated. But more recent investigators following this line of thinking suggest that there are openings or gaps in the monolithic immensity of language and culture. To take the preceding example, if you did make up a word for something and you did get people's attention and get them to go along with it, you could actually make a dent, a move in the direction of change in the structures of the language. Even the history of changes in spoken and written English over the years suggests that such alterations can and do take place with some regularity. The main question is whether individuals are responsible for such changes.

Although it seems clear that no one individual can create changes singlehandedly, a number of people might. The prevailing thrust of modernist criticism, then, is to raise the consciousness of enough individuals so that significant change might take place. To take an example not strictly from semiology but from feminism, one of the critical stances that has accepted semiology's view of cultural determination, we can see the process in action, how an increased self-consciousness about the effects of language use might change that use, with the result, it is hoped, of changing the attitudes embedded in that use. Feminists have brought to the public's attention the fact that the customary use of the masculine personal pronoun when referring to "anyone" implies the culture's consistent valuation of males over females. The construction used to look like this:

- The director has to know how to handle lighting, editing, and other techniques so *he* can make good cinematic choices.

Perhaps we didn't intend to imply that all directors were male, but the repeated and automatic use of this construction does have such an effect. Today, after the consciousness raising of the feminist movement, we are more likely to see alternate ways of handling this grammatical problem:

- The director has to know how to handle lighting, editing, and other techniques so *he or she* can make good cinematic choices.

Or:

- Directors have to know how to handle lighting, editing, and other techniques so *they* can make good cinematic choices.

To anyone who has grown up accustomed to using *he* automatically, such changes may seem awkward and unnecessary. And the question of whether or not these changes in grammar will catch on until they seem natural is not answerable in the short term. Whether such changes in the language, even if they become common usage, will help alter the culture's prevailing discrimination against women is also uncertain. But the example does show that criticism of culture, the raising of consciousness about the way language and culture determine our values and attitudes, can go beyond the simple recognition of the case—explaining "the way it is"—to the possibility of effecting change. All the post-modernist critical theories assume that awareness can lead to change. In fact, making changes in the culture—what has been termed "cultural politics"—is a primary aim of most modernist critiques of film.

The first semiologists to apply their discipline to film, however, were more descriptive and analytical in their aims. They attempted to understand how meaning is created by film's visual and auditory representations. What at first appears simple and natural—we see a photographic likeness of persons, places, and things and hear sounds they make—semiologists found to be governed by a complex set of rules and codes. More interested in how codes of lighting worked, or how certain editing patterns created meanings, semiologists focused on film in general, rather than on individual films. Christian Metz, a French scholar, devoted an incredible amount of energy and research to the task of trying to find out if cinema is in fact a "language," whether it can be broken down to discrete units of meaning like the words in a verbal language. He ultimately decided that cinema is not a language because the single shot is always overdetermined—for instance, the meaning of a close-up of a telephone is never just "Here is a telephone." Metz explained it this way:

> Even the most partial and fragmentary "shot" (what film people call the closeup) still represents a complete segment of reality. The closeup is only a shot taken closer than other shots. . . . The filmic "shot" therefore resembles the statement rather than the word. Nevertheless it would be wrong to say that it is equivalent to the statement. For there are still great differences between the shot and the linguistic statement. Even the most complex statement is reducible, in the final analysis, to discrete elements (words, morphemes, phonemes, relevant features), which are fixed in number and nature. (Rosen, pp. 40–41)

But you can't reduce a shot in the same way to any such arbitrary, discrete units. The meaning of such a shot in a film is derived from a confluence of a number of codes and not a single one. Nevertheless Metz, in his several lengthy works, isolated certain codes that were specifically cinematic. In *Film Language* (1974), he described a typology of various ways shots and sequences can be combined, the *grande syntagmatique,* as well as discussing types of editing devices—straight cuts, wipes, dissolves—that could join them.

Seeing a film as a system of conventions and codes, a set of structures dictating and circumscribing the ultimate possibilities of any individual film, reduces the emphasis on the individual artists making the films. If the general structure of language limits any individual's potential utterances, so much more so does the structure of film communication limit the potential of the filmmaker. Despite the fact that one could photograph anything and combine the shots in any imaginable way (the avant-garde or experimental filmmaker does this, of course, showing that it can be done), most filmmakers wish to communicate to an audience. And the precedents, the conventions, the genres are fully established for mainstream films. If nothing else, audience expectation, in a medium that depends explicitly on a large mass of viewers, cannot help but pressure filmmakers into "speaking" in comprehensible ways. Or we might put it another way: it is not the individual artist whose film it is, who makes the meaning, but the culture's. The culture creates the films.

They come out of the context—social, cultural, economic, historical—and hence undue praise for film auteurs is something that semiology avoids. Semiology's interests, as mentioned above, are in the processes of signification, processes that are not manipulable by the individual artist. Semiologists see film as just one of the many ways that society "speaks." Signification is more important than any single example of it. Thus for semiology there is no distinction between art and nonart, between artisans and artists. All are caught in the web of the signifying practices that determine the ultimate possibilities of meaning in any text.

Structural Practices

Structuralism as a modern intellectual discipline has defied easy definition, although its major tenets and assumptions can be catalogued. Developed from studies in comparative anthropology, structuralism locates the existence of basic patterns—structures—in human life that underlie what appear to be a diversity of surface manifestations. Narratives, rules of etiquette, dress codes, holiday rituals, and so forth, when examined carefully, reveal these patterns to the diligent observer. Thus the founding epic story told in every culture, from the South Sea Islanders to the East Indians to the Greeks, though different in particulars, exhibiting characteristics of the specific geography, climate, and life style of the group telling the story, also has a pattern that is basically the same as the others: a hero challenges the gods and wins a victory of some sort that preserves the integrity of the group. The relationship of the hero to the community, the obstacles to be overcome, the rewards to be gained, the methods to be employed are remarkably similar from one story to another. Thus we can speak of a universal structural base for such narratives upon which an individualized superstructure is built, similar to the consistent way steel girders are invariably put together for any skyscraper no matter how different the outside of the building will eventually look.

Structuralism seeks to peel away the outer wrapper of any cultural activity in order to reveal what the core looks like; it attempts to identify the consistent principles that organize and give meaning to human activities. For the most part, structuralism has identified those principles as a system of bipolar opposites that include such categories as male/female, light/dark, raw/cooked, civilized/barbarian, individual/community, and so on. Like other modern approaches, structuralism assumes a strong deterministic effect that emerges as these basic underlying patterns operate unconsciously on all members of a community. Writers who think up plots and characters for a story may believe they are fashioning a brand-new narrative. The structuralist suggests that the patterns of narrative are already there in the culture; the writer follows them unconsciously. The culture, then, and not the individual artist, determines the shape of the narrative.

The emphasis on cultural determinism is similar to semiology's, but structuralism's interests are broader. Semiology investigates the smallest possible units of communication and meaning, whereas structuralism investigates large patterns and ways of organizing experience. The semiologist looking at film might focus on the meanings generated by the use of the wipe as an editing device; the structualist would be more interested in the way the protagonists in film deal with the opposite sex or whether a film's narrative can be broken down into discrete action units that are similar to those in other films. Like semiologists, structuralists have shown that the phenomena of human activity are based on complex rules and conventions that are learned unconsciously, the way we learn the grammar of our native tongue, but that pervade all our communicative acts.

Claude Lévi-Strauss, the French anthropologist who is considered the founder of structuralism, investigated the life styles of many tribal cultures. His findings led him to the idea that the seemingly different aspects of social life—such as art, religion, customs—were, in fact, organized like languages. He discovered that these activities, too, though apparently diverse and various in their manifestations, were in fact reducible to a set of finite codes. The activities themselves made sense to the participants only because they shared an unconscious understanding of those codes. In a given culture, the eating of some foods raw and others cooked has little to do with personal tastes, group hygiene, or physiological necessity; rather, cultural statements are being communicated by the ritualized behavior. One group is saying to itself, "We are the people who eat carrots raw; we are not the others who don't," every time they eat carrots raw. In other words, an unconscious adherence to a set of well-defined rules organizes the eating habits of a group to such an extent that any individual's eating habits are a product of this structuration. Lévi-Strauss went on to say that the same principles are to be found operating in the much more elaborate customs of sophisticated cultures (our own industrialized society of the West, for example). Our music, painting, literature, and film, of course, could also be understood as rule-bound activity communicating group relationships.

The structural approach to narrative analysis was practiced in literary criticism even before the term "structuralism" was coined. Literary critic Northrop Frye, for example, used the structuralist method of finding opposites as basic organizing patterns in literature, relating myth, folktales, and archetypes from Jungian psychology to the study of narrative. As far back as the 1930s, Vladimir Propp, a Soviet literary critic, analyzed hundreds of folktales to find a consistent underlying plot structure. Joseph Campbell reduced the world's great epics to a single universal pattern in which he discerned "the hero with a thousand faces" who is, in fact, the one, true, single, generic hero, whether he's called Odysseus or Gilgamesh, or, ultimately, John Wayne.

Because it is concerned with large patterns of organization, structuralism can be particularly illuminating when applied to genre films. Looking for deeper structures, this approach can go beyond simple surface analysis of obvious and conscious structures as revealed by plot, theme, character, and icon to find those principles of organization that are psychologically and culturally determined and neither consciously created nor perceived. As mentioned in Chapter 4, most of the western films Will Wright examines in *Six Guns and Society* (1975) were made as popular entertainment, to bring in a commercial return on their investment. Audiences accepted them as such. Nevertheless, Wright's argument—basically structural in terms of how the films are organized and how the audience understands the hidden meanings dependent upon that structure—allows us to see the way general human conflicts become embedded in particular narrative complexes. Obviously the organizing principles of all narratives operate on any film narrative, but there are particular ones that coalesced around the western. Seeing the western hero as a person who exemplifies the general human concern about being in or out of society, seeking both freedom and security, relating such freedom to social responsibility or irresponsibility, with the benefits or disadvantages of civilization or the wilderness, enlarges our understanding of the individual films, the genre, and the way these patterns of actions and conflict structure the process of making films.

Jim Kitses's opening chapter in *Horizons West* (1970) (see Chapter 4) employs a structuralist approach, although the remainder of the book relies more on auteur theory. Thomas Schatz, in his introduction to the whole issue of genre film, *Hollywood Genres* (1981) (see Chapter 4), reveals the influence of structuralism on his material. Peter Wollen, though associated with the semiological approach, uses a blend of structural and auteur approaches in his discussion of Howard Hawks, in *Signs and Meaning in the Cinema* (1972). For him, an auteur is identified not by biography, personal style, or psychology, but by certain structures that are visible in a body of work. Thus a Howard Hawks film is not one directed by that historical person, but rather a film that is part of a body of films that all exhibit certain unifying structural elements, both on the surface and at a deeper level. Wollen says:

> In the films of Howard Hawks a systematic series of oppositions can be seen very near the surface, in the contrast between the adventure dramas and the crazy comedies. If we take the adventure dramas alone it would seem that Hawks's work is flaccid, lacking in dynamism; it is only when we consider the crazy comedies that it becomes rich, begins to ferment: alongside every dramatic hero we are aware of a phantom, stripped of mastery, humiliated, inverted. (pp. 93–94)

In this way Wollen shows that the comedies of Howard Hawks are structurally the reverse of his adventure, western, and war films insofar as they reveal a certain pattern of male/female relations that always gives form and substance to Hawks's work no matter the genre. Hawks (and other film artists) can be then regarded as the embodiment of structural oppositions found in the culture at large.

Marxist Practices

Karl Marx authored a critique of capitalist culture in the middle of the nineteenth century. Like others of his time, he saw grave social, political, and economic consequences for a system that has the profit motive as its mainspring. He saw inevitable conflict between the working classes and the owning classes until a classless society came about. He was one of the first to suggest that the industrial way of producing goods and services creates alienation in the worker—a person doesn't feel any connection with the product of his or her labor. Cash is the only interface between people where it counts—in the marketplace. Anyone who adheres to these basic principles, who sees the ills of contemporary society—war, poverty, pollution, overpopulation, the nuclear threat—stemming from the dominant economic system is a Marxist, even though contemporary Marxism is a much more sophisticated critique of culture today than it was even fifty years ago.

For years the foes of capitalism had simply been rephrasing the work of Karl Marx. He had stated that the ruling classes, the owners of the means of production, though a minority in a given country, maintained their power and control through the production of an ideology that fooled the masses into believing that the place they occupied in the world was the best it could be, thus discouraging change. "Religion is the opiate of the masses," he had written, meaning that the church—all religions—by promising people a better time of it in some other world, especially if they were meek and docile in this one, kept people in a condition in which they could be exploited by those who had the power to do so. He suggested that all the fine ideals of civilization were just a cover-up for the brute economic realities that lay beneath.

The Marxist critique does not single out the economy of the United States, but attacks all systems built on the profit motive and wealth accumulation. Twentieth-century Europe and America, however, fit the model very well. Marxists argue that the owners of giant corporations and huge financial institutions have formed a "ruling class" as powerful as any ruling body of aristocrats in the past by acquiring domination over a nation's means of production. The vast majority of citizens "own" only their own labor, which they must "sell" to the "ruling class," who own the factories and corporations and financial institutions. As the elite pursue greater wealth, they exploit more and more people. The economy goes through cycles of boom and bust, inflation and recession, which keep the workers (most of the citizens) always in a position of trying to catch up, but never getting far enough ahead to actually accumulate wealth. In most industries a few firms, controlled by the "ruling class," dominate the market, exploiting consumers as well as their own workers. In the area of moviemaking, for example, eight corporations have dominated the business from the 1920s on. Whereas millions have paid to see Hollywood films, only a small number of people have controlled production, distribution, and exhibition.

Karl Marx called the economic realities the base of all social relationships. The *real* relations between people in a society are economic: how basic necessities are produced and exchanged, what a given amount of labor is worth in securing the goods and services thought necessary, and how that exchange is regulated. In every period of history, a superstructure of ideas, attitudes, and beliefs has been erected upon this base. This *ideology*—the system of laws, the accepted relationship of individuals to the group, social organization itself, ultimately the specific form of government—arises, Marx would say, primarily to legitimate and support the power of the "ruling class." Particular forms of social discourse, political, ethical, aesthetic, and religious, develop in order to promote the ideas and beliefs that will enable the dominant class to continue its rule. Clearly, then, mainstream films, made by the corporations that run the business, financially dependent on banking institutions that run the country, can be expected to take part in this ideological discourse. These films tend to reaffirm and not challenge the dominant ideas and beliefs of the society, those ideas and beliefs most favorable to the "ruling class."

At times it appears Marx was suggesting a kind of social conspiracy between the church, the state, and the rich and powerful, a conspiracy that, by controlling all forums of discourse, all media, could in a sense brainwash the vast majority of a population into accepting a situation that was not in its best interests. Even in a strict totalitarian regime, however, where the press, radio, and TV are literally controlled by the state, channels of communication develop that are not subject to state control. People exchange views orally here, there, and everywhere. Letters, essays, and underground literature circulate. How much more apparent in our Western pluralistic societies must it be, then, that such a conscious, deliberate conspiracy does not exist? The Warner Brothers made movies, not to reinforce dominant attitudes and beliefs, but to deliver a product to an audience and make a profit thereby.

Modern Marxists recognize this fact and have adjusted their ideas of ideology accordingly, by using insights semiology and structuralism have discovered about the nature of cultural determinism. Louis Althusser, for example, suggests that ideology is the glue that holds a society together. "Human societies secrete ideology as the very element and atmosphere indispensable to their historical respiration and life" (Harvey p. 95). In other words, there must always be an ongoing relationship between the ideal and the real in any social organization. Man (or woman) does not live by bread alone, but also by discourse, the interaction with others, and this takes place through the communication of thoughts, feelings, and ideas. The relationship between Marx's base and superstructure appears less simple than it once was.

Nevertheless, we can recognize certain mainstream, dominant ideals that are a part of a cultural system, a set of ideals that are perpetuated by all forms of discourse. The Marxist film critic finds those ideals produced in the cinema in two ways: the values found in the diegesis (the narrative, the characters, their conflicts, their outcomes) and in the material basis of the cinema itself—the mechanical, material apparatus for making movies as well as the way they are produced, distributed, and exhibited. In both cases, Marxists seize upon the fact that illusions are created, giving false messages to the viewers. At the level of content, the stories revolve about individuals who ultimately solve their problems through individual effort, presenting the idea that life's problems are individual and not the result of larger forces that might require group action to correct. Even in a war film, for example, the social and political problems are minimized in favor of examples of individual heroism or cowardice. At the level of the material, the cinematic apparatus is viewed as a machine of illusion that hides its own activity, masks the work involved in creating the illusion of a coherent time and space which are presented as "real." And, of course, few films openly admit to their viewers the terms of economic exchange that caused them to come into existence. True, as spectators we must pay at the door for the privilege of experiencing the film, but once past the ticket booth, we are urged to forget that the film exists as much for the maker's profit as for our pleasure.

One of the editors of *Cahiers du Cinéma,* Jean-Louis Comolli, has analyzed the development of the cinematic apparatus from this perspective. He said that the cinema is the interaction of two forces—the ideological and the economic (the Marxist basic assumption). The ideological desire, coming out of the nineteenth century's interest in the scientific and pragmatic, is to see life as it is, without subjective interference, objectively. The economic desire that causes the cinema to "happen" is profit maximization. But the ideological motive is tainted from the start (here Comolli, like other modern Marxists, relies heavily on the ideas of semiology and structuralism that assume you can never see the world "as it is" without the filter of your language and culture) because the technology of cinema is never neutral. It was invented to reproduce the world as it was perceived by the inventors. It follows a long tradition of representation in the Western world which goes back to the discovery of perspective in Renaissance painting (Rosen, pp. 421–43). And, of course, the economic motive for cinema's way of being-in-the-world precludes making films whose form or content would disturb the paying audience. Therefore the movies are inevitably bound up with an ideology that supports capitalism and all the ills that one can attribute to that form of economic organization.

At one level, then, the Marxist critical approach to film may seem to have as its one drive the unmasking of all the illusions inherent in the form so that the audience can simply stop supporting films altogether. It is difficult to imagine any change within the current system of film production and distribution that would make a significant impact on the films. At first glance, mainstream films appear to be simply all bad because they inevitably promote a system that the Marxist sees as pernicious and wicked. On the other hand, Comolli and his co-editor, Jean Narboni, suggested that the aim of the criticism in *Cahiers* was not merely to condemn mainstream cinema but also to point out those kinds of cinema which in one way or another do not totally promote the values of the dominant culture. In their article "Cinema/Ideology/Criticism," setting up the guiding principles behind their editorial policy for the magazine, they made a list of various kinds of films that do offer an alternative cinema (Nichols, *Movies and Methods,* pp. 22–30). One of the fundamental modern beliefs about ideology in any society is that it is not absolute. Clearly there would be no Marxist ideas in a capitalist culture if the dominant ideology had no cracks. But in any ideological system a counterideology, a minority ideology, can and will take root. The dialectic works. If you have a set of values that leans toward the conservative, the liberal seems to crop up. If you have expressions of fascist ideals, then communist ideals will arise.

Thus the work of the Marxist critic is twofold. First, the critic seeks to unmask the illusions of cinema both at the story level and at the level of signifying practices—the codes of lighting, editing, and so on that create the illusions of temporal and spacial continuity—and, second, the critic praises and supports those films that somehow are truly radical or revolutionary either in their subject matter or in their form. Bill Nichols, in his *Ideology and the Image,* for example, shows, through a very close textual analysis of specific films (Chapters 4, 5), that both Joseph von Sternberg and Alfred Hitchcock, though nominally mainstream directors, made films that revealed dissatisfaction with the norm. Nichols sees in *Blonde Venus* (1932) and *The Birds* (1963) evidence that "the sense of coherent plausibility normally fabricated within the diegesis of classical narrative is noticeably flawed."

In *Blonde Venus,* for example, the usual role of the woman in Hollywood films is reversed. Marlene Dietrich's Helen, spurned by her husband for presumably immoral activity, eventually becomes an international entertainer who can have any man she wants and finally decides not to have any at all. She refuses the charming, wealthy Cary Grant, who, we are led to believe, truly loves her. Ordinarily, if a man makes this declaration of love, the woman must accept him as her lord and master. Dietrich sits in her dressing room backstage in Paris, dominating the conversation with Grant. She is wearing a top hat and a white tail suit, the very image of a female with male power. She dismisses Grant and he leaves. The scene ends. This is the way von Sternberg would have ended his film, with Dietrich triumphant and totally independent, in charge of herself and her world. Unfortunately, the studio insisted on a different ending. As Nichols says:

> Helen relinquishes control and reaffirms the principle of availability for the other. She is reunited with Ned [her husband] and her child, and the zippered-up suggestiveness of the fur coat she wears when she arrives with Nick [Grant] is abandoned for the erotic dress she displays only for Ned (and her son—a matter of some small interest in more than one sense). A new but more trivial game, one of reconciliation, of forgive and forget, attempts to gloss over the more basic game of hide-and-seek, desire and denial, performance and control, narrative and style—that complex game played by Joseph von Sternberg and Marlene Dietrich alike. (p. 132)

The more complex game is played throughout the film and clearly there is nothing in the narrative thrust to suggest the obviously tacked-on ending. Viewers of the film surely sensed something extremely uncomfortable, something not quite ordinary in this film. Nichols and others indicate that if the norm is challenged in this subtle way, it may lead viewers to begin to look not only at films but at all other forms of ideological production in the community in a more discerning way, to seek constructive changes in the system as a whole.

Feminist Practices

With the rise of feminism as a social movement in the late 1960s came an interest in the way women were portrayed by the culture in all forms of images. Novels, advertising, manners, television, and films were examined in order to find out what kinds of messages were being broadcast to the public at large. As noted above, traditional language usage came under scrutiny as well and was found to carry sexist overtones: the use of the masculine personal pronoun to mean "anyone" has been denounced by feminists for reinforcing the notion that males are more important to a society than females. Common words such as "stewardess," "mailman," "chairman," and "mankind" have been changed to "flight attendant," "letter carrier," "chairperson," and "humankind" to eliminate any hint of sexual evaluation. Clearly, then, feminists have assumed the basic tenet of semiology, that a society reinforces its values through its various discourses. Like Marxists, they also assume that a male-dominated society uses these modes of discourse to maintain itself in power. Thus the aim of the feminist critic is to uncover the hidden structuring devices in any medium whereby the male maintains dominance and reduces the female to a passive position.

The earliest feminist writings about films contended that the role of women in the bulk of Hollywood films presented a very unsatisfactory image. Molly Haskell, in *From Reverence to Rape* (1974), charted the history of women characters in the movies and found that, by and large, they were very unrealistic. In fact, she suggests they are little more than male fantasies, stereotypes of what men want to believe about women. She found most characters typed as either demure virgins or passionate but evil prostitutes. The plot dynamics of American genre films revolve around male heroes who are the active agents. Women play passive roles as maidens in distress, comforting mothers, objects of sexual desire, or obstacles to the male's success. When women are the protagonists, their successes are always compromised. In *film noir*, they are devious, power-hungry bitches who dupe men into criminal activities; in family melodrama, they may be capable enough to get ahead in a career, but they cannot have the security and love of a family as well.

Even the briefest glance at the content of Hollywood films confirms the feminist position. Women as women, women as they actually exist in the everyday world, are hard to find. They do play either secondary roles or negative ones. This, of course, is not surprising considering the fact that nearly all the decision-making power in the film industry has been in the hands of males. Most major studio executives, producers, directors, screenwriters, and directors of cinematography have been men. The female point of view has not been represented. And this, too, is a situation that feminist film critics have written about. They have urged more acceptance of women in the production process, have argued for screenplays that accurately depict the role of women in the world, have sought for more admission to the craft unions, equal pay and equal opportunity for women in all phases of the industry. Like all social revolutions, this takes time. Today, the independent film—low budget and not subject to industry control—has made it possible for women screenwriters, producers, and directors to take control of their own productions and to fashion narratives that represent the female point of view. *Desert Hearts* (Donna Deitch, 1986), *Heartland* (Richard Pearce, 1981), and *Smithereens* (Susan Seidelman, 1983), crafted by women, were very successful in portraying the female side of existence. Though not box office smashes, they demonstrate that feature-length narratives made by women about women's concerns can be successful.

Nevertheless, for every independently made film that becomes available, the mainstream of film narratives still seems saturated with male action adventure films like *Top Gun* or *Rocky,* in which women characters enact the age-old stereotypes. What is it that makes female viewers support these films when there seems to be no possibility of identifying with the characters? Is there something about the motion picture that is basically male-oriented? Do women, though it may be against their personal interests, actually identify with the jaw-busting, ruthless, active male protagonist because that is what they must do in order to get any pleasure out of the cinema experience at all? The most recent development in feminist film criticism has been to investigate these questions primarily from a semiotic theoretical perspective, to understand how the codes of cinema produce sexually loaded meaning.

Women and Film, Camera Obscura, and *Wide Angle* are three journals that have published this newest form of film criticism. Without a firm understanding of the way the very form of classical film narrative projects a sexist vision of the world, the feminists argue, there is little hope of changing the stereotypical characters portrayed. For example, it has been noted that the "look" or the "gaze" of the camera is essentially masculine in character, not simply neutral. The proof, feminists contend, lies in the way subjective point-of-view shots of male characters looking at women abound, whereas there are very few of women looking at men. Women are the objects of the male gaze in film. They are a spectacle, something to see from the male's point of view. In this sense they are turned into mere objects of voyeuristic pleasure. This becomes true, then, for the audience as well, since no matter what the sex of the viewer, it is the only image provided. Women as well as men in the audience are forced to participate in this practice.

The analogy, of course, in this filmmaking practice, is to the general notion in the world outside the theater, that men are "lookers" at women—they look at women with a sexual gaze, taking pleasure in the physical appearance of the female, usually whether the female wants it or not. Women usually do not use their gaze to trap, hold, or single out men for sexual attention. Their gaze seems less sexually loaded, less sexually aggressive. Thus the look of the camera appears to have the characteristics of the male gaze (again, in most mainstream narrative films) rather than the female or a neutral one. The conclusion for some feminist critics, then, is that the ideology of the cinema, the message sent to the audience, is not simply in the content of the film—the lack of realistic female characters—but in the signifying practices of the medium itself. It remains a question, as it does for a Marxist critique of the cinematic apparatus, whether these basic principles of narrative construction can be changed to reflect a more egalitarian ideology. Some feminist film critics, like Laura Mulvey in her article "Visual Pleasure and Narrative Cinema" (Rosen, pp. 198–209), merely wish through analysis and consciousness raising to destroy any pleasure the spectator might take in mainstream narrative film. Others, however, suggest the possibility that a feminist cinema, an alternative cinema, can be produced.

Neo-Freudian Practices

When Jean-Luc Godard had a character in one of his films announce that we in the twentieth century were the children of Marx and Coca-Cola, he might have added Freud to his list to be more accurate and inclusive. There is no contemporary intellectual position that has not been influenced by Freud. His notion that a large part of the mechanisms of life lie hidden from direct observation, that there is an unconscious element behind every conscious action, seems to inform every modern critical discourse. As we have seen in the brief summaries above, semiotic, structural, Marxist, and feminist critical theory all agree with this basic assumption.

The answer to what is hidden, to what lies behind, differs in each case, yet the aim of each of these critical stances is to reveal or uncover what does not appear to be the case on the surface, to get down to the underlying motives and activities that are the "real" reasons for human behavior, to lay bare the truth, which has been covered over by custom or design. And like psychoanalysis itself, the object of this uncovering is to produce a cure, to make life better, to improve our interrelationships with other human beings, to bring about a better social matrix.

In one of his later writings, *Civilization and Its Discontents,* Freud expresses some doubts about the possibility of ever solving the problem inherent in the conflict between individual desires and group desires. The necessary constraints of the social reality instituted for humankind's well-being will always cause repression, frustration, and anxiety, leading to aggressions that have to be expended. The new Freudianism, founded chiefly by Jacques Lacan in France but carried around the world by his students, seems less absolutely pessimistic. In fact, it might be possible to see in the Neo-Freudian revisions of the original concepts of Freud a greater hope that an understanding of the nature of the unconscious reality might lead to positive ends.

How does Lacanian Freudianism depart from the original? Freud said the individual personality or psyche was formed as a relation between the inner, physical drives of the material body and the outside world. Loosely, the inner, hidden drives constitute the id, and the volitional, acting element that tries to satisfy the id's desires (food, warmth, sexual pleasure) is called the ego. In some sort of a natural state, the ego would simply act when the id signaled a need. The id wants food; the ego directs the body to pick an apple and eat it. The ego, however, does not have to deal simply with an external physical reality but with the social one as well. Other people (family, society) create certain conditions for satisfying the id's desires, like waiting to eat, or not eating certain things at certain times, or eating things in a particular way. Taken together, all the rules and regulations imposed by society are called the superego, because they are *above* any individual's ego needs. The super-ego of the community becomes a part of the individual's psyche, operating there to control the ego's activities. The ego then must constantly accommodate the often conflicting demands between the id and the superego, leading to a whole host of inner mechanisms trying to lessen the effects of the inevitable frustrations. "I want that apple now!" says the id. "You can't have it now!" says the superego. The ego is caught between conflicting imperatives. In a properly functioning psyche, the energy produced by this frustration is channeled elsewhere into useful activities; when the balancing act of the ego is less successful, the energy may become destructive.

Lacan, leaning heavily on the basic presumptions of semiology, rewrote the basic Freudian categories. Most important, he suggested that the id is not a biological entity but a linguistic one. It is clear that Freud's superego is a set of rules and regulations articulated in language—we are *told* what we should or should not do. And the ego of Freud is also linguistic insofar as the "I" represents it. The ego's capacity to will and to judge and to define an individual's responses is, at least on the conscious level, a matter of the self "speaking" to the self and "speaking" to the outside world. Lacan's positing that the id is in fact also a linguistic entity has far-reaching implications, however. It clearly makes the self, the subject, the "I" that any individual feels exists, a product of the language of the culture into which a person is born. Gender differences—for example, the awareness that one is female or male—become less a matter of biological reality than of cultural conditioning. This is not to say that biology has nothing to do with it, but that, at the point at which the male self comes into being for any male, the sign system which constitutes maleness for a given culture will be of more importance than the amount of testosterone in the person's body.

Since Lacanian psychoanalytic theory embraces the fundamental assumptions about the relationship of culture to the individual, it should be easy to see why it has been applied to modernist film theory. It dovetails neatly with the semiological, structural, Marxist, and feminist positions. Like these other views, Lacan's position is that language, in its broadest sense of a structured system of symbolic representations, determines the psyche or self of every individual. Thus film, a "language" of a sort, operates on its viewers in a similar way, positioning the self, giving it substance, symbolically representing to the self the self's own inner working, imitating not the world but the self's very own construction.

For film theorists who follow Lacan, the motion picture is an imaginary construct that caters to the desires and needs implanted in the individual by the original psychic structuring of the self by the language/culture. In a sense the film is a mirror of the psyche, a Freudian dream, which speaks to the viewer in unconscious ways. It offers surface satisfactions, but their acceptance may hide the true relation of the individual to the dream, a relation which is seen as harmful, neurotic. For example, an alcoholic's immediate pleasures in drinking may hide the fact that the desire for such pleasures comes from an inability to handle relational problems in the alcoholic's life. Similarly, the immediate pleasures of narrative for the spectator may be only illusions that cover over important problems of the spectator's relations with the actual. If the unconscious mechanisms of film can be revealed, then perhaps the patient can be cured, give up the addictive and pernicious habit. Thus psychoanalysis of the film/viewer relationship may bring about a change in the viewer's perceptions of the signifying practices of films and/or the culture that produces them.

Lacan may be described as a "conventionalist"—that is, a person who believes that there is no external "real" which can be verified. What people call the "real"—the outside world, other people, the way things would be if there were no perception of them—is merely a verbal construct. Language (the only way we can "know" the world) always is one step removed from reality. As noted in the discussion of semiology above, the modernist position assumes we always deal in *signs* of that world, but never with the world itself. For Lacan this means that individuality, a person's self, comes into existence only when the child begins to grasp language. At the moment of language acquisition, a child is thrust out of the "real" world, into a constructed world of social and cultural relationships defined by language. One cannot refer to one's self as a self, making the differentiation between the self and others, between inner and outer states, without a language. The "I" we use to define ourselves is a linguistic counter. But so are all the other ways we are positioned in society: "the daughter of," "John Brown," "six feet tall, blonde hair, blue eyes." Every child must submit to this loss of contact with the actual world and enter into the social order, the system of symbolic relationships. At the same time as it allows the individual to become an entity, it also traps that individual in the preexisting coordinates dictated by the society; the individual is defined in specific terms by the society.

At the psychic level this means that certain universal constructs and relations are waiting to snare the individual. It is not simply a matter of being born into a high or low position in society, but rather of being born into the human family. Here Freud's original concepts about the psychosexual development of the child are shown to be part of the linguistic order of all human society. The child's need to resolve the Oedipal complex is still primary. Lacan says that prior to the acquisition of language, to a sense of individuality, the child sees itself as connected to the world that appears as an extension of its own self. This relation with the outside world Lacan calls the *imaginary*. At this time the infant is fixed in an undifferentiated world that it controls and possesses, centered on the source of food and security—the mother. The child has a sense of plenitude and unity. But as time passes and the child grows, it soon becomes aware that this relation is an illusion. It perceives that the breast is not there all the time. The mother plays "peek-a-boo" and leaves the child. This separation from the source of all pleasure and satisfaction produces anxiety and an intense desire not to be separated from that source. But it is the awareness of this "lack," the sense of absence, the not being whole and united with the world—represented by the mother—that is the first step toward individuation. It is thus the "lack" that originally structures the self.

The infant, however, still yearns to be restored to the prior condition of wholeness. It desires the mother, but recognizes the ultimate impossibility of having the mother. The first attempt at substitution for the mother comes when the child sees itself in the mirror and believes that the mirror image is itself. For a brief period—the "mirror stage" usually takes place just before language acquisition occurs—the child makes the *imaginary* transposition that the other in the mirror constitutes a perceived wholeness of the inner subjective self. But as soon as the child begins speaking and has grasped the elusive quality of the "I"—it can be used by anyone, it does not in fact define specifically any one "I" but indicates only a relative position between speakers—the child becomes a fragmented subject. Lacan has called this stage of development the *symbolic,* for now the individual self understands that the "I" which is occupied by the self of any individual is only one among many such symbolic entities. Communication takes place between all the "I"'s without ever fixing on any one of them. They are known to each other only through a process of accommodation and relative position between individuals. "I" may be pleased with myself—I define myself as a "good boy"—whereas at the same time my teacher may say "I" am a "bad boy." When I understand myself as operative in the symbolic realm, I realize that I am neither one thing nor another. I am in a floating and ever-changing set of relations with others constructed out of our linguistic exchanges. Hence the use of the word "fragmented" in regard to the self operating in symbolic exchange.

But this apprehension of the self, though considered the most mature and adult stage, is of course fraught with anxiety. It is farthest away from the security of some sort of fixed definition. If one cannot ever regain the *real,* lost forever with the construction of the self, nor the image of that world, the mother or the self caught in the mirror, there is still a hunger and a desire for such a meeting. In standard Freudian terms it would be called *regression.* For Lacan it is the inherent desire to return to the realm of the *imaginary,* where the illusion of wholeness can occur when we see ourselves in a mirror. And what better analogy for that desire than the images in a film? Looking at the frame is often likened to looking at a window, but what if that window were perceived unconsciously as a mirror? That is, the figures up there are not simply others, but the Other through which I seek to define myself. Lacan says we do that in real life by trying to find a Significant Other who will relieve us of the responsibility of always existing in the Symbolic register where we must suffer from not knowing for sure who we are. The desire for wholeness and completeness can take the form of letting others define us and fix us in a phrase, in a look. We let job, family, and public opinion form an imaginary self for us that may be comfortable or uncomfortable, but being fixed seems preferable to an ambiguous self, the symbolic one.

Lacanian film critics have suggested that the relation between the viewer and the screen, the very act of viewing films, can be seen as an assumption of the imaginary condition. The desire for wholeness and plenitude, the desire to rid ourselves of the sense of lack, of separation, can be satisfied in two ways while watching films: (1) The classical narrative film unrolls before us as if we were in charge; we seem to be organizing the world we see. It goes the way we want it to; we have the illusion that we have created a world and that it is under our control. (2) Classical editing style, allowing us to see through the eyes of a character in the point-of-view shot, permits a strong identification with the characters on the screen. In a sense we thus "become" the hero, take on the well-defined attributes of the powerful, dynamic, resourceful protagonist. Though an illusion, this kind of psychic transposition of identity assuages our feelings of unease, gives us a wholeness that we cannot enjoy in life outside the theater.

Colin McCabe, in his article "Theory and Film: Principles of Realism and Pleasure," maintains that all human subjects swing back and forth between the imaginary (the notion that we are in control of our lives and that we give meaning to the world) and the symbolic (the often painful recognition that we are not in control and that meanings are imposed on us by forces outside our control). He goes on to say that the classical Hollywood narrative film style caters to the imaginary wishes of the viewer, primarily by positioning the viewer at the point of omniscience, the third-person-objective camera view. He then argues that editing, particularly the point-of-view shot, robs us of that position of omniscience. But almost immediately it is restored to us again, since the objective, God-like view is always dominant. Any potential entry of the symbolic level, the possible notion that we are not in control of the world that lies before us, is smoothed over. This, of course, includes any hint that the film is a product made by someone else; the marks of the work that went into the film are erased from the film viewed (Allen, pp. 168–69).

Like others, McCabe then connects the illusion of plenitude and fullness created by the formal devices of classical narrative with the illusions of ideology noted by Marxist critics. Just as Hollywood's signifying practices give us imaginary pleasures without anxiety and contradictions on the level of the psyche, so do most Hollywood films mask or displace certain basic contradictions in the capitalist world represented in the diegesis. An illusion of personal power and control over the narrative is handed the spectator in the film's form; similarly, the characters in the film's world (which seems to represent the everyday world) present the illusion that they have power and control over their success of failure. Seldom are social, economic, or political forces to blame for a character's rise or fall in mainstream narratives. The Hispanic hero of *Scarface* (Brian DePalma, 1980), for example, rises to the top of the underworld and falls from power seemingly because of his greed and lust for power. It is scarcely suggested that the reason for such activity may be the unwillingness of white America to offer equal access to the good life to our most recent immigrant population.

Lacanian psychoanalytic theory is extremely complex and controversial. This brief summary of its application to film theory has barely dented the surface. Nevertheless, the post-modernist critical approach to film has been deeply influenced by this revision of Freud. The main impulse of film scholars like Colin McCabe, Stephen Heath, Laura Mulvey, and others, however, is clear: films function to articulate attitudes and ideas that are not available at the conscious level, and it is the job of the film critic to psychoanalyze the film and the spectator's relations ot it. The act of film viewing is analogous to the way we negotiate the social world entered at the time of language acquisition. Psychoanalytic critics use film to explain how elements of our experience are buried in the unconscious and later appear in disguised form in language, ritual, myth, and art. Invariably the basic assumptions of semiology, structuralism, Marxism, and feminism are conjoined in their work, since all of these disciplines suggest a basic agreement about the way the social formation operates: the individual is determined by forces outside his or her control, but is led to think the opposite by every discourse (except modernist criticism) available in the culture. Thus the aim of the modernist critic, like that of the psychoanalyst for the individual patient, is to rend the curtain hiding the truth, and thereby effect a cure.

What shape movies would be in after such a cure, however, is hard to imagine. The vague but general agreement of modernist film criticism is that a radical cinema needs to be supported, one that would not follow the "illusionist" principles of classical narrative. Such cinemas, alternative cinemas—either the documentary of radical content or the antinarrative, experimental, avant-garde—are available today, but their products are clearly not popular with the mass of moviegoers. Some modernist film critics do suggest that there is a third way, a narrative cinema that would do justice to radical ideas and practices in form and content that could still attract an audience. They point to the independent feature film movement of the last several years as a place where such films might be made. But as of yet the impact of such films on the general public has been small. Only the future can tell if the psychoanalysis of film will change the expectations of the filmgoer and filmmaker. Until then we can use this approach only on the classic films of the past and the present.

THEORETICAL APPROACHES
AND PRACTICAL CRITICISM

At first glance there may appear to be little connection between modern film theory and the writing of film criticism, particularly for the student. The theories seem too abstract, too general, too far removed from the experience of watching films. How can the beginning student of film expect to make use of any of this material? how apply it to his or her own work? Though a thorough understanding of the modernist practices may have to wait for an immersion in the primary texts, our short summary of the basic tenets of these positions may open up some intriguing possibilities for interesting papers.

Assessing the depiction of women in current films from a feminist perspective would surely be a possibility. Nearly all mainstream narrative films hide the work that goes into their production. You could describe how that takes place in a number of recent releases or seek out alternative films— independent, avant-garde, documentary, self-reflexive—that attempt to show their construction. You could examine both genre and auteur issues from a structural point of view. Or you could attempt the simple level of Marxist analysis: How are the economic systems of capitalism promoted in some films? Are there any films that critique that system? How do films highlight the ideal of personal achievement—the protagonist always solves the conflicts—without suggesting the restrictions on personal action inherent in a highly structured, technological, corporate world? Finally, you could try a little Neo-Freudian analysis by looking closely at the positioning of the audience and speculating on how films manipulate the viewer into an "imaginary" identification with both the characters in a narrative and the authorial view implied by the camera.

These possibilities for translating film theory into criticism about particular films can enlarge your view of the whole field of film. Seeing movies in a new way, learning to find more meanings in a given text, trying to read behind, in back of, around, and between the lines from some theoretical stance can only enlarge your pleasure and satisfaction in the moviegoing experience. Thinking and writing about films in any context—film criticism, that is—assumes a point of view, a position about what film is and what it means. In a sense, film theory is always present when you write film criticism. But with your new knowledge, you can now be articulate about the assumptions that underlie your relationship to the movies.

GUIDELINES FOR WRITING IDEOLOGICAL/ THEORETICAL FILM CRITICISM

I. Sources
  A. Primary

Having a good sense of all the periods and kinds of films, some experience of silent films, classic American studio pictures, and foreign, independent, documentary, and experimental films, is essential. You need to have a grasp of the whole of cinema, even if you don't write about particular films. If you haven't seen representative films in all these categories on your own, take a comprehensive survey class in film history.

  B. Secondary

Surely the writings of classic and contemporary theorists must be placed under secondary sources, but in one sense, they feel like the primary sources. Read first all the anthologies mentioned in the chapter or the bibliography. Then you can branch out with readings in semiology, literary theory, structuralism, and so on. To do this kind of criticism well, you will have to immerse yourself in serious philosophical writings.

II. Method

Reading, reading, and reading is absolutely essential. Seeing representative films from all countries, eras, and schools of thought is very important. You can try to understand the new concepts and then see if you agree or disagree with the pronouncements in the books and scholarly journals. Then be prepared to argue your case with exceptional thoroughness. Be precise. Avoid the jargon (which, unfortunately, much of the sources are full of) and try to get a handle on the main points of a particular position. Though feminist, Marxist, and Neo-Freudian views are closely connected, as a beginner try to stick to just one and master it.

III. Questions a Writer Using the Ideological/Theoretical Approach Might Ask
  1. What is the basic structure of the film medium, realist or formalist?
  2. What is the relation of the spectator to the film? Where is the viewer positioned psychologically?
  3. How does a movie affect an audience at a deep psychological level? How is audience desire manipulated by film structure?
  4. In what ways does the film contain the evidence of its production? Do we always know "it's only a movie"? Or can we be subtly primed to accept the dominant ideology through the seemingly harmless mass entertainment of the picture show?

5. How are women represented in the movies? Is this good or bad? Is it true to life?

6. Do movies show us the real complexity of the world or continue to suggest that individuals can solve their basic problems? If this is not an accurate picture of the way things really are, who stands to benefit from the audience's acquiescence in this fiction?

7. How do empathy and identification with characters really work in a film?

8. What kinds of bipolar opposites, like light and dark, good and evil, male and female, individual and group, structure genre films?

9. What is the basic cinematic language and how does it work?

10. Can you locate films that vary from the norm, even though at the surface they appear to be simply conventional? Are these films clever enough to fool most of the public and thus become successful at the box office, or are they too obvious in their critique of the norm and thus alienate the mass audience?

Appendix
Sample Student Papers

JOURNALISTIC APPROACH: THREE REVIEWS

Scott Rivers

House of Games
Orion
Produced by Michael Hausman
Directed by David Mamet
Starring Lindsay Crouse, Joe Mantegna

An original American classic and the ultimate cinematic con game. Pulitzer Prize-winning playwright David Mamet has written and directed this stunning psychological thriller with more twists and turns than Chubby Checker.

While critics and viewers squander their time praising a ludicrous nonentity such as *No Way Out,* they miss the hidden treasures such as *House of Games*—which is superb, carefully calculated filmmaking through and through. Mamet's directorial debut is an auspicious occasion indeed, as the texture and detail of this manipulative study in human compulsion resembles the work of an experienced master such as Alfred Hitchcock and Fritz Lang. You're left with the impression that Mamet has been a filmmaker for years.

Never being one to spoil the fun, I'll keep plot details to a minimum. Dr. Margaret Ford (played by Lindsay Crouse, Mamet's wife) is a successful psychiatrist trying to help one of her patients—in this case, a compulsive gambler who owes $25,000 to a poker professional named Mike (Joe Mantegna). Going against her principles, Ford decides to visit Mike in an attempt to wipe her patient's debt clean . . . and that's when this marvelous con game begins.

There are so many levels to Mamet's ingeniously crafted screenplay that one viewing doesn't necessarily provide all the answers. The script is so intricate and tightly layered, it's somewhat akin to dissecting a pomegranate. No wonder Mamet wanted to handle the directorial duties.

The performances of Crouse and Mantegna are so coolly controlled and self-assured that their underplaying becomes a polished art form itself—it's certainly one of the more notable screen pairings in recent years. Juan Ruiz Anchia's cinematography adds the perfect *film noir* touch to the proceedings.

If I were to recommend only a half-dozen films to see this year, *House of Games* would definitely be on that list. It's a knockout.

The Dead
Vestron Pictures
Produced by Wieland Schultz-Keil, Chris Sievernich
Directed by John Huston
Starring Anjelica Huston, Donal McCann

Sheer perfection. John Huston's final motion picture ends on a haunting, spellbinding note—not as a last gasp, but rather as a parting, heartfelt glance at an extraordinary body of work and the director's love for Ireland.

Based on a short story from James Joyce's *Dubliners, The Dead* is a small, intimate, and finely drawn portrait of a post-Christmas family gathering in 1904 Dublin—an Epiphany supper full of warmth, humor, and a heartbreaking revelation for the visiting Gretta, who unlocks a secret from her past she can't bear to face—but does.

This is one of the rare Huston films that display his meticulous penchant for ensemble acting. The casting resembles a graceful masterstroke, with Anjelica Huston (Gretta), Donal McCann (Gabriel, Gretta's husband), and Donal Donnelly (the lovably sloshed Freddy), among several others, in memorable form. Each actor blends into Huston's framework with effortless precision. Danny Huston's screenplay is remarkably faithful to Joyce and letter-perfect throughout.

At eighty-five minutes, *The Dead* is over before you know it—as though you, too, had a relaxed, soulful holiday visit. More than anything, John Huston's valedictory film captures the moodiness and beauty of the Irish countryside in a breathtaking manner. Its chilling climax reveals the words that eloquently sum up Joyce's story and provide a fitting coda to Huston's life and career: "Better pass boldly into that other world in the full glory of some passion than fade and wither dismally with age."

Frantic
Warner Brothers
Produced by Thom Mount, Tim Hampton
Directed by Roman Polanski
Starring Harrison Ford, Emmanuelle Seigner

Without a doubt one of Roman Polanski's dullest, emptiest films. The fact that *Frantic* was made by the same man who brought us *Chinatown, Tess,* and *Rosemary's Baby* really hurts.

"Imitation Hitchcock" it isn't, because there's little sign of the master's influence (or even Polanski's) in this slow, tedious thriller that runs two hours, but could easily be trimmed by thirty minutes. Rather than take a few quick detours, the writer/director travels the scenic route.

Harrison Ford plays an American doctor whose wife (Betty Buckley) disappears from their Paris hotel room. He looks everywhere, but gets little help from the incompetent members of the U.S. Embassy or the hotel's polite but patronizing staff.

It turns out that the disappearance is linked to an accidently exchanged suitcase belonging to a youthful smuggler (Emmanuelle Seigner). Once Ford tracks down Seigner (which takes an excruciating hour!), the film becomes more intriguing but—before we know it—Polanski again takes some wrong, predictable turns that we've come to expect from a pseudo-Hitchcock effort.

Ford gives an excellent, convincing performance; though the movie is a jumbled mess, he's always worth watching. Seigner makes an impressive English-language debut as she develops an offbeat, sometimes amusing rapport with Ford. Their chemistry, however, is the only aspect that clicks.

At times, you're not sure whether Polanski intended this to be a thriller or a slapstick farce. The suspense and tension are virtually nonexistent, despite Ford's credible playing. By the time *Frantic* reaches its ho-hum, bullet-riddled climax, I found it hard to believe that Polanski actually put this clichéd hodgepodge together. I think Warner Brothers made him a big-budget offer he couldn't refuse—but it's too bad we're stuck with this paint-by-numbers guide to filmmaking. Roman, wake up, the parade has passed you by.

RATING GUIDE: ***** Superb
                         ****   Excellent
                         ***   Good
                         **   Fair
                         *   Poor
                         No Stars Self-explanatory

HUMANIST APPROACH: AMERICAN PIE VS. PUMPERNICKEL RYE

Kelly Ioane

I always feel so good after watching *Singin' in the Rain*—confident, optimistic, buoyant—and I feel sure that my talent and perseverance will eventually be rewarded, and that I, too, will have my slice of the American pie.

This feeling does not last very long. The world seems somewhat flat and dull after all the vibrant energy and color of film; nobody smiles at me as I walk through the parking lot to my beat-up '69 Chevy Impala. No one bursts into song—indeed, what's there to sing about, anyway?

My enthusiasm dwindles quickly, my hopes for fame and fortune fade or, worse, seem a bit ridiculous in the harsh light of day. Success like that only happens in the movies. Real life is so different, with so many scenes that should be cut—too long, too boring, too corny. Would that life could be more like the movies! (I hate that thought as soon as it comes out.)

Movies are our Greek myths and through them we experience rage and revenge and murder and lust and love and sorrow. As we sit in the darkness, we dream together, we dance and sing and leap, we defy our earthly limitations for an hour or two and become superhuman. Except that really we are just sitting there, perhaps eating popcorn, but really just sitting there.

Are we inspired, or are we simply pacified? Do movies create energy or do they drain it? The Romans had the circus, and we have the movies.

In *The Purple Rose of Cairo* Woody Allen examines the ethical problems which surround the enterprise of filmmaking. The film closes with a shot of Mia Farrow's face as she becomes absorbed by the image of Fred and Ginger dancing gracefully across the screen. We know that she will go home to Monk, because, as she's told us, she doesn't want to be alone. She goes to movies to escape the boredom of her life, to avoid the abuse of her husband, who reminds her that "You'll be back. It ain't the movies out there; it's real life."

Movies are easy—all they want are a couple of bucks and a couple of hours from us—and we get so much in return. Life is hard, so what is wrong with escaping for a few hours? As Tom Baxter says, "Life's too short to think about life." Our movies today seem full of this mindless message, and Allen is courageous in his criticism of both audience and filmmaker. Allen's courage is his genius, it is what makes him a great artist. In *Purple Rose* he tells us that our lives will not improve while we sit passively in the movie theater, wishing or believing that our lives could be different.

For Farrow's character, movies are more real than real life. It is a problem when we believe in movies too much. We go with the surface high, the original rush, and ignore the message which is always there, especially in popular genre films. Our films are filled with capitalist propaganda. In *Top Gun* the message is "American is good, powerful, invincible, and every patriotic young man who will willingly die for his country deserves a comely armful like Kelly McGillis." In *Rambo,* more of the same, but the thing that waves around the phallic symbols is bigger and greasier. In *Romancing the Stone,* the message is that "true love conquers all, *and* goes hand in hand with great wealth." (You either have it all or have nothing at all. The sweet life is to cruise around on a yacht and never have to work again in your life. The sweet life does exist, just beyond our grasp.)

The messages are so taken for granted that we never question them, we just accept them or ignore them or, most dangerously, ingest them unconsciously. In other words we are brainwashed by a constant barrage of movies that present a reality which does not exist. In this reality, which should always be *seamless,* people have a lot of fun in glamorous settings. In real life I've never had a very good time at a cocktail party, and I feel a bit short-changed. I want to experience a real Hollywood cocktail party, where everyone is either very beautiful or very witty and charming. In movieland people fall in love, at first glance and forever, and their love lifts them above the cares of everyday reality. Money does not matter. What a disappointment love in real life is in comparison! Real love is messy and unbearably complex, and you are lucky if it lasts a year, let alone a lifetime.

An hour or two after seeing *Singin' in the Rain* I feel vaguely depressed and strangely guilty. Why am I such a failure? Why am I still just a mousy little nobody? Could there be another message in *Rain,* besides the obvious one?—work hard, keep singing, don't let 'em get you down, and you'll be rewarded in the end—a message that seems to say, "If you are not a success, it's because you haven't worked hard enough, smiled brightly enough, or been good enough." "Good" is personified by Debbie Reynolds, a girl almost too nice to hate, and the thing that makes her so good is her ability never really to question and never really to think. She is easily swept into the Hollywood world which treats her kindly, of course, since she is no threat to it. There might be a few sort-of-mean people in Hollywood, like Lina, but basically it is fair and just and good, and hard work will be rewarded.

Every film contains layers of meaning, and most Hollywood films are like chocolate-covered balls of monosodium glutamate. Self-reflective cinema is an attempt to reveal what goes on behind the scenes, behind the camera, in the minds of the filmmakers. It is the degree of honesty which varies from film to film. *Singin' in the Rain* is beautiful and amusing, but it lacks the honesty which makes *Purple Rose of Cairo* a truly great film. Wonder Bread versus pumpernickel rye—I'll take the rye.

AUTEUR APPROACH: JOSEPH von STERNBERG

Angie Kelson

In Sadoul's *Dictionary of Film Makers,* Joseph von Sternberg is quoted as having said, "My background was in another world than that of films: that of literature and the plastic arts." Upon viewing his films, one can easily see that this is true and that his particular background aided in the development of his personal style of filmmaking.

Von Sternberg's films have a certain literary feel to them. One qualification for literature is that it present a cohesive view of life along with a theme and often a moral. Many films lack an easily identifiable theme, much less a moral which can be substantiated, but von Sternberg consistently manages to express themes and morals in his films. One of them von Sternberg deals with is the individual's fall from grace, as in *Blue Angel* or *Blonde Venus*. Love conquers all is another theme explored again in *Blonde Venus* as well as *Morocco*. These are both classical literary themes von Sternberg translates to film with finesse.

This eloquent translation from literary to filmic form is partially due to von Sternberg's undisputed mastery of light and form. Von Sternberg was partial to expressionistic techniques: backgrounds filled with shapes, framing within the screen, and looming shadows are just a few techniques utilized. Yet von Sternberg never overuses or abuses this stylistic device. Instead he uses it to further deepen tension and meaning in the individual scenes and throughout the film.

In *Blue Angel* Professor Rath's home is filled with stacks of books. More than just a device to fill the screen with small rectangular shapes, the books have another purpose. Stacked everywhere, they represent the seemingly ordered professor's chaotic state of mind. He appears to be a strict authoritarian in the class, but he has little real control over his students, who tease him mercilessly. He is also an apparently lonely man, crushed when his small songbird dies. Surrounded by the hodgepodge of books, Professor Rath is separated from humanity behind an academic tangle. A confused and lonely man, he is easily overcome by the brassy charm of Lola.

In *Morocco* von Sternberg utilizes framing within the picture to highlight and intensify the movie's ending. Aimee Joli has finally decided she wants to be with her true love and follows the foreign legion out of town. As she leaves the city, she passes under a huge archway that fills the screen, framing her. This final framing of Aimee is in keeping with the stylization of the whole film. As love and romance are idealized, the sets are also stylized to echo the thematic idealization. Framing Aimee turns her into a picture: a perfect picture for a picture-perfect ending.

The third device used by von Sternberg, shadows, is obvious in *Blonde Venus*. One example occurs when Ned, upon his return from Europe, is creeping up the stairs to the apartment. He has learned from neighbors that his wife has not been living at home, and he has become suspicious. Shadows from the staircase are thrown against the wall forming bars around him, trapping him in his suspicion and distrust of his wife. The shadows also heighten the tension; will Helen be there or will she not? The shadows give an effective portrayal of Ned's state of mind and add suspense to the scene.

Joseph von Sternberg was undoubtedly a master of light and shadow as he used these elements to manipulate film into expressing his themes and emotions of characters as well as adding thematic meaning to the scene. He never abused expressionistic techniques but used these styles to enhance and elevate his films.

GENRE APPROACH: THE COMIC BOOK HERO—A NEW SUBGENRE

Dale K. Intveld

Throughout the years of the twentieth century there has been a continual evolution of the industry called film. The technology of this industry has evolved to meet the demands of the audiences that it serves to entertain. The technological demands have increased dramatically with the passage of years and decades. Though the technology of the medium has continued to change and become increasingly complex, the basic themes or plots of the stories have remained relatively the same. With the exceptions of changes in the everyday objects, practices, and rituals that the public is shown in these films, most stories have remained based on plots that were developed over the centuries past.

The stories that have survived have done so because of their popularity with the public. Here is where the story of film in today's society for the demanding public begins. Throughout this evolving history of film certain types of films have developed in similar patterns so as to fit into categories. These categories are called *genres*. The definition of *genre* is: a group of films that are extremely similar in their subject matter, thematic concerns, characterizations, plot formulas, and visual settings. This paper will touch on a new category of films that seems to be emerging in this society. This new type of film seems to have been created to deal with the decline in popularity of films with complex meaning and to attract younger and younger audiences that are paying for expensive tickets that allow them into the fantasy worlds of their favorite heroes. The new type of film comes under the heading of genre melodrama. This new category is the comic book hero melodrama.

First, we must define the term *genre melodrama*. The melodrama comes from the context of the romance in medieval literature. It follows a basic pattern: a society is found to be in grave trouble and a hero must be located who has great and special skills; with few exceptions traditionally male, he is charged with the task of saving the society by overcoming obstacles and solving problems, and he does so in a series of encounters that often culminate in one big struggle, at which point the society is returned to a state of harmony. The primary struggle of a hero who embodies good against the forces of evil pervades nearly all melodramatic genres.

The new subcategory that falls under this larger category is that of the comic book hero melodrama. Although it displays the properties of the larger category of genre melodrama, it tends to become more specialized in its simplistic construction of characters and its similar plots and something called "the vindication principle." The comic book hero melodrama subgenre is a new and different approach to the newly created and downgraded group of American society called "the younger viewer with the ticket price." Moviemakers have long been looking for ways to capitalize upon this group that has freely been spending its more affluent parents' money in vast quantities. Although this is true, there has been a decline in the education level of many of those same American youngsters and their peers. To capitalize on this fact of society there was created a level of movie that could be accommodating to this same group. This is where the new comic book hero melodrama subgenre comes in.

In the last five to ten years there has steadily emerged the simplistic story that can be related to this new society subgroup with relative ease. There are no intense meanings, no deep intellectual subtleties, no complex plots, and certainly no complex dialogues written for these new movies. What is similar in this new category are the following properties: simple easily grasped plot for low-intelligence or younger audiences, single hero upon which the world's hopes ride, a hero who starts out as a simple everyday person, but is turned almost superhuman from some freak chance of nature or event, constant challenges requiring fantastic action, and the simple "blow them up or capture them and put them in jail" endings that satisfy the "vindication principle." Also, these shows all have similar icons in them. They have the machine guns, the explosions, and the "simple hero dialogue."

Let us look at four movies that belong to this new category. Although these movies belong to many other categories, they all seem to fit the pattern of this new subgenre. The movies are *First Blood* (1984), *Missing in Action* (1984), *Rambo: First Blood II* (1985), *The Running Man* (1987). All these movies have in them the elements that are listed above. Let us examine the points below.

As for the simple plots for younger audiences and people of low intelligence, these are the perfect examples. All these movies contain plots that are derived from the survival films.

These plots follows either the line of a lost group of people (in this case the MIA's) or the contestants of the survival game as in *The Running Man*, all forming a minisociety in which the group can accomplish a specific function successfully with the aid of the superhero. The plots of these movies go like this: heroes or other people are wronged by society, the hero goes in or breaks free to help, he runs into a series of trials by fire and wins them all, he becomes more self-powered, the enemies fall down around him or he conquers them all in the final battle at the end. This is the standard plot of the basic survival film. It is also the same plot that all the comic book hero subgenre films share.

There is, of course, in all these films a hero on whom the down-and-out must depend in order to survive. Only that hero has enough strength and agility to get them out of the fix they are in. In *The Running Man,* only Arnold Schwartzenager can save the poor slobs from the plight that has befallen them at the hands of a society gone mad. The game show that has imprisoned them stands for the society around them that has warped itself through the catastrophes that have occurred over the years of decline. It is this injustice that Arnold must conquer in order to save the girl at his side (after the deaths of the two friends at the hands of the evil superheroes). In *First Blood,* it is Rambo who must gain strength in order to battle the injustices of a town that has acted hostilely toward him and the cause that he fought for in Vietnam. Only he can conquer the awful hatred and discrimination that is plaguing the town. Again in *Rambo: First Blood II,* it is Rambo who must free the lowly MIA's from their exile in Viet Nam. He has achieved the power and super-human strength and endurance that will allow him to conquer the hostiles who have imprisoned his buddies. The plot and character are similar in *Missing in Action,* in which Chuck Norris plays the superhero. One has to wonder if the comic book hero GI Joe was the role model for these movie characters.

It is amazing the way an ordinary citizen (built like a tank) can miracu-lously emerge with the power of ten grown men and the agility of the helicopter that he sometimes rides in. The heroes in these films copy each other and become the same type of hero to all those younger movie au-diences.

The strong-men heroes of these films all embody the power of those ten grown men but they have lost the power of speed. The most one of these characters ever says in a scene is a single line of dialogue. Sometimes this is not even the case, as with Schwartzenager in *The Running Man* and also in a similar movie, *The Terminator* (1986). In these two movies (in one he plays a good hero and the other a dark-force hero) his most intelligent line is "Fuck you, asshole!" The fact is that in most of these films there is a lot of profanity and senseless violence that trigger the ratings people to drop the ratings to PG or lower. This is a disturbing trend, since these movies are designed to appeal to a young audience.

In all the movies in this subgenre there is a definite lack of morality regarding the use of violence. Sure, the bad guys get their just desserts, but it is also true that there is too much just desserts getting dealt out. These movies are prolific with the violence associated with war and crime.

In accordance with this penchant is the violent ending that must accom-pany the action. All these movies contain a violent final battle in which the superhero conquers the foes. It is he alone and not the ones he is helping who have saved the day for society. These finales are usually accompanied by an even larger show of gunfire and pyrotechnics. Without that final set of explosions at the end of the film, the audience would not feel as if the hero had vanquished the enemy.

This leads to the ending called the "vindication principle." If the hero does not sufficiently punish or kill the enemies in order to pay them back for the injustices they have heaped on the poor helpless subjects, the audience would not have the satisfaction of seeing good triumph over evil. Good must triumph over evil as it does in the comic books that younger audiences read.

A set of icons usually accompanies these movies. It includes machine guns, violent actions, and pyrotechnics. Without such icons there would be no action or story and the movies would not draw such a crowd. The machine guns symbolize the meaning of law and justice to the audience. Without law and justice the world would be a terrible place to live.

One needs only to read an adventure comic book in order to appreciate the validity of these arguments. A comic book has a simple plot that is easy for young audiences to follow. There is no depth to the characters in those comic books either. If they had depth, they could then feel the pain that is inflicted on their enemies and themselves. Instead, they see only the need for retribution that is attached to their goal of straightening out the wronged society in which they live. If one could give life to a comic book, then one would have created this subgenre of films.

With their simple characters, plots, violence, gunplay, pyrotechnics, poor language, and the vindication principle, these movies fit into an ever-increasing group of films that are similar enough in construction and nature to be in their own category: the comic book hero subgenre.

SOCIAL SCIENCES APPROACH: MOVIE MUSICALS AND THEIR EFFECT ON AUDIENCES

Holly Vestal

In the late 1970s into the 1980s, movie musicals were experiencing a change. But contemporary film musicals still have the familiar formula plots that were found in the movie musicals of the 1930s and the 1950s. The society that is reflected in current musicals is one of action and driving ambition. The protagonists have a dream to make it big. The audience is witness to the struggles and disappointments the protagonists face. The movie usually is pumped up with a fast-beat soundtrack and elaborate choreography. With luck, talent, and desire, the protagonists usually get what they want. This burst of stardom is generally displayed by a grand finale of lights, music, and dance. This type of movie musical can be called musical melodrama, for the movies rarely end with a wedding but usually end on an upbeat note. Our society has changed its viewpoint toward love and marriage. No longer do the hero and heroine marry, but instead the new star usually stands alone, independent of everyone.

Saturday Night Fever (1977) paved the way for other films akin to its plot and conventions. *Fever* produced influences on culture and society. The movie sparked an explosion of discotheques, disco music, white three-piece suits worn open-necked with gold chains, and new dance steps. *Fever*-mania spread to records, posters, and T-shirts. Other movie musicals, like *Fame* (1980), *Flashdance* (1983), and *Footloose* (1983), turned out film parapher-nalia and new fashions. The movies focused their attention on the young and their dreams of fame and fortune. The movies become an acted-out version of our own dreams and hopes. We root for the protagonist and are bedazzled by the energetic and creative talents of the hero.

Saturday Night Fever, the parent of spawning offspring, relates the story of an average youth who lives only for the dance floor. Tony has a dreary, menial, 9–5 job; he lives for Saturday night. He escapes from his life in Brooklyn to the discos in Manhattan, where he becomes a wizard on the dance floor. The audience can identify with an ordinary person such as Tony. He represents the great American hope that, with hard work and a dream, anything is possible. A sequel to *Fever, Stayin' Alive* (1983) is the continuing story of Tony. He is in the big city trying for a break into Broadway. Again, dramatic episodes and intense musical sequences help develop the protagonist's quest. With the last musical number, the audience knows that he is well on his way to success and fortune. He has climbed up from a repressive and boring life to that of fame. The audience can leave the theater in an upbeat mood, secure in the knowledge that dreams can come true.

Fame was probably made with a specific audience in mind—those with aspirations to success. *Fame* follows the four years of several students through the High School of Performing Arts. The audience gets an insider's look into the bright, talented youth who are in search of dreams. The film emphasizes the toughness of the arts: many people fail or never gain the recognition they so desperately seek. However, the students' creativity and energy probably fired the ambitions of many a youth. The film also produced a very popular sound track and a not so popular hour-long television series. The film showed young people putting on a production that was not only entertaining but proved there is hope for the up-and-coming adults in our society.

Flashdance and *Footloose* also were influential to many in fashion, music, and dance. *Flashdance*'s heroine is a dewy young woman who is also street-smart. She is a steelworker during the day and a dancer with dreams at night. She is independent and ambitious; she serves as a role model for other young women. Even if some of the storyline is a bit hard to swallow, one is caught up in the hypnotic dance and music. Besides the obvious commercial tie-in of the original sound track, the film inspired fashion. People everywhere were sporting the "*Flashdance* look." Sweatshirts purposely cut up so that they could slide seductively off the shoulders became the fashion craze of the 1980s. While *Flashdance* had a female protagonist, *Footloose* had a hip and rebellious hero. The hero moves to a small town which has outlawed dancing. Our hero, a boy filled with pent-up emotions and a very good dancer, fights the adults of the town to have the ban lifted. This move shows that it is okay for males to be able to outdance their partners, that dance can be used to strut their stuff, as Tony did in *Fever.* This movie also had a musical sound track that influenced the popular-music charts.

Current movie musicals use the power of music and choreography not only to provoke feelings of fear, anger, and hope but also to influence the audience to imitate the characters' dress, music, and life style. They are fast-paced and slick portrayals of how ambition, based on a dream and with lots of hard work, can mean success. This genre provides an escape for ninety minutes. One can forget his or her troubles and the horrors of contemporary world problems, be entertained, and leave the movie house in an uplifted mood probably humming the title song, and then go directly to a record or clothing store in order to be just like those wonderful, successful people in the movies.

HISTORICAL APPROACH: THE POLITICAL IMPLICATIONS OF *THE ADVENTURES OF ROBIN HOOD* (MICHAEL CURTIZ, 1938)

Verna Huiskamp

It is this paper's contention that the effects of the Depression and the impending war in Europe had explicit political implications in the 1938 version of *Adventures of Robin Hood*. According to Bergman (Davies and Neve), in any period of stress there are certain tensions that permeate a society and affect the majority of society's members, including the artists. Because of this, Bergman believed, the moviemakers of the 1930s mirrored the tensions of the post-Depression era, and reflected an encompassing fear of brewing turmoil in Europe.

The Adventures of Robin Hood is a fundamentally conservative film, concerned with the efforts of the charismatic individual to restore responsible government and economic stability to his country. *Robin Hood* promotes the individual hero against the corrupt powers that have improperly assumed control over the world. The hero's quest is the defeat of tyranny and the restoration of the social order.

Being inherently political, the swashbuckler genre films are concerned with the individual in his relationship to society and government. *The Adventures of Robin Hood* fits the expectations of the genre; it takes a firm stand against aggression and oppression by promoting an activist hero fighting injustice and cruelty in the world. While commenting on the impoverished conditions of the subjects under Prince John, the film goes beyond economic problems and primarily focuses on the more threatening concern of tyranny festering in Europe. Robin Hood's battle with Prince John and his followers predicted the struggle between the United States and the dictator of Germany.

The military tactics displayed in this film reflect a novel approach to the defeat of the overpowering, evil rulers. Robin and his merry men have been credited with being one of the first guerrilla armies (Callenbach). Like the citizens of the Depression, Robin's men are forced into their actions because of the conditions in their environment. The merry men are uprooted from their villages because of hard economic realities. And there, rejected by the better-off and harassed by the tax collectors, they drift into crime and guerrilla tactics in order to survive. The group hides out in the impenetrable Sherwood Forest and makes hits against the rich and then quietly retreats into the safety of the forest.

The justification for Robin's acts of terrorism and guerrilla warfare is his goal of returning the true and supposedly just king, King Richard, to the thrown. Robin makes clear that only John's misuse of power can justify taking the law into his own hands and curses the fact that Richard's absence has forced him to take such extraordinary measures. He condemns Richard and the situation that would leave the task of saving England to an outlaw like him. The people Robin robs are shown to be vile wrongdoers, and the people he kills are the defenders of the corrupt elite intent on usurping the power from Richard. Robin's guerrilla tactics of having his men drop from overhanging branches onto their victims and hiding behind trees to shoot unsuspecting horsemen riding through the forest are depicted as being justified in the interest of a higher and a more just system of law and order.

Several political elements exist in *Robin Hood,* so that the viewer of the late 1930s could accept the guerrilla tactics used by the merry men to change the social order. First of all, Robin is a nobleman, not a common man fighting for power from the elite. Sir Robin of Lockesley sees his king as a father figure and does not look upon himself as a peasant leader intent upon confiscating and dividing land among the poor, hanging the nobility, and creating a new republic. In the story of *Robin Hood* society is a family, not meant to be totally disrupted, merely adjusted.

Second, in *Robin Hood,* problems of society are fought on a personal and emotional level, represented by the protagonist, and the struggle is not depicted as an overt political and economic battle involving the masses. In *Robin Hood* the true remedy for society's brutalities comes from above, not below. Robin is an aristocrat, not a peasant, who is merely serving as a surrogate of the absent monarch.

According to the class readings, although the hero in a swashbuckler is invariably from noble stock, as in the case of *Robin Hood,* the hero temporarily aligns himself with the poor when faced with the injustice of society. The hero dramatically moves from aristocracy to democracy and freely expresses the notion that all men should be treated equally—as when Robin pronounces that he is fighting a battle for all Englishmen ("It's injustice I hate, not the Normans") (Hark).

Robin's symbolic move to democracy can be seen in his relationship with the Saxon peasantry, as shown in the feast in the forest. During the feast everyone seems to be involved in the preparation of the meal, people are dancing in the background, and the captured adversaries are given peasant clothing to wear so that all may appear equal. Everyone shares in the meal, even using the same despicable table manners. There is no obvious division between master and servant in Sherwood Forest.

Another example of a product of democracy is the forest hospital Robin has established for the poor and suffering peasants. Robin, trying to convince Marion of the evils of Prince John's rule, introduces her to the peasants hiding in the forest. This sanctuary Robin has established for those displaced and maimed by Norman tyranny reflects a close parallel to similar camps erected by our democratic government during the Depression.

The most important element of Robin Hood's goal of retaining social order is that he calls for equality of treatment among the kingdom's subjects. According to Bergman's essay (Davies and Neve), film in the 1930s revealed the popular assumptions of the time. As in the case of *Robin Hood,* it was the glorification of democracy, depicting America as a classless, melting pot nation. The swashbuckler genre by definition focuses on this similar ideal of social unity (class readings).

After Robin Hood's struggle against opposing forces, the viewer is returned to the idea of social conformity, reinforcement of the status quo, and the regularity of the social order. Critics on the left believed it was a conspiracy of movie producers and government that films during this tense period in American history did not advocate dramatic changes in the social structure. Some believed that revolutionary change in the 1930s was subdued and sapped of radical energies by the organized deceit of Hollywood. The resulting movie fare encouraged the muting of class anxieties and stressed the need for victims to endure within the existing social structure (Davies and Neve).

Robin Hood was a film to be criticized by the left because it also advocated no change in the existing social structure. The film did not call for anarchy over established government. By showing the deadly flaws of Prince John, the message was that it is individuals, not systems, that are to blame for tyranny and social injustice.

Robin Hood worked well in articulating the political and economic concerns of the ruling class in the late 1930s and served as a catharsis, a diversion, and an affirmation of values necessary for the continuation of the democratic system in power. The genre film helped define a moral and social world that spoke against the evils of tyranny while encouraging a retention of social order under the established political systems.

Our hero reinforces the acceptance of the status quo when he throws off his democratic disguise once social order has been restored. He remains above the masses and reenters the aristocracy. The swashbuckling hero returns society to a just social order, but never fully assimilates with the common people. The idea of democracy is worth fighting for, but our swashbuckling hero will never be one of those who enjoys mere equality.

References

Callenbach, Ernest. "Comparative Anatomy of Folk-myth Films: *Robin Hood* and *Antonio das Mortes." Film Quarterly,* vol. 23, no. 2, 1969, pp. 41–47.
Davies, P., and Neve, B. *Cinema, Politics and Society in America.* Manchester: Manchester University Press, 1981.

Hark, I. R. "The Visual Politics of *The Adventures of Robin Hood*." *Journal of Popular Films,* vol. 5, no. 1, 1976, pp. 3–17.
Robinson, D. "The Hero." *Sight and Sound,* vol. 42, no. 2, 1972, pp. 62–68.

THEORETICAL APPROACH: SPECULATIONS ON THE PHENOMENON OF AUDIENCE POSITIONING

Allan Godwin

It is no coincidence that narrative cinema is vastly more popular than either documentary or experimental cinema. This is due partly to the idea that narrative cinema is the best suited of the three categories to satisfy the viewer's desires or expectations.

To understand how this occurs, it is first necessary to posit the notion of audience positioning. Watching films is a mostly voyeuristic activity, as opposed to being actively participatory. Much film theory has used the psychoanalytic implications of this notion to develop an understanding of how cinema "works" within the viewer's mind. A thorough overview of this notion is far beyond the scope of this essay. Yet it will be useful to cite Christian Metz's writings to support a few of the subsequent statements.

Metz asserts that "it is not so much the distance kept, . . . as the absence of the object seen" that specifically defines the scopophilia inherent in the practice of cinema. In other words, it is the illusory nature of the representation of reality in film that distinguishes cinema from more intimate voyeuristic activities such as those related to sexual exhibitionism or perversity. Presumably all voyeurism as defined along psychoanalytic lines is somehow connected to humankind's obsession with sexuality.

Much of the impact of cinema lies in its power to use voyeuristic tendencies within the viewer to coax him or her into suspending disbelief in the illusory representation on the screen and accepting it as "real," however subliminally. The viewer is then rewarded with the feeling of having been transported without risk to a time or place other than the present. This is why we as cinema spectators are so willing to believe so soon what is being shown on the screen. Although we seem to think all too often that seeing is believing, somewhere in the back of our minds remains the conviction that what is being seen is also absent. We are relieved of participatory responsibility. The irony then becomes that, as we are detached from the film, we are also accepting the invitation to be "sucked-in" or veritably engrossed in the narrative. Alfred Hitchcock liked to open his films by taking the viewers into someone's house or apartment in a smooth, gliding shot which seemed designed to underlie the feeling of nonintrusiveness. We are so willing to accept this invitation that we are not disappointed when it is only a local bloke like Jimmy Stewart we come upon doing nothing particularly interesting or if we get there just a few minutes too late, as in *Psycho* to find the couple getting dressed after making love.

Yet not all film openings have to depend on a voyeuristic shot to captivate the viewer. The opening of *The French Lieutenant's Woman* (1981) shows the character of the actress about to step into her role for what seems is the actual filming of a sequence. The viewer arrives at a pivotal point in time. At this juncture the "reality" of the viewer's suspension of disbelief, the "reality" of the film within the film, and the "reality" of the scene being filmed all meet at a crossroads.

It was extremely interesting to get a false start into the screening of the film during class since the sound was absent for the first few minutes. This experience now seems to have been deliberately set up as an exercise because it strongly underlined the dimension of the sound track and what it adds to the conglomeration of "multiple realities" that characterize this film. The sound track included the noises of the set overlaid with the beginnings of a string orchestration while the opening credits were still rolling. Thus we get two overlapping and conflicting positions from both the sound track and the images. We are uncertain whether we have begun to watch a movie of the novel or a movie about the making of that movie. Eventually we learn to reposition ourselves each time these "movies" alternate.

The sophisticated execution of the opening scene of *The French Lieutenant's Woman* relies on the advanced level of film literacy on the audience's part. To the uninitiated this can conceivably be a very confusing scene. But to those of us who have already lost our innocence, this was a particularly effective and economical way to lay the expository groundwork for the story. But what does the confusion of time and place, the revelation of positioning, do for the average viewer? Perhaps it helps alert the audience, through violation of expected conventions, to understand their true relation to the images on the screen.

One can then argue for the value of such self-reflexive cinema—film about the making of film, one that makes the viewer aware of positioning. It can ultimately serve an educational end by raising the level of filmic understanding among general audiences, who can theoretically then be more aware of what is happening before their eyes in films that follow conventional continuity. Understanding the nature of film's positioning power is certainly a byproduct of the self-reflexive film. Anything that raises public consciousness about the nearly invisible ideological and behavioral effects of a mass medium is surely valuable.

Chronology of Film Reviewing, Criticism, and Theory

1896   The *New York Times* publishes the first English-language article about film, a report on the "Projecting Kinetoscope" exhibition at Koster & Bial's Music Hall theater.

1896–1906   New film programs are "reviewed" in daily newspapers in synopsis form, with very little evaluation or criticism.

1906–1907   Trade papers make their first appearance: *Views and Film Index, The Moving Picture World, Moving Picture News*. Though intended for trade audiences, these publications contained columns and articles that begin to discuss the motion picture critically.

1908–1912   Frank E. Woods, writing under the pseudonym "The Spectator" for *The New York Dramatic Mirror* (a trade paper), becomes America's first influential film critic.

1915   THE BIRTH OF A NATION (D. W. Griffith, USA). This epic motion picture attracts so much attention in intellectual as well as popular circles that it fires a critical consciousness. The first film to fully utilize the artistic possibilities of the medium, it gives impetus to film criticism and reviewing as a professional activity practiced by daily newspapers and monthly magazines.

1916   *The Art of the Moving Picture* (Vachel Lindsay, USA). The first book-length attempt to distinguish the properties of film from those of the other arts is written by an American poet. It argues for a recognition of cinema as an art form and is the first attempt at a film theory.

            The Photoplay: A Psychological Study (Hugo Münsterberg, USA). Also arguing for film's status as an art, this major work of early theory approaches the medium psychologically and perceptually. Pre-Freudian, the book explores the relationship between the viewer and the screen image, foreshadowing current contemporary theoretical explorations.

1919–1920   *Cinéma et cie* and *Photogénie* (Louis Delluc, France). These two early French theoretical works are by the founder of the film-club movement. With Léon Moussinac, Delluc is responsible for making film reviewing a serious occupation rather than a forum for gossip, publicity, or mere plot synopses.

1920   *Exceptional Photoplays* is founded by the National Board of Review as a magazine devoted to discussions and reviews of current films. (The title is changed in 1926 to *The National Board of Review Magazine*.)

1920–1930   American film criticism is primarily limited to individual reviews of current films, although such reviews are increasingly written by distinguished authors like Robert E. Sherwood and Edmund Wilson and begin appearing in prestigious magazines like *The New Republic* and *The Atlantic Monthly*.

            As an outgrowth of the Dadaist and Surrealist movements, many essays and manifestoes are published in France articulating the need for more "art" and less story in films. They are written by such practicing artists and filmmakers as Germaine Dulac, Jean Epstein, René Clair, and Abel Gance.

1924   *The Visible Man, or Film Culture* (Béla Balázs, Germany). Written by a Hungarian filmmaker and theorist, this early theoretical work on the properties and strengths of the silent cinema may have influenced the practical and theoretical work of Soviet filmmaker V. I. Pudovkin. It is also one of the few works predating World War II that indicates a "realist" persuasion.

1925   The London Film Society is founded.

            Film study begins to develop in France.

1926   *Film Technique* (V. I. Pudovkin, USSR). The first major work by this seminal theorist and filmmaker, influenced by his studies in editing at the Kuleshov Workshop, is published. This theoretical work develops the "linkage" theory of film editing or montage.

1928   Sergei Eisenstein begins publishing the first of his many theoretical essays on film form in Soviet Russia. He outlines the montage through conflict and dialectic theory in opposition to Pudovkin. His output is prodigious and often based on interdisciplinary approaches to art. These essays are finally collected and published in English in the 1940s as *The Film Sense* (1942) and *Film Form: Essays in Film Theory* (1949).

1929   Two English-language journals appear that are devoted to the serious consideration of the "artistic" film: *Close-Up* and *Experimental Cinema*.

1930   *The Spirit of Film* (Béla Balázs, Germany). This theoretical work responds to the introduction of sound to the cinema, arguing for the use of asynchronous sound.

1930–1940   Documentary filmmakers in Britain, like John Grierson and Paul Rotha, write numerous essays relating the social consciousness of their cinematic approach to reality. A concern for "realism" and a great respect for the "raw material" of life begin to arise that counters the notion of film as "art."

            American film criticism, always more practical than theoretical, takes a sociological and political cast in the work of Harry Alan Potamkin and Otis Ferguson.

1933   *Film als Kunst (Film as Art)* (Rudolf Arnheim, Germany). This major work codifies the formalist position that film is a plastic art whose aesthetic should be based on its limitations, its very inability to reproduce reality prescribing that its aesthetic function be antirealist and expressive. The work, thus, denigrates the representational functions of cinema and decries the advent of sound.

The British Film Institute is founded.

1935   *Film Acting* (V. I. Pudovkin, USSR). The second major theoretical work by this influential Soviet filmmaker not only explores film performance but also continues discussion of film form.

1936   Henri Langlois founds the Cinématèque Française, the continual and rotating film archive/exhibition that is to have such an influence on contemporary French filmmakers.

1940–1950 Cesare Zavattini and other Italian Neorealists write numerous essays and manifestoes promoting a realistic approach to filmmaking and film's function as a social and political force.

Practical American film criticism reflects social and political concerns in the work of Robert Warshow, who sees film genres as indicative of a covert American mythology; Walter Benjamin, whose "The Art in the Age of Mechanical Reproduction" recognizes the effect production and technology have on art; and James Agee, whose social humanism is reflected in film reviews collected for book publication in 1946.

1945   *Theory of the Film: Character and Growth of a New Art* (Béla Balázs, Germany). This major work is the culmination of the Hungarian theorist's practice and thought and balances certain formalist principles of film as art with certain realist predilections, particularly in its discussion of the close-up.

In France, filmmaker, film critic, and journalist Alexandre Astruc publishes an essay positing the concept of "camera stylo," or camera-pen, the cinema as a medium as fluid and as able to deal with abstract ideas as written language. It called for film to express thought and go beyond a primary dependence upon its visual elements.

1951   *Cahiers du Cinéma* is founded in France by André Bazin, Jacques Doniol-Valcroze, and Lo Duca. Bazin becomes the major "realist" film theorist, publishing many essays questioning the nature of film and exploring cinema's realistic capability in essays on *mise-en-scène* and deep-focus photography. Many contemporary French filmmakers, like François Truffaut and Jean-Luc Godard, begin their careers as film critics for the magazine.

1954   "Une certaine tendance du cinéma français" by François Truffaut is published in the *Cahiers du Cinéma.* It attacks the stagnant French film industry and praises the work of American directors, establishing the groundwork for the auteur theory.

1956   "Montage, mon beau couci," by Jean-Luc Godard, is published in the *Cahiers.* It is the first work of contemporary film theory that attempts to erase the division between formalist/expressionist aesthetics and realist aesthetics, between montage and *mise-en-scène.* The article focuses on film as something perceived and understood by a participant viewer.

1959–1962   *Qu'est-ce que c'est le cinéma?* (André Bazin, France). Four volumes of Bazin's essays are collected and published, later translated into English as *What Is Cinema?* and published in 1967 and 1971. The collected essays are less a coherent theory than theory in practice.

1960   *Theory of Film: The Redemption of Physical Reality* (Siegfried Kracauer, USA). This massive work attempts a coherent film theory based on the representational qualities of the photographic image. It is the antithesis of aesthetic theories such as Arnheim's and represents the realist aesthetic.

1960–1970   An outpouring of books, magazines, journals, and theoretical writings on all aspects of film, from memoirs to scholarly studies, marks the decade. Film study becomes a serious subject in American universities. American film criticism is still primarily review-oriented and practical, as evidenced in the work of Dwight Macdonald, Manny Farber, John Simon, Andrew Sarris, and Pauline Kael—the most influential and popular film critics.

1963–1965   *Esthétique et psychologie du cinéma* (Jean Mitry, France). A masterwork of contemporary film study focused on theoretical inquiry, the book delineates the position of former film theory and functions almost like an anatomy in its scrupulous detail.

1967   The American Film Institute is founded.

1968   *Essais sur la signification au cinéma* (Christian Metz, France). Translated into English as *Film Language: A Semiotics of the Cinema* in 1974, this theoretical work introduces the application of linguistic sign theory to the exploration of film's capacity to convey meaning. It initiates an entire new approach to film theory that leaves questions of realism/formalism behind to explore viewer/film relationships.

            Le Gai Savoir (Jean-Luc Godard, France). Perhaps the first film theory proposed in film form rather than in written form, this film essay overtly questions and demonstrates cinematic language and methodology.

1969   *The American Cinema: Directors and Directions 1929–1968* (Andrew Sarris, USA). This book brings the *auteur* theory to America and posits its use as a means of approaching film history in a systematic manner. It also creates a hierarchy of film directors determined by their personal style.

            Signs and Meaning in the Cinema (Peter Wollen, USA). Published in America by a British author, this book is the first in English to apply semiotic theory to film.

1975   Umberto Eco, an Italian semiologist, addresses a conference of American film scholars at the City University of New York, stating that work in modern film criticism must be based on the recognition that any sign system is culturally and ideologically based, thereby turning away from Metz's apolitical semiotics. He suggests the connection between film theory, sign theory, and neo-Freudian psychoanalytic theory propounded by Jacques Lacan.

1976   *Movies and Methods* (ed. Bill Nichols, USA). This anthology of film criticism brings together a number of seminal articles of post-structural modernist approaches, including the essays by Jean-Louis Comolli and Jean Narboni of *Cahiers du Cinéma* on Ford's *Young Mr. Lincoln* and "Cinema/Ideology/Criticism."

1980   *May '68 and Film Culture*. Sylvia Harvey, of the influential British film journal *Screen,* produces a volume that explains the roots of ideological film criticism in the events of the student uprising in Paris in 1968 at the government's closure of the Cinémathèque. She summarizes the views of neo-Marxist Louis Althusser and shows how his view of ideology underpins modern film theory.

1981   *Questions of Cinema* (Stephen Heath, England). This collection of Heath's articles posits film as a psychoanalytic/ideological system that regulates the spectator's desire.

   The Imaginary Signifier (Christian Metz, France). Metz continues his analysis of the cinema, but here he has clearly incorporated Lacanian psychoanalysis into his method.

1983   *The Subject of Semiotics* (Kaja Silverman, Canada). This book makes clear the feminist position that cinema is a patriarchal apparatus that uses woman as the signifier of lack, the object of spectacle, a topic first raised by Laura Mulvey in her 1975 article in *Screen,* "Visual Pleasure in Narrative Cinema."

1984   *Concepts in Film Theory* (Dudley Andrew, USA). This work is a complete and thorough summary of all major aspects of contemporary film theory.

1985   *Film History: Theory and Practice* (Robert C. Allen and Douglas Gomery). This book applies modernist critical methodologies to all areas of film history. Indeed, the authors subject film history itself to the rigors of the latest concepts of historiography.

   [As *An Introduction to Film Criticism* goes to press, the situation in film criticism remains remarkably stable. Each critical approach has its forums, its journals, its place of interaction with its readers. Conferences are held yearly at which papers are read. New books appear at any time. Reviewers in print and on television are happy to let the world know what they think of the latest releases. Academics still are compelled to publish. The discourse of film criticism will never cease until films lose their ability to mesmerize an audience with their power and brilliance. Old movies, new movies, movies on big screens or small—if they mean anything at all, people will continue the attempt to find more meaning through new readings, new ways of seeing these most fascinating texts.]

Works Cited and Selected Bibliography

Note: Original publication dates for books are given in the text. In some cases the dates in this Works Cited section are more recent, indicating reissues or paperback versions more likely to be available to students.

CHAPTER 1: JOURNALISTIC APPROACHES

Current reviews of films are available in all major daily and weekly newspapers as well as weekly and monthly magazines. *The Readers' Guide to Periodical Literature* lists reviews of older films by title and tells where they can be found in back issues.

The following list contains collections of journalistic reviews and books that are written from a journalistic approach.

Adler, Renata. *A Year in the Dark: Journal of a Film Critic 1968–1969*. New York: Random House, 1969.

Agee, James. *Agee on Film. Vol I, Reviews and Comments*. New York: McDowell, 1958.

Crist, Judith. *The Private Eye, the Cowboy and the Very Naked Girl*. New York: Paperback Library, 1970.

Crowther, Bosley. *Hollywood Rajah: The Life and Times of Louis B. Mayer*. New York: Holt, 1960.

———. *The Lion's Share: The Story of an Entertainment Empire*. New York: Garland, 1985.

Farber, Manny. *Negative Space*. New York: Praeger, 1971.

Ferguson, Otis. *The Film Criticism of Otis Ferguson*. ed. Robert Wilson. Philadelphia: Temple University Press, 1971.

Grau, Robert. *The Theater of Science*. New York: Broadway Publishing, 1914.

Kael, Pauline. *5001 Nights at the Movies*. New York: Holt, 1984.

———. *I Lost It at the Movies*. Boston: Little, Brown, 1964.

———. *Kiss, Kiss, Bang, Bang*. Boston: Little, Brown, 1968.

Kauffmann, Stanley. *Figures of Light: Criticism and Comment*. New York: Harper, 1971.

———. *A World on Film: Criticism and Comment*. New York: Harper, 1966.

———, with Bruce Henstell, eds. *American Film Criticism*. New York: Liveright, 1972.

Macdonald, Dwight. *Dwight Macdonald on Movies*. Englewood Cliffs, N.J.: Prentice-Hall, 1969.

Mount, Douglas N. "Authors and Editors." *Publishers Weekly,* 24 May, 1971.

Murry, Edward. *Nine American Film Critics*. New York: Ungar, 1975.
The New York Times Film Reviews, 1913–1970. 7 vols. New York: Arno, 1971.
Ramsaye, Terry. *A Million and One Nights*. New York: Simon & Schuster, 1964.
Reed, Rex. *Big Screen, Little Screen*. New York: Macmillan, 1971.
Sarris, Andrew. *Confessions of a Cultist: On the Cinema, 1955–1969*. New York: Simon & Schuster, 1970.
Simon, John. *Movies into Film*. New York: Dial Press, 1971.

CHAPTER 2: HUMANIST APPROACHES

Andrew, Dudley. *Concepts in Film Theory*. New York: Oxford, 1984.
Braudy, Leo. *The World in a Frame*. Garden City, N.Y.: Doubleday, 1976.
Cavell, Stanley. *Pursuits of Happiness: The Hollywood Comedy of Remarriage*. Cambridge, Mass.: Harvard University Press, 1981.
———. *The World Viewed*. Cambridge, Mass.: Harvard University Press, 1971.
Durgnat, Raymond. *Films and Feelings*. Cambridge, Mass.: MIT Press, 1967.
Eisner, Lotte. *The Haunted Screen: Expressionism in the German Cinema and the Influence of Max Reinhardt*. Berkeley: University of California Press, 1969.
Film Quarterly. Ernest Callenbach, ed. Berkeley: University of California Press.
Fletcher, John. "Bergman and Strindberg." *JML*, vol. 3, no. 2, April 1973, pp. 173–190.
French, Brandon. *On the Verge of Revolt: Women in American Films of the Fifties*. New York: Ungar, 1978.
Huss, Roy, and Norman Silverstein. *The Film Experience: Elements of Motion Picture Art*. New York: Harper, 1968.
Lawson, John Howard. *Film: The Creative Process*. New York: Hill & Wang, 1964.
Linden, George W. *Reflections on the Screen*. Belmont, Calif.: Wadsworth, 1970.
Lindgren, Ernest. *The Art of the Film*. London: Allen & Unwin, 1949.
Lindsay, Vachel. *The Art of the Moving Picture*. New York: Liveright, 1916.
Literature/Film Quarterly. Thomas L. Erskine, James M. Welsh, eds. Salisbury State College, Salisbury, Maryland.
Mast, Gerald. *Film/Cinema/Movies: A Theory of Experience*. New York: Harper, 1977.
McConnell, Frank D. *The Spoken Seen: Film and the Romantic Imagination*. Baltimore: Johns Hopkins University Press, 1975.
———. *Storytelling and Mythmaking*. New York: Oxford, 1979.
Münsterberg, Hugo. *The Photoplay: A Psychological Study*. New York: Dover, 1970.
Perkins, V. F. *Film as Film*. Baltimore: Penguin, 1986.
Pressler, Michael. "The Idea Fused in the Fact: Bergman and *The Seventh Seal*." *Literature/Film Quarterly*, vol. 13, no. 2, 1985, pp. 95–101.
Richardson, Robert. *Literature and Film*. Bloomington: Indiana University Press, 1969.
Robinson, W. R., ed. *Man and the Movies*. Baltimore: Penguin, 1969.
Ross, T. J., ed. *Film and the Liberal Arts*. New York: Holt, 1970.
Simon, John. *Movies into Film*. New York: Dial Press, 1971.
Sontag, Susan. *Against Interpretation*. New York: Dell, 1966.
———. *Styles of Radical Will*. New York: Farrar, 1969.

Stephenson, Ralph, and J. R. Debrix. *The Cinema as Art*. Baltimore: Penguin, 1965.
Warshow, Robert. *The Immediate Experience*. New York: Atheneum, 1970.
Wood, Michael. *America at the Movies*. New York: Basic Books, 1975.
Wood, Robin. *Hitchcock's Films*. New York: Barnes, 1967.

CHAPTER 3: AUTEURIST APPROACHES

Bogdanovitch, Peter. "The Kane Mutiny." *Esquire,* 77 (Oct. 1972).
Capra, Frank. *The Name Above the Title*. New York: Macmillan, 1972.
Durgnat, Raymond. *Nouvelle Vague: The First Decade*. Loughton, England: Motion Publications, 1963.
Film Comment.
Graham, Peter. *The New Wave*. New York: Doubleday, 1968.
Henderson, Robert M. *D. W. Griffith: His Life and Work*. New York: Oxford, 1972.
Kauffmann, Stanley, with Bruce Hensell, eds. *American Film Criticism*. New York: Liveright, 1972.
Kitses, Jim. *Horizons West*. Bloomington: Indiana University Press, 1970.
Narboni, Jean, and Tom Milne, eds. *Godard on Godard*. New York: Viking, 1972.
Rothman, William. *Hitchcock: The Murderous Gaze*. Cambridge, Mass.: Harvard University Press, 1982.
Ross, T. J., ed. *Film and the Liberal Arts*. New York: Holt, 1970.
Sarris, Andrew. *The American Cinema: Directors and Directions 1929–1968*. New York: Dutton, 1969.
Schrader, Paul. *Transcendental Style in Film: Ozu, Bresson, Dreyer*. Berkeley: University of California, 1972.
Sight and Sound.
Talbot, Daniel. *Film: An Anthology*. Berkeley: University of California Press, 1966.
Truffaut, François, with Helen G. Scott. *Hitchcock*. New York: Simon & Schuster, 1984.
Wollen, Peter. *Signs and Meaning in the Cinema*. Bloomington: Indiana University Press, 1972.
Wood, Robin. *Hitchcock's Films*. New York: Paperback Library, 1970.
———. *Howard Hawks*. Garden City, N.Y.: Doubleday, 1968.
Books on individual directors not cited in the chapter are too numerous to list here. They can be looked up in a library's Subject catalogue under the director's name.

CHAPTER 4: GENRE APPROACHES

Altman, Rick, ed. *Genre: The Musical*. London: Routledge & Kegan Paul, 1981.
Baxter, John. *The Gangster Film*. New York: Zwemmer and Barnes, 1970.
———. *Science Fiction in the Cinema*. Zwemmer and Barnes, 1970.
Cawelti, John G. *The Six-Gun Mystique*. Bowling Green, Ohio: Bowling Green University Press, 1984.
Clarens, Carlos. *Crime Films*. New York: Norton, 1980.
———. *An Illustrated History of the Horror Film*. New York: Capricorn Books, 1968.

Fenin, George, and William K. Everson. *The Western from Silents to Cinerama.* New York: Bonanza Books, 1962.

Feur, Jane. *The Hollywood Musical.* Bloomington: Indiana University Press, 1982.

Grant, Barry, ed. *Film Genre Reader.* Austin: University of Texas Press, 1986.

Kaminsky, Stuart M. *American Film Genres: Approaches to a Critical Theory of Popular Film.* Dayton, Ohio: Pflann, 1974.

Kauffmann, Stanley, with Bruce Henstell, eds. *American Film Criticism.* New York: Liveright, 1972.

Kitses, Jim. *Horizons West.* Bloomington: Indiana University Press, 1970.

Schatz, Thomas G. *Hollywood Genres: Formulas, Filmmaking, and the Studio System.* New York: Random House, 1981.

Shadoian, Jack. *Dreams and Dead Ends: The American Gangster/Crime Film.* Cambridge, Mass.: MIT Press, 1979.

Sobchack, Vivian C. *Screening Space: The American Science Fiction Film.* New York: Ungar, 1986.

Solomon, Stanley. *Beyond Formula: American Film Genres.* New York: Harcourt, 1976.

Warshow, Robert. *The Immediate Experience.* New York: Atheneum, 1970.

Wright, Will. *Six Guns and Society: A Structural Study of the Western.* Berkeley: University of California Press, 1975.

Other books on individual genres can be located through the Subject index in a library's catalogue.

CHAPTER 5: SOCIAL SCIENCE APPROACHES

Bach, Stephen. *Final Cut: Dreams and Disasters in the Making of Heaven's Gate.* New York: Morrow, 1985.

Biro, Yvette. *Profane Mythology: The Savage Mind of Cinema.* Bloomington: Indiana University Press, 1982.

Blumer, Herbert. *Movies and Conduct.* New York: Macmillan, 1933.

Boorstin, Daniel. *The Image, or What Happened to the American Dream.* New York: Atheneum, 1962.

Cline, Victor B. *Where Do You Draw the Line?* Provo, Utah: Brigham Young University Press, 1974.

Glucksmann, Andre. *Violence on the Screen.* London: British Film Institute, 1972.

Huaco, George. *The Sociology of Film Art.* New York: Basic Books, 1965.

Jarvie, I. C. *Movies and Society.* New York: Basic Books, 1970.

Jowett, Garth. *Film: The Democratic Art.* Boston: Little, Brown, 1976.

Kauffmann, Stanley. *Figures of Light: Criticism and Comment.* New York: Harper, 1971.

Kracauer, Siegfried. *From Caligari to Hitler: A Psychological History of the German Film.* Princeton: Princeton University Press, 1957.

McClintick, David. *Indecent Exposure.* New York: Morrow, 1982.

Monaco, Paul. *Cinema and Society.* New York: Elsevier, 1976.

Powdermaker, Hortense. *Hollywood the Dream Factory.* New York: Grosset & Dunlap, 1950.

Riesman, David, with Revel Denny and Nathan Glazer. *The Lonely Crowd*. New Haven: Yale University Press, 1968.

Sklar, Robert. *Movie-Made America: A Cultural History of American Movies*. New York: Random House, 1975.

Tyler, Parker. *The Hollywood Hallucination*. New York: Creative Age Press, 1970.

————. *Myth and Magic in the Movies*. New York: Holt, 1970.

Wolfenstein, Martha, and Nathan Leites. *Movies: A Psychological Study*. Glencoe, Ill.: Free Press, 1950.

Wright, Will. *Six Guns and Society: A Structural Study of the Western*. Berkeley: University of California Press, 1975.

CHAPTER 6: HISTORICAL APPROACHES

Allen, Robert C., and Douglas Gomery. *Film History: Theory and Practice*. New York: Knopf, 1985.

Balio, Tino. *The American Film Industry*. Madison: University of Wisconsin Press, 1976.

Bergman, Andrew. *We're in the Money*. New York: N.Y.U. Press, 1970.

Bohn, Thomas, and Richard Stromgren. *Light and Shadows: A History of Motion Pictures*. Palo Alto, Calif.: Mayfield, 1986.

Brownlow, Kevin. *The Parades Gone By*. New York: Knopf, 1968.

Ceram, C. W. *Archaeology of the Cinema*. New York: Harcourt, [n.d.]

Ellis, Jack. *A History of Film*, 2nd ed. Englewood Cliffs: Prentice Hall, 1985.

Fielding, Raymond, ed. *A Technological History of Motion Pictures and Television*. Berkeley: University of California Press, 1967.

Grau, Robert. *The Theater of Science*. New York: Broadway Publishing, 1914.

Guback, Thomas H. *The International Film Industry: Western Europe and America Since 1945*. Bloomington: Indiana University Press, 1969.

Hendricks, Gordon. *The Edison Motion Picture Myth*. Berkeley: University of California Press, 1961.

Kindem, Gorham. *The American Movie Industry: The Business of Motion Pictures*. Carbondale: Southern Illinois University Press, 1982.

Knight, Arthur. *The Liveliest Art*. New York: Mentor, 1957.

Limbacher, James L. *Four Aspects of the Film*. New York: Russell & Russell, 1968.

Macgowan, Kenneth. *Behind the Screen: The History and Techniques of the Motion Picture*. New York: Delacorte, 1965.

Mast, Gerald. *A Short History of the Movies*, 4th ed. New York: Macmillan, 1986.

O'Connor, John, and Martin Jackson. *American History/American Film*. New York: Ungar, 1979.

Panofsky, Erwin. "Style and Medium in the Moving Pictures." In *Film and the Liberal Arts*, T. J. Ross, ed. New York: Holt, 1970.

Ramsaye, Terry. *A Million and One Nights*. New York: Simon and Schuster, 1964.

Salt, Barry. "Film Style and Technology in the Thirties." *Film Quarterly*, vol. 30, no. 1, Fall 1976, pp. 19–32.

Talbot, Daniel. *Film: An Anthology*. Berkeley: University of California Press, 1966.

CHAPTER 7: THEORETICAL/IDEOLOGICAL/ APPROACHES

Allen, Robert C. and Douglas Gomery. *Film History: Theory and Practice*. New York: Knopf, 1985.

Andrew, Dudley. *Concepts in Film Theory*. New York: Oxford, 1984.

——. *The Major Film Theories: An Introduction*. New York: Oxford, 1976.

Arnheim, Rudolf. *Film as Art*. Berkeley: University of California Press, 1957.

Balázs, Béla. *Theory of the Film: Character and Growth of a New Art*. London: Dobson, 1952.

Bazin, André. *What Is Cinema?* vols. I and II. Berkeley: University of California Press, 1967 and 1971.

Cadbury, William, and Leland Poague. *Film Criticism: A Counter Theory*. Ames: Iowa State University Press, 1983.

Eco, Umberto. *A Theory of Semiotics*. Bloomington: Indiana University Press, 1976.

Eisenstein, Sergei. *Film Form: Essays in Film Theory*. New York: Harcourt, 1949.

——. *The Film Sense*. New York: Harcourt, 1942.

Harvey, Sylvia. *May '68 and Film Culture*. London: British Film Institute, 1980.

Haskell, Molly. *From Reverence to Rape: The Treatment of Women in the Movies*. New York: Holt, 1974.

Hawkes, Terrence. *Structuralism and Semiotics*. Berkeley: University of California Press, 1977.

Heath, Stephen. *Questions of Cinema*. Bloomington: Indiana University Press, 1981.

Kaplan E. Ann., ed. *Women in Film Noir*. London: British Film Institute, 1978.

Kracauer, Siegfried. *Theory of Film: The Redemption of Physical Reality*. New York: Oxford, 1960.

Kuhn, Annette. *Women's Pictures: Feminism and Cinema*. London: Routledge & Kegan Paul, 1982.

Lindsay, Vachel. *The Art of the Moving Picture*. New York: Liveright, 1916.

Lotman, Juri. *Semiotics of Cinema*. Ann Arbor: University of Michigan Press, 1976.

Lovell, Terry. *Pictures of Reality: Aesthetics, Politics, and Pleasure*. London: British Film Institute, 1978.

Mast, Gerald, and Marshall Cohn. *Film Theory and Criticism: Introductory Readings*. New York: Oxford, 1979.

Metz, Christian. *The Imaginary Signifier*. Trans. by Alfred Guzzetti et al. Bloomington: Indiana University Press, 1981.

——. *Language and Cinema*. The Hague: Mouton, 1974.

Mulvey, Laura. "Visual Pleasure and Narrative Cinema." *Screen*, vol. 16, no. 3, 1975.

Münsterberg, Hugo. *The Photoplay: A Psychological Study*. New York: Dover, 1970.

Nichols, Bill. *Ideology and the Image*. Bloomington: Indiana University Press, 1981.

——. *Movies and Methods*. Berkeley: University of California Press, 1976.

Propp, Vladimir. *Morphology of the Folk Tale*. Austin: University of Texas Press, 1968.

Pudovkin, V. I. *Film Technique and Film Acting*. New York: Grove, 1960.

Rosen, Philip, ed. *Narrative, Apparatus, Ideology*. New York: Columbia University Press, 1986.

Tudor, Andrew. *Theories of Film*. New York: Viking, 1974.

Wollen, Peter. *Signs and Meaning in the Cinema*. Bloomington: Indiana University Press, 1972.

Film Terms

abstract film. A film that uses mass, line, and color to create shifting and changing patterns; also, loosely, any nonrepresentational film.

adaptation. The transformation to the screen of a story, novel, play, or other work suitably treated so as to be realizable through the motion picture medium.

art director. The person who assesses the staging requirements for a production and arranges for and supervises the work of set design and preparation.

aspect ratio. The width-to-height ratio of a motion picture frame as photographed; also, the ratio of the frame dimensions as projected on a screen.

asynchronous sound. Sound derived from a source not in the image on the screen at the time it is heard—that is, sound not in synchronization with corresponding lip movement or object movement in the film.

auteur theory. A theory that says there is a person primarily responsible for the entire style and treatment of the content of the film. Generally used in reference to a director with a recognizable style and thematic preoccupation, the theory covers other production personnel (writers, performers, cinematographers, editors) who are seen as the major force behind a given film. More particularly, film auteurs function within the boundaries of studio production systems and are distinguishable from film artists, who have nearly total control over all aspects of production.

background music. Nonindigenous music that accompanies a film, usually on the sound track, but maybe from a live performance of one or more instrumentalists, or from records or tapes. Most background music in nontheatrical films is not scored to fit the action; in theatrical films the music is usually written to reinforce and emphasize the action.

backlighting. Light coming from behind objects or performers being photographed.

camera angle, angle. The physical relationship between camera and subject. If the

222

camera is low, tilted up toward the subject, the result is a low-angle shot. If the camera is high, tilted down toward the subject, the result is a high-angle shot. If the camera is tilted neither up nor down, the result is a normal-angle shot. If the camera is not tilted but is placed at the eye level of a person standing or seated, the angle is called an eye-level shot. If the camera is tilted off its horizontal and vertical axes, the result is a tilt angle or dutch-tilt angle.

camera movement.   Any motion of a camera during a shot, such as panning, tilting, dollying, or craning.

camera speed.   The rate at which film is run through a camera in frames per second (fps) or feet or meters per minute. The normal speed for sound film today is 24 fps; for silent films, 18 fps.

characters, characterizations.   The fictional people within a narrative film, not to be confused with the actors who play them.

CinemaScope, Scope.   Trade name (Metro-Goldwyn-Mayer) for wide-screen films made and projected by the use of anamorphic lenses on camera and projector.

cinema verité.   (French, literally "film truth") A style of filmmaking begun in Europe in the 1950s involving the use of portable sound cameras and recorders, and the cinematography of interviews and events on location. Commentary, sometimes obtained from interviews, is used, as well as lip-synchronous sound. Cinema verité films often express strong, sometimes radical, opinions.

close-up shot, close-up, CU, close-shot, CS.   A shot in which the image of the subject or its most important part fills most of the frame. A close-up shot of a person usually includes the head and part of the shoulders.

code.   The rules or forms that allow a message to be understood, to signify. Codes are the rules operating on the means of expression and thus are distinct from the means of expression.

color film.   Film that carries one or more emulsions in which, after processing, brightness values of a scene are reproduced in terms of color scales.

color saturation.   The measure applied to how vividly a color appears on the film— that is, whether it seems washed out or dense.

comedy.   Generally, a work of literature, drama, or film that has a nontragic ending and creates a climate considered humorous by a majority of viewers. There are many different types of comedy (slapstick, parody, screwball comedy), and comedy may be created around any subject matter.

compilation film.   A film made by editing together large amounts of footage shot for other purposes—that is, old movie clips, home movies, newsreels, and so forth.

composition.   The arrangement, balance, and general relationship of masses and degrees of light and shade, line, and color within a picture area.

contextual criticism.   A form of criticism that sees film in relation to the context in which it created and in which it is shown. Considerations of specific films and groups of films touch on history, politics, sociology, psychology, and other disciplines.

continuity.   The appearance in a fiction of an autonomous, temporal flow of events. It refers to the standard Hollywood editing practices of hiding the fact that film scenes are built up out of shots that are normally filmed out of sequence.

contrapuntal sound, counterpoint.   Sound, especially music, that contrasts or conflicts within the action in a motion picture.

convention.   A recurrent unit of activity, dialogue, or cinematic technique that is used in films and is familiar to audiences—for example, the shootout in a western, the line "There are some things man was not meant to know" in a horror film, the editing of a chase scene.

counterpoint.   See **contrapuntal sound.**

credits, credit titles.   The listing of script writers, costume designers, art directors, cinematographers, actors, electricians, carpenters, assistants to the assistants, and so forth.

cross-cut.   A cut from one line of action to another. The term also applies as an adjective to sequences that use such cuts.

cut-away shot, cut-away, CA.   A shot of action occurring at the same time as the main action, but that is not part of the main action. A cut-away shot may be preceded by a definite look or glance out of the frame by an actor or actors. Conversely, it may show something of which actors in the preceding shot are unaware. During a chase, for example, there may be a shot of what is going on back at the ranch.

deep-focus cinematography, deep-field cinematography.   Filming technique that renders objects in focus at both near and far distances.

depth-of-field.   The distance in front of a camera and its lens in which objects are in apparent sharp focus.

dialogue.   Lip-synchronous speech in a film, with the speaker usually, but not always, visible.

direct cinema, uncontrolled documentary.   A type of location, nonfiction, close observation cinema in which lightweight cameras and sound recorders are used to record events as they actually happen, with indigenous sound only. The origin of the term, used to distinguish this kind of filmmaking from *cinema verité,* is attributed to Albert Maysles.

director.   The individual who interprets the script in terms of performances and cinematic technique, and who supervises all phases of the work involved in achieving a coherent, unified film presentation.

dissolve, lap dissolve.   An optical edit that results when one shot fades out at the same time that a second shot fades in.

documentary.   A nonfiction film. It uses images of life as its raw material and may be of many different types and for many different purposes.

dolly.   (1) A small, sturdy wheeled platform built to carry camera and camera operators to facilitate movement of the camera during shooting. (2) To move the camera by means of a dolly while shooting.

dramatization.   The acting out and its realization in images on the screen of a fictional or factual event. Narration tells what happened; dramatization shows it as it happens.

editing, cutting.   The process of assembling, arranging, and trimming film, both picture and sound, to the best advantage for the purpose at hand.

epic.   A film that stresses spectacle and large casts, often with a historical or biblical plot. The emphasis is on scope, and so, appropriately, many epics have been filmed in various wide-screen processes.

epic documentary.   A recent form of documentary distinguished by its great length, its combination of interviews and stock footage, and its attempts to be accurate and fair through its complexity and scope.

establishing shot.   Usually, a long shot that shows the location of the ensuing action, but may be a close-up or even a medium shot that has some sign or other clue that identifies the location. It is sometimes called a *cover shot*.

experienced time.   The time the film seems to take to the viewer, generally felt as a sense of rhythm and pacing—that is, the film is felt to be long and boring or excitingly fast. The concept is not to be confused with subjective time, which belongs to a screen character rather than the viewer.

experimental film.   An independent, noncommercial film that is the product of the personal vision of the filmmaker.

expressionism (adjectives: **expressionist, expressionistic**).   Fantasy and distortion in sets, editing, lighting, and costumes used as a means of conveying the inner feelings of both filmmaker and characters.

extended image.   Composition within the film frame that draws the viewer's eye and consciousness beyond the frame itself and suggests the completion of the image outside the camera field. For example, an image of half a face in the frame will provoke the viewer to complete the image mentally, and so to extend the face beyond what is shown in the actual image.

fade.   An optical or sound effect in which the screen or sound track gradually changes from black to an image or silence to sound *(fade-in)* or the reverse *(fade-out)*.

fast motion.   Action that has been photographed at a filming rate less than normal, then projected at normal speed. It is sometimes called *accelerated motion*.

feature film, feature.   Usually, a fictional narrative film lasting more than 80 minutes, made for showing in commercial theaters.

film.   (1) A strip of flexible, transparent base material, usually cellulose triacetate, having various coatings such as photographic emulsions and iron oxide, and usually perforated. (2) To photograph a motion picture. (3) The cinema in general. (4) A movie, a motion picture.

film artisan.   A filmmaker who realizes a given film on the screen competently and aesthetically, in accordance with production dictates of a studio or other commercial considerations. Generally not the originator of the story the film artisan does not develop a personal style, but matches his or her style to the needs of a particular production.

film artist. Generally, a filmmaker who has as much control over the idea, production, realization, and final form of a released film as is possible, given the collaborative nature of the commercial medium. Unlike the film auteur, who faces many studio-determined obstacles in realizing his or her personal vision on the screen, the film artist often works independently and with personally chosen collaborators. (The term is often loosely used as a synonym for film *auteur.*).

film criticism. The analysis and evaluation of films, usually in relation to theoretical principles including aesthetics, philosophy, history, economics, and so on.

film movement. The films and filmmakers who constitute a cinema (usually national) at a given period of historical time. Most often, social and political factors cause a film movement, bringing together artists who have common aesthetic and political goals and who recognize themselves as a group.

film noir. (French, literally "black film") A group of films that share a common cinematic style and related themes dealing with corruption, generally in urban settings. The term is most often used in reference to a group of films made in Hollywood during the 1940s and 1950s.

film review, review. A summary of the content of a film, usually accompanied by information about the cast and the production, and often by the reviewer's judgment as to the worth of the film, published in print media or delivered orally on radio or television.

film speed. (1) The general term used to indicate a film emulsion's sensitivity to light; the higher (or faster) the film speed, the better it is able to record an image with low illumination. (2) The rate of speed at which the film progresses through the camera and the projector, measured in frames per second or feet or meters per minute.

film theory. General principles that explain the nature and capabilities of film. It refers to the ongoing discourse that attempts to uncover such principles.

filmic time and space. The expansion, condensation, or elimination of time and space, as well as shifts from a film's present time to past time, through flashbacks, and to future time, through flash-forwards.

final cut. The editing of the film as it will be released in theaters. The filmmaker who has the right to final cut will guarantee that his or her version of the film is not tampered with prior to its release.

flashback. A shot or sequence (sometimes quite long) showing action that occurred before the film's present time.

flash-forward. A shot or sequence that shows future action or action that will be seen later in the film.

flash pan, swish pan. An extremely rapid pan in which the subject becomes blurred.

focus.   (1) The sharpness or definition of the image. (2) To adjust the sharpness and clarity of the image by adjusting the lens or light source so as to create sharp or soft focus or to change focus.

foreground music.   Music, often synchronous, that finds its source within the actual narrative of the film. It can be heard realistically over the radio or from a television set, or performed on screen by the narrative characters (both major and minor) or by performers in the background.

formalism (adjective: **formalist**).   A cinematic or critical approach to film that stresses form over content in the belief that meaning occurs in the way that content is presented.

formula.   A pattern of dramatic actions or plot (for example, the reluctant hero of a western forced to take up his guns once more for the final shootout) that becomes familiar as it is repeated with minor variations from film to film.

frame, framing.   (1) One individual picture, as defined by the limits of the camera aperture, on a piece of motion picture film. (2) To compose a shot.

freeze frame, stop frame, hold frame.   A frame that is printed repetitively so that although the projector is still operating, the image in the print can be seen without movement for a desired length of time.

futurism.   An art movement around the time of World War I, emphasizing speed and dynamism in its forms as a response to modern life in the machine age.

genre.   A film type, such as a western or science-fiction film, that usually has conventional plot structure and characters; loosely, a formula film.

German Expressionism.   A film movement in Germany from 1919 through the 1920s, peaking about 1925. Following earlier expressionist movements in fine art and literature, filmmakers used decor, lighting, and cinematic technique to express interior states of being and feeling rather than to record an objective reality.

hand-held.   Referring to a shot with a camera held by a camera operator, and to the somewhat wobbly image on the screen that results from such shooting.

high contrast.   The appearance of an image in which tones grade quickly from white to black with a few intermediate values.

icon, iconography.   An object, landscape, or performer that accrues symbolic as well as particular meaning and conveys that meaning through recurrent presence in a group or genre of films. The term is not to be confused with a motif, which accrues such meaning in a single film only.

independent filmmaking.   Film production initiated by a person or persons not under contract to a commercial studio. Some independents may produce without making use of union personnel or commercial facilities, other than a laboratory. Others may subcontract the production to union personnel and commercial facilities. They may be off-Hollywood features made on low budgets. With the demise of the studio system in the 1960s, nearly all theatrical films today are independent productions.

insert shot, insert.   A shot of some detail of the main action or parallel action that can be made at any time during production, then inserted into the action during the editing process.

intellectual montage.   An assembly of shots through editing that results in conveying an abstract or intellectual concept. A group of people being menaced and beaten by mounted police next to a shot of cattle being butchered in a slaughterhouse provokes the idea that the people in the first shot are being victimized and are helpless, considered no better than dumb animals by their oppressors. The idea itself is not pictured; it is suggested by the relationship of the two shots.

invisible editing, invisible cut.   A cut made during the movement of a performer, achieved either by overlapping the action or by using two cameras and then matching the action during editing. Such cuts make shifts of camera position less noticeable. Invisible editing is a conventional Hollywood narrative structure.

jump cut.   An instantaneous advance in the action within a shot or between two shots caused by the removal of a portion of film or by poor pictorial continuity. It is sometimes an intentional reminder to the viewer that editing is taking place.

light, lighting.   (1) Illumination (the lamps) used in connection with filming. (2) To arrange illumination for shooting.

live action.   The action of living things, as distinguished from action created by animation.

location shooting.   Shooting done away from a studio.

long shot, LS.   A shot that shows all or most of a fairly large subject (for example, a person) and usually much of the surroundings.

long take.   A single shot (or take, or run of the camera) that lasts for a relatively lengthy period of time before it is juxtaposed with another shot. It reveals information within an unbroken context of space and time, and through camera and subject movement rather than through editing.

mask.   A device used to block or limit the passage of light from one area while admitting whole or reduced illumination of another area. A mask is used to create a wider ratio image on 35mm film by cutting off the top and bottom of the original nearly square image.

master shot, master scene.   A long shot or moving shot that includes all the action in a particular sequence, with the camera fairly distant. After it is made, if only one camera is being used, medium shots and close-ups are made of the repeated action and are inserted into the master shot during editing.

medium shot, MS.   A shot that shows part of a person or an object. A medium shot of a person is usually considered to include head, shoulders, chest, and enough additional space for hand gestures to be seen.

melodrama. In Aristotle's terms, a work of literature or film that treats serious subject matter (often life-and-death situations) but that is distinct from tragedy because the ending is always happily resolved, with the protagonist overcoming all obstacles to achieve his or her desired goal. In those cases where the protagonist does not fully have the audience's sympathy (for instance, the socially unacceptable ambitious female of the 1940s or the gangster hero of the 1930s), the happy ending for society, not the protagonist, may be somewhat ambiguous. The term is also used to refer to soap operas—that is, the family melodrama.

minimal film, minimal cinema. A type of experimental film that attempts to reduce film to its basic properties (its recording of actuality in continuous space and time), with minimal intervention by the filmmaker.

mise-en-scène. A term generally used to describe those elements of the film image placed before the camera and in relation to it, rather than to the process of editing that occurs after the interaction between camera and subject. The term also refers to the images in which context and relationships are revealed in units that preserve continuous space and time.

montage. The assembly of shots—hence, editing—and especially the portrayal of action and creation of ideas through the use of many short shots. In the 1920s, the Russians formulated several kinds of montage styles. Later, in the United States, *montage* came to refer to a series of shots, often with superimpositions and optical effects, showing a condensed series of events—for example, a crime wave in a city.

motif. An object or sound that becomes linked to a film's narrative in a meaningful way so that it becomes symbolically identified with a character or action. The glass paperweight in *Citizen Kane* and the attack music in *Jaws* are motifs. The term should not be confused with an icon, which functions from film to film, whereas motifs convey specific meaning in a single film only.

multiple track, multiple channel. More than one recording source for motion picture sound. For easier control in sound mixing, dialogue, music, and effects are recorded on separate tracks, which are then mixed into one track, or several tracks for stereophonic sound. As many as eight tracks can be used for the final optical sound track.

narration. Commentary spoken by an off-screen voice. In informational films, the voice is usually that of an anonymous expert. In dramatic films, it may be the voice of one of the characters.

Neorealism, Italian Neorealism. A style of filming and kind of film content that became prominent in Italy after World War II. It is characterized by concern for human struggles against inhumane social forces, is filmed mostly on location with untrained actors, and uses unsoftened realism throughout.

nonfiction film. Any film that does not use an invented plot or characters.

objective time. Time as it is recorded and revealed through camera movement and editing, unallied with any specific character in the narrative, or with a narrator.

The camera functions as an omniscient third-person narrator, and the viewer is to perceive the time the camera perceives as undistorted by emotion or personality. Objective time often coincides with screen time.

off-screen space.   Space that is out of the camera field but is implied by the film through the movement of the camera and subject movement into and out of the field of vision.

optical sound.   Sound recorded on or reproduced from photographic sound tracks, as distinguished from sound recorded on or reproduced from disks, tapes, and magnetic film.

out-take.   In general, any shot that is not used in a film.

overhead shot.   A shot made from a position directly above the action.

pan, pan shot.   A movement of the camera from left to right or right to left along a horizontal plane. Unlike the tracking shot, in which the camera moves with the subject, the pan is shot from a stationary point.

parallel editing, parallel action, cross-cutting.   The intercutting of shots of two or more simultaneously occurring lines of action.

persuasive documentary.   A form of documentary that is aimed at persuading the viewer to accept a given thesis. Raw footage is assembled so as to make that point, and narration is not uncommon. At its most extreme, persuasion is attempted through dramatization presented on screen as actuality, or distortion of actual fact through editing or commentary; this form of persuasion is called *propaganda*.

point-of-view shot, p.o.v. shot, POV.   A shot made from a camera position close to the line of sight of a performer who is to be watching the action in the shot.

process shot.   A shot made of action in front of a rear projection screen having on it still or moving images for the background.

producer.   The entrepreneur who initiates and/or manages film production activities; also the administrator who is assigned to manage the production of a contract film.

propaganda film.   A type of film used for persuasive purposes (often political) that tends to manipulate and distort actuality and to appeal to emotion rather than to rational thought.

puppet animation.   Animation of puppet figures that often have numerous heads and body parts with slightly different expressions and positions.

rack focus, pull focus, shift focus.   To change the focus of a lens during a shot.

raw footage.   Exposed film that has recorded desired subject matter but has not yet been assembled into any kind of narrative or informative order, or been selected on the basis of technical qualities.

reaction shot.   Any shot, usually a cut-away, in which an actor reacts to action that has just occurred.

realism, realistic film.   The use of scripts, staging, costuming, and camera coverage that renders action as if it were real, not fantasy. Attending to the conventions of realism—that is, the promotion of ordinary human figures in lifelike situations concerned with everyday problems—and maintaining a high degree of plausibility.

running time.   The time of the film's duration on the screen—that is, length (for example, 2½ hours).

satire.   A work of literature or film that ridicules or exposes the vices, follies, foibles, and shortcomings of its subject, most often society and its institutions.

scene.   A dramatic unit composed of a single shot or several shots. A scene usually takes place in a continuous time period, in the same setting, and involves the same characters.

screenplay.   See **script**

screen time, diegetic time.   The time covered by the film's story, or narrative time—for instance, a lifetime, a week, two days.

screenwriter, script writer.   One who prepares stories, treatments, and scripts for motion pictures.

screwball comedy.   A kind of American feature film that got its start in the 1930s, characterized by satire, sexual candor, romance, and comically impossible and incongruous situations, featuring likable people from different social classes, and involving fast-moving events.

script.   A set of written specifications for the production of a motion picture. There are several different kinds of scripts, and they contain specifications for settings, action, camera coverage, dialogue, narration, music, and sound effects, in varying degrees of explicitness.

selective sound.   A track in which some sounds are removed while others are retained. It can sound realistic, but it can also be so selective that its lack of ambient sound makes it seem artificial or expressionistic.

semiotics, semiology.   The study of signification via codes or systems in texts; the general science of signs, of systems of signification.

sequence.   A dramatic unit composed of several scenes, linked together by their emotional and narrative momentum. A sequence can span time and space so long as its dramatic elements and structure are unified.

setting.   The location for a film or parts of a film.

setup.   One camera position and its associated lighting; also, loosely, any arrangement of settings, lights, and cameras.

shooting ratio.   The amount of film shot compared to the length of the edited film, with the edited film having a value of 1.

shooting script.   A final script that is followed by performers and the director during filming.

shooting time.   The time it takes to set up, perform, and record photographically the images and sounds of a motion picture.

shot.   A single run of the camera; also, the piece of film resulting from such a run. Systematically joined together in the process of editing, shots are synthesized into sequences, and the sequences in turn are joined to form the film as a whole.

simultaneous time.   Time created by the parallel editing or cross-cutting of events that are narratively understood to be occurring at the same moment—for example, the heroine being tied to the railroad tracks, cut back and forth with the hero riding to her rescue. Simultaneous time can also be created through multiple-image and split-screen technique, in which different events actually do occur in simultaneous running time and screen time.

slapstick comedy, slapstick.   Violent, acrobatic comic acting, generally depicting aggressive and destructive behavior.

soft focus.   An effect in which sharpness of image is reduced by the use of an optical device, usually a soft-focus lens, diffusion disk, or open-weave cloth over the lens. The technique is usually confined to close-ups. The term also indicates an image or parts of an image that are slightly out of focus.

sound bridge.   A segment of sound track (dialogue, music, effects) that continues from one shot into another, quite different shot—that is, time, space, or characters change radically enough for the two shots to be part of two separate scenes. The sound track thus acts as a unifier, or bridge, between the two, and the transition is less abrupt.

sound effects, SFX.   Any sounds from any source other than synchronized dialogue, narration, or music.

sound track, track.   The portion of the length of film reserved for the sound record, or any recording so located; also, any length of film bearing sound only.

Soviet Social Realism.   A film movement in postrevolutionary Russia that joined ideology and aesthetics to celebrate the new Soviet Union cinematically. The emphasis was on documentary realism illuminated by artistic and purposeful editing and camera technique.

special effects.   Shots unobtainable by straightforward motion picture shooting techniques. In this category fall shots requiring contour matting, multiple image montages, split screens, vignetting, models, and the like. The term also applies to explosions, ballistics effects, and mechanical effects.

splice.   The act of joining two pieces of film by any of several methods—by cementing, butt-welding, taping, or, for processing, by stapling or grommeting; also, the resulting lapped or joined portions of film.

split-screen effect, split screen, split-screen shot.   The division of film frame into two or more separate, nonoverlapping images, done either in the camera or in an optical printer.

star system.   The system of developing audience appeal through publicity stressing a leading performer rather than other elements of a film. Begun in the second decade of this century with such stars as Mary Pickford and Charlie Chaplin, the system allows star actors to command extremely high salaries.

Steadicam.   Trade name for a camera support attached to the operator's body. A movement-dampening mechanism holds the camera steady, and the outfit uses a small television monitor as a viewfinder.

stock shots, stock footage, SS.   Film footage of scenery and action catalogued and stored for possible future use.

storyboard.   A pictorial outline of a film presentation, with sketches or photographs representing shots, and usually having in writing the speech, music, and sound effects that are to go with each shot.

straight cut.   Referring to two shots butted together with no optical effects.

structural film, perceptual film.   Films using slow or fast camera movements, repeated loops, extended zooms, flickers, or images photographed from the screen on which they are projected in order to explore the structures of the medium.

structuralism.   The study of how human institutions and art forms are structured on basic notions of conflict and opposition (for example, light and dark, good and evil) and how those structures are repetitive and archetypal.

subjective camera, subjective viewpoint.   A situation in which the audience involvement with a scene is intensified through identification with the camera point of view. In some dramatic films, the camera has taken the place of an actor, with other actors looking directly at the lens.

subjective time.   The time experienced or felt by a character in a film, as revealed through camera movement and editing. For example, a fearful character climbs a flight of stairs to find out what is making a noise, and the climb is prolonged to match his terror, or a character dreams and time has no meaning.

subtitle, subtitling.   A title superimposed over action, usually at the bottom of the frame, used to translate a foreign language or to identify the scene.

surrealism.   An art movement of the 1920s that attempted to tap the world of dreams and the unconscious for its sources. Incongruity, shock, and a rejection of causality were its major characteristics. Because of its ability to move instantaneously in time and space, film greatly interested surrealist artists.

synchronous sound.   Sound whose source is apparent in the picture, and that matches the action.

take.   A shot; also, a term used to indicate the number of times a given shot has been made. Takes are usually numbered sequentially and identified in picture by slate and in track by voice.

theme.   The story subject matter from which the general value or idea forming the intellectual background for a film is evolved.

360-degree pan.   A pan shot that makes a complete circle.

tone.   The mood or atmosphere of a film (for example, ironic, comic, nostalgic, romantic) created as the sum of the film's cinematic techniques.

tracking shot, traveling shot, trucking shot.   A shot made while the camera and its entire support are moving.

tragedy.   A work of literature or drama that focuses on the downfall of an admirable character whose defeat (physical or moral) usually is brought about through a flaw in an otherwise noble nature.

treatment, treatment outline.   A short summary of a proposed film, giving information about the kind of production and describing the main sequences to be developed.

typecasting.   The selecting or casting of actors because of their looks or type rather than for their acting experience.

underground cinema.   A term often used synonymously with independent film, avant-garde film, and experimental film. It also, however, connotes films that deal with shocking subject matter, or are purposefully antitraditional.

universal time.   Time created through imagery (often edited in a montage sequence) that abstracts its subject matter from a specific temporal or spatial context. The actions perceived could occur, therefore, anywhere and at any time, and the experiences on the screen are universalized.

viewer's script, cutting continuity script.   A script, often published after the critical and commercial success of a film, that is a recording in dialogue or frames of the film as it appears on the screen in its final release. It may differ quite a bit from the actual shooting script.

viewpoint.   The apparent distance and angle from which the camera views and records the subject. The term is not to be confused with point-of-view shots or subjective camera shots.

voice-over, VO.   A sound and picture relationship in which a narrator's voice accompanies picture action; also, any off-screen voice.

wide-angle lens, wide-angle shot.   A short lens able to capture a broad field of action. It appears to create depth and, in its extreme forms (such as the fisheye), distorts linear perspective so that the edges of the image may appear bowed.

wipe.   An optical effect used to join one shot to another. In its commonest form, scene A appears to be wiped off the screen by the progressive revelation of scene B, as a vertical dividing line separating the two advances across the screen from left to right. Many modifications of this basic form have been used, such as vertical, diagonal, iris, spiral, and even "atomic bomb" wipes.

writer's script.   The screenplay for a motion picture conceived by the writer and recorded to best represent the story and characters to potential commercial backers. Such a script will have a minimum of camera direction, lighting information, or technical specificity, but will attempt instead to convey mood, tone, plot, and characterization.

Index